When art meets science in the world of coaching, you k [ ] *interesting read! In* Evoking Greatness, *Megan and* [ ] *coach and education leader dancing in an evocative learning relationship toward an openness to designing experiments for transformative practice. The book is packed with coaching skills and tools for listening, questioning, storying, and illuminating the way forward in leadership with a strengths-based approach. Through a process of storytelling with the heart and language of compassion, the coach respectfully and skillfully brings the education leader to a deep understanding of professional practice and into the flow of inspired being. This book is so important in today's turbulent, complex, and ever-changing education environment—education leaders deserve coaches who have read this book!*

Dr. Jan Robertson, Author of *Coaching Leadership:*
Building Educational Leadership Capacity Through Partnership
Wellington, New Zealand

This book reminds us how essential coaching is to the development of effective school leaders who are committed to equity. I recommend this book to novice coaches as they begin to develop a coaching stance, as well as to veterans who are seeking to refine and extend their practice. The Tschannen-Morans' strengths-based, design-oriented approach makes this book particularly important for those who supervise school leaders—theirs is fundamentally a coaching relationship, and the wisdom of these pages will inspire and accelerate their efforts.

John Hall, Professor of Educational Leadership
Temple University
Philadelphia, Pennsylvania

Megan and Bob Tschannen-Moran have taught me a lot about coaching, trust, and leadership, and their new book might have taught me the most. Anyone interested in coaching will learn a lot from this book, no matter how long they have been coaching, and the book's topic—leadership coaching—is critically important. On top of all that, the book's stories and vignettes provide a great picture of what coaching can do; in telling those stories the book should inspire anyone to feel hope. If you're interested in coaching or leadership, or if you just want to know that better possible futures exist, you should get this book.

Jim Knight, Author of *High-Impact Instruction*
Lawrence, Kansas

Leadership coaching has arisen as a powerful intervention to support the professional learning of leaders. In this book Megan and Bob Tschannen-Moran invite us to see into their world of evocative coaching. They demonstrate how coaching conversations can lead to a flow of energy, enthusiasm, and possibilities that bring out movement in people. The authors combine their theoretical knowledge with their experience as coaches, exemplified in wonderful stories and practical examples. As a coach myself I could not stop reading because I was so curious about the next chapter. The book is a great example of how high-quality professional learning can enhance educational leaders' daily leadership practice.

Marit Aas, Associate Professor
University of Oslo
Oslo, Norway

We expect a lot from principals. They have to be managers as well as instructional leaders and work with a variety of stakeholders—all at a time when we ask them to do more with less. Fortunately, coaching is a way to help them negotiate these waters. It is a tried and true method of professional development that helps leaders grow as learners and become better leaders. As usual, Megan and Bob Tschannen-Moran do an amazing job of providing a case for coaching and offering a step-by-step process on how to make it impactful. The authors are among my favorite researchers because of their extensive work in the area of self-efficacy and collective efficacy, and when you read Evoking Greatness *you will see why their work will continue to be important for decades to come.*

Peter DeWitt, Ed.D., Author of *Collaborative Leadership:*
6 Influences That Matter Most and the *Finding*
Common Ground blog (*Education Week*)
Albany, New York

Not much is known about administrative coaching. This is a great book to inform and help more teachers understand a different coaching focus.

Brian E. Fernandes, Grades 4/5 Reading Specialist/Literacy Coach
Hampden Meadows School
Barrington, Rhode Island

Anyone who reads this book and applies the concepts will increase their effectiveness as a coach.

Jennifer Wiley, Instructional Coach
Park Hill School District
Kansas City, Missouri

There is a definitely a need for effective coaches to serve inexperienced school administrators. This text provides a guidebook and resources to support these coaches. It provides a model that emphasizes strengths and a positive approach. Furthermore, the authors build a strong case for the use of the story as the vehicle for the educational leader to examine possibilities and reflect on what can be changed.

Martin J. Hudacs, Educational Consultant
Martin J. Hudacs Consulting, LLC
Quarryville, Pennsylvania

Evoking Greatness

Coaching to Bring Out the Best in Educational Leaders

Megan Tschannen-Moran

Bob Tschannen-Moran

CORWIN
A SAGE Publishing Company

FOR INFORMATION:

Corwin

A SAGE Company

2455 Teller Road

Thousand Oaks, California 91320

(800) 233-9936

www.corwin.com

SAGE Publications Ltd.

1 Oliver's Yard

55 City Road

London EC1Y 1SP

United Kingdom

SAGE Publications India Pvt. Ltd.

B 1/I 1 Mohan Cooperative Industrial Area

Mathura Road, New Delhi 110 044

India

SAGE Publications Asia-Pacific Pte. Ltd.

3 Church Street

#10–04 Samsung Hub

Singapore 049483

Executive Editor: Arnis Burvikovs

Senior Associate Editor: Desirée A. Bartlett

Editorial Assistant: Kaitlyn Irwin

Marketing Manager: Nicole Franks

Production Editor: Veronica Stapleton Hooper

Copy Editor: Shannon Kelly

Typesetter: C&M Digitals (P) Ltd.

Proofreader: Annie Lubinsky

Indexer: Judy Hunt

Cover Designer: Anupama Krishnan

Printed in the United States of America

Library of Congress Cataloging-in-Publication Data

Names: Tschannen-Moran, Megan, author. | Tschannen-Moran, Bob, author.

Title: Evoking greatness : coaching to bring out the best in educational leaders / Megan Tschannen-Moran, Bob Tschannen-Moran.

Description: Thousand Oaks, California : Corwin, 2017. | Includes bibliographical references and index.

Identifiers: LCCN 2017012440 | ISBN 9781506377803 (pbk. : alk. paper)

Subjects: LCSH: Educational leadership. | School management and organization. | School administrators—In-service training.

Classification: LCC LB2806 .T82 2017 | DDC 371.2—dc23

LC record available at https://lccn.loc.gov/2017012440

This book is printed on acid-free paper.

SUSTAINABLE FORESTRY INITIATIVE

Certified Chain of Custody
Promoting Sustainable Forestry
www.sfiprogram.org
SFI-01268

SFI label applies to text stock

17 18 19 20 21 10 9 8 7 6 5 4 3 2 1

Contents

Preface

PURPOSE

This book is designed to equip those who coach educational leaders at the building and central office levels with the tools to host engaging and inspiring coaching conversations that contribute to the improvement of the leadership practice of their coachees. The leadership coaches who read this book will be introduced to the evocative coaching model, a robust model framed for a leadership orientation using the acronym LEAD, which stands for listen—empathize—appreciate—design. This model helps to guide meaningful and productive coaching conversations and invites people to explore and dream together, in a judgment-free space, in order to awaken a new and higher interest for change. Through collaborative dialogue that assesses and builds on a leader's strengths, people enhance not only their performance but also their enjoyment and engagement with their work. The evocative coaching model starts with the stories that coachees bring to their work as educational leaders and to the coaching contexts in which they work. By spending time with these stories, skillful coaches unearth the values and fears that both motivate and block educational leaders from achieving all they hope to achieve. The evocative coaching model then incorporates a concrete, skills-based process for expressing empathy. Once connection, trust, and rapport have been established, coach and coachee engage in a search for capabilities on which to build and together design an experiment for moving forward.

The evocative coaching model is a person-centered, no-fault, strengths-based coaching model, which is a refreshing change from the deficit mindset that has disheartened and demoralized so many educators in this era of accountability. It has been well received by those who coach teachers, and this book was written in response to colleagues who asked us to apply the model to the coaching of educational leaders. This model rests on several principles. As evocative coaches, we give clients our full, undivided attention, listening for the meaning embedded in their stories. We maintain an upbeat, energetic, and positive attitude. We dialogue with clients regarding their higher purpose. We accept and meet clients where they are right now, without judgment or blame. We enable them to appreciate the positive value of their own experiences. We harness the strengths clients have to meet challenges and overcome obstacles. We reframe difficulties and challenges as opportunities to learn and grow. We assist clients to draw up a personal blueprint for professional mastery. We support clients in brainstorming and trying new ways of doing things. We collaborate with clients to design and conduct targeted learning experiments. We inspire and challenge clients to go beyond what they would do alone.

A key concept in the evocative coaching model is that the coach is careful not to take too much responsibility for the professional learning of a client; the coach instead inspires a robust curiosity and sense of purpose in the client that drives the ongoing professional learning essential to what it means to be a professional. We ask and trust clients to take charge of their own learning and growth. We invite clients to discover possibilities and find answers for themselves. We ensure that clients are talking more than we are. By using the principles and practices described in this book, paying careful attention to LEAD, and working in evocative ways with individuals and their environments, we have the privilege of sharing in the joy of discovery, the passion born of self-efficacy, the cultivation of trust, and the productive shifts in energy and direction that results.

The Need for Better Coaching Models

Over the past three decades, performance coaching has grown in popularity in a wide variety of fields and has become especially important in supporting the work of leaders. An entire performance-coaching industry has emerged, as represented by the International Coach Federation and the International Association of Coaching, with a rich knowledge base grounded in positive psychology and adult learning theory. This book brings that knowledge base to bear in the context of supporting the work of educational leaders.

Coaching is an increasingly popular form of job-embedded professional development used to address the unprecedented pressures of the accountability movement that educational leaders face. While the first wave of the accountability movement focused on the work of teachers as essential to reform efforts, the focus most recently has turned to the vital role that educational leaders play in fostering success in schools. With this growing awareness, there is greater recognition of the need for high-quality, individualized, professional development for educational leaders. This development is increasingly coming in the form of leadership coaching. Schools and districts have found coaching to be much more effective in bringing about lasting change than other, more traditional forms, such as bringing in an outside expert to give a speech or providing training to a large group of educators at once.

Although leadership coaching has proven to be a highly effective intervention, it is also expensive. It is therefore essential to ensure meaningful results. Unfortunately, the literature and practices for coaching in education have not kept up with the advancing body of knowledge on leadership coaching in other fields. In fact, many people who function as leadership coaches in education have no coach-specific training and no working model to guide their interactions with their clients. In the absence of such training, many revert to a tell-and-sell approach, recounting stories of their own years in the field and giving advice as to how they would handle situations similar to those faced by their coachees. Some may try nondirective forms of coaching that too often fail to advance thinking and improve performance. Or they may toggle between facilitative and directive forms of coaching that leave clients unsure of the coach's stance and therefore interfere with the safety needed for risk-taking and growth. With the increased use of leadership coaching for both building-level and central office leaders, there is a need to prepare and equip those who fill these coaching roles with theories and methods to increase their success. This book provides a powerful model for training leadership coaches in how to engage the educational leaders they are charged with supporting.

The need for better models to support the professional learning of educational leaders is widely recognized. In its publication *Model Principal Supervisor Professional Standards 2015,* the Council for Chief State School Officers suggested a shift away from a compliance orientation to that of a coach. This document noted, however, that those asked to coach school leaders "often lack the right training and support to help principals build their capacity as instructional leaders" (p. 2). Furthermore, the Wallace Foundation has recognized the crucial roles principals play in the improvement and success of schools and has invested heavily to study, develop, and utilize better models for those who supervise and support school principals. Those who hire and supervise leadership coaches in education are among those who have encouraged us to write this book. Many states and districts are investing in coaching for both building and district leaders, and with these initiatives comes the need for trained professionals to provide the coaching. *Evoking Greatness* helps coaches to fill this need.

ORGANIZATION

Resting on strong, evidence-based practices, the evocative coaching model offers coaches the help they need to foster the capacities of educational leaders. The genius of this model is the way it brings together disparate resources and bodies of knowledge through an easy-to-remember coaching model. As Kurt Lewin famously said, "There is nothing so practical as a good theory." This book is chock-full of well-grounded, well-researched theories that support the work of coaching in schools. And yet readers have not found it to be so theoretical as to be impractical. Each chapter is framed around a robust theory that undergirds the strategies presented with strong evidence to back up its effectiveness. These bodies of knowledge include adult learning theory; positive psychology; Nonviolent Communication (Rosenberg, 2003); appreciative inquiry; design thinking; flow (Csikszentmihalyi, 1990); immunity to change (Kegan & Lahey, 2009);

and reflective practice. With the help of these bodies of knowledge, the model evokes fresh insights and new approaches for improving schools one conversation at a time.

Chapter 1: Introduction provides an introduction and overview of the evocative coaching model. **Chapter 2: Coaching Presence** explores the importance of our presence as coaches and of adopting a stance of mindfulness that is calm, playful, and open. Between Chapter 2 and Chapter 3 is an interlude in which we explore the fascinating qualities of a Möbius strip, the analogy we use to depict the evocative coaching model. In this interlude we introduce the first two stages of the evocative coaching model: story listening and expressing empathy. We frame these two phases as the no-fault turn of the coaching model, highlighting the judgment-free space we try to create with our clients. In **Chapter 3: Listening for Stories**, we explore methods for evoking coachable stories and how to deepen their impact through a process we call imaginative story listening. **Chapter 4: Expressing Empathy** presents a cogent and skills-based model of empathy called compassionate communication. Between Chapter 4 and Chapter 5 is another interlude in which we introduce the strengths-building turn, which is made up of appreciative inquiry and design thinking. In this interlude we also introduce the learning brief as a mechanism through which coaches and clients can articulate and agree upon the parameters of their work together. **Chapter 5: Appreciative Inquiry** introduces readers to the theory and research that supports adopting a thorough, strengths-based orientation in coaching, while in **Chapter 6: Design Thinking**, elements of the design thinking process are brought to bear in the development of learning experiments. In this phase, coaches invite their clients to design a SMARTER learning experiment in which they test a hypothesis in support of their own professional learning and growth. **Chapter 7: The Dynamic Flow of Change** considers what it takes to assist our clients to get into the state of flow and explores the dynamics of honoring ambivalence and rolling with resistance. We also investigate the use of coaching to plan and implement systems-level change. Finally, **Chapter 8: The Reflective Coach** invites us to take all that we have learned about coaching and to turn inward to reflect on our own learning and development as a coach. Alone or with a mentor coach, we are invited to explore our own stories, attend to our own feelings and needs, and investigate our strengths and capabilities. Then we are encouraged to design learning experiments of our own.

Throughout this book we use the terms *educational leader, client,* and *coachee* interchangeably. By *educational leader* we mean leaders at both the school and district level, whatever title they may hold. When we refer to school leaders, we are generally speaking about a leader at the school level, often a principal or assistant principal, but it could also be a person in a teacher-leader or coaching role.

SPECIAL FEATURES

Evoking Greatness has a number of special features to support the learning and growth of the leadership coaches who are inspired to implement this model.

- Each chapter provides concrete guidance and specific suggestions for questions to ask, things to listen for, and ways to generate new ideas and motivation in the leaders we coach.

- Templates and supportive materials are available for each stage of the coaching process.

- The book is further enriched by real-life vignettes of coaches who have used the evocative coaching model as a guide for their coaching conversations with educational leaders.

- At the end of each chapter we summarize the key points and offer questions for reflection and discussion, thus making the book a robust tool for both individual reflection and group study.

- An appendix brings together lists of coaching questions from each phase of the coaching model to serve as a resource for coaches as they plan their coaching sessions and as a guide to use in the midst of those sessions.

As you begin to implement the ideas in this book, we invite you to visit our companion website, www.SchoolTransformation.com, where you will find templates, related articles, and additional resources to support the evocative coaching process. There you will also find opportunities for coach training so that you can better apply and engage the transformational principles and practices of evocative coaching in your own life and work.

We dedicate this book to
Jeanie Cash, George Manthey, and Michael Bossi,
whose passion and enthusiasm in supporting the work
of educators has inspired us.

Acknowledgments

We want to start by expressing our deep gratitude to Jeanie Cash, George Manthey, and Michael Bossi. Without your encouragement this book would never have been written. We treasure your friendship and have been sustained by your caring. We are so grateful for your partnership in training educators in evocative coaching through Lead Learner Associates. You beautifully embody the principles of evocative coaching in all you do.

We also want to express our gratitude to an amazing group of coaches: Donni Davis-Perry, Susan MacDonald, Amy Piacentino, Kathleen Pietrasanta, Butler Knight, Sara Miller, Daphane Carter, Regina Armour, Leslie Anderson, Stephanie Baker, Eric Stone, Drew Schwartz, and Richard Streedain, as well as Fran Cohee-Chandler, Diane Hansen, and Nancy Harms ("the T-Mobiles"). The wisdom you've gleaned from your coaching experiences and shared with us has filled us with delight.

Special thanks to Davis Clement, Jennifer Wallace, John Hall, and Dabney Morriss, who read drafts of this manuscript and offered helpful suggestions on how it might be more concise. Your questions, comments, and suggestions helped us to convey what we wanted to say more effectively.

The Howell Creative Group developed the graphic designs in this book, including the Möbius strip diagram, the compassionate communication model, and the wheel of needs. It is wonderful to have partners who can take a sketch, an idea, a concept, and turn it into a graphic that illustrates the intended meaning in a beautiful and compelling way.

Finally, we want to express our love and gratitude for Maura Rawn, who helps our lives to run more smoothly in so many ways and whose love and caring are a precious gift.

Publisher's Acknowledgments

Corwin gratefully acknowledges the contributions of the following reviewers.

Martin J. Hudacs, Educational Consultant
Martin J. Hudacs Consulting, LLC
Quarryville, Pennsylvania

Jacie Maslyk, Assistant Superintendent
Hopewell Area School District
Aliquippa, Pennsylvania

Angela M. Mosley, High School Principal
Essex High School
Tappahannock, Virginia

About the Authors

Megan Tschannen-Moran (Ph.D., The Ohio State University) is a professor of educational leadership at the College of William & Mary. Inspired by her fourteen years as a school leader of a nonpublic school serving primarily low-income and minority students in a distressed neighborhood of Chicago, she is motivated to work at the intersection of theory and practice so that schools grow in their capacity to serve all students well. The coaching model presented in this book sits squarely at this intersection. Megan's scholarly research focuses on relationships of trust in school settings and how these relationships are related to important outcomes, such as the collective efficacy beliefs of a school faculty, teacher professionalism, and student achievement. Her book *Trust Matters: Leadership for Successful Schools, 2nd ed.* (2014, Jossey-Bass) reports the experiences of three principals and the consequences of their successes and failures to build trust. Another line of research examines principals' and teachers' self-efficacy beliefs and the relationship of those beliefs to educator performance. Megan has published more than 60 scholarly articles and book chapters.

Bob Tschannen-Moran (M. Div., Yale University) served as the president of LifeTrek Coaching International (www.LifeTrekCoaching.com) and as CEO of the Center for School Transformation (www.SchoolTransformation.com). Bob is a past president of the International Association of Coaching (www.CertifiedCoach.org). He trained as a business and life coach through Coach U, CoachVille, FastTrack Coaching Academy, and Wellcoaches Corporation. He served on the faculty of the Wellcoaches Coach Training School and coauthored *Coaching Psychology Manual, 2nd ed.* (2015) with Margaret Moore and Erika Jackson. His work on skills and performance coaching is included in *The Complete Handbook of Coaching, 3rd ed.* (2017, Sage Publications). Using a variety of strengths-based approaches, Bob has assisted many individuals and organizations, including schools, congregations, and corporations, to build positive relationships and to achieve positive results.

Together Megan and Bob published *Evocative Coaching: Transforming Schools One Conversation at a Time* (2010, Jossey-Bass), which presents a person-centered, no-fault, strengths-based model for supporting teacher professional learning. They have also published articles in *Educational Leadership* and the *Appreciative Inquiry Practitioner.*

Introduction

Dan Lyons was kind of an accidental school leader. A popular wrestling coach and social studies teacher in a rural desert town, Dan was asked to serve as assistant principal at the middle school. Although he had no formal administrative training, he passed the administrative licensure exam, which was all his state required for certification, and assumed his leadership duties at the middle school. The following summer he was asked to fill an opening as assistant principal of Desert Flower High School—a dubious honor, as Desert Flower had a terrible reputation as being a rough, dangerous place for students and teachers alike. Rival gangs provoked fights during almost every passing period, creating an atmosphere of fear and intimidation. Suspension rates were among the highest in the state. The teachers were demoralized and held a low opinion of both the capacity and future prospects of their students. Without effective direction or governance, teachers did as they pleased when it came to instruction. The school secretary pretty much ruled the roost, doling out insults and foul language to get things done. The school was out of compliance with state and federal regulations, and no one could remember a time when the high school had been fully accredited.

Early one morning, just a week before the opening of the school year, Dan got a call from the superintendent. Late the night before, an e-mail trail had revealed an inappropriate romantic relationship between the high school principal and another employee in the district. The principal had been fired, and Dan had been named the new principal of the high school. The only bright spot was that he was offered a leadership coach, Diane, to help him navigate the turbulent waters ahead.

(Continued)

(Continued)

Dan was feeling pretty overwhelmed the first time he and Diane met. Diane listened to the story of his journey as an educator and the turn of events that had led to his new leadership role. Throughout, Diane offered Dan empathetic reflections of the many feelings and needs stirred up for Dan by both the challenge and the promise in what he faced. Diane then began exploring what Dan perceived to be his own outstanding strengths as well as the strengths, however latent, of the school itself. Diane invited Dan to make three wishes for the school. His first wish was to create a sense of safety and calm in the school so as to overcome the climate of fear and intimidation. He also wanted to increase student engagement by improving the quality of instruction. Finally, he wanted to put the school on the path to state accreditation.

In collaboration with Diane, Dan decided building positive relationships in the school would be his first focus. He began by interviewing each staff member, asking strengths-based questions similar to those Diane had asked him. Dan took careful notes during these meetings, and from these collective wishes he framed a vision of the school culture to share at his first staff meeting. Diane and Dan carefully planned that first staff meeting and subsequent meetings to model the kind of engagement he hoped to see in the classrooms. For example, Dan stood at the door of the meeting and greeted each staff member by name with a smile or a handshake. Dan then invited the teachers to do the same with their students. This one small change cut down on fights during passing periods, thus reducing the number of suspensions.

With Diane as his thinking partner, Dan began to transform the school culture. He instituted a well-supervised intramural sports program and a debate club. The first debate nearly ended in a fistfight, but with training the students' discipline and the clarity of their arguments grew. The debate team began to debate at regional and state events, increasing their confidence and pride. During a field trip to a local courthouse, the judge came out in his robe to greet the students and told them, "I am where I am today because of my high school debate team." As Dan and Diane walked the school, visiting classrooms, they also noted the need to improve the instructional skills of the teachers. Diane helped Dan identify resources focused on levels of rigor and the Common Core. Teachers were introduced to the four Cs of communication, collaboration, critical thinking, and creativity. They were then asked which they would like to focus on first. Greater student engagement fueled greater innovation and risk-taking on the part of teachers.

With a state accreditation visit looming in January, Dan appointed a team of teachers different from those who had served before. Diane assisted Dan in carefully planning for these meetings. She also assisted Dan with planning a presentation to the school board outlining the initiatives underway at the school. They rehearsed the points he would make and how he would respond to questions. On the night of the presentation, Dan stood before the board well prepared and confident. In January, just five months after that early-morning phone call, the school passed its accreditation visit and the faculty and staff celebrated the changes that were occurring. At the end of the year, a faculty member marveled that as a school they had begun to have hope and to believe in themselves again. From such a discouraging and desolate place, she noted, the school was turning into an amazing place!

Results like those Dan achieved with Diane are what have made coaching such a popular approach for fostering skills and performance improvement. Coaching facilitates learning that sticks. Educators increasingly recognize the limitations of traditional forms of professional development, such as trainings and demonstrations. Regardless of how inspiring and memorable such experiences may be, they seldom translate into sustained attitude and behavior changes. Leadership coaching has arisen, then, to fill the professional development gap. It does this not only by getting leaders to think about their own experiences and to practice new behaviors but, more importantly, by getting them excited about the prospect of learning new things and becoming masterful educational leaders.

Leadership coaching can be a powerful intervention. At its best, coaching enables people not only to make incremental improvements in technique but also to make quantum leaps forward in their ways of working and being in the world. And it does so through the age-old art of conversation. In partnership with a trained coach, educational leaders who aspire to greatness can achieve that goal for both themselves and the schools they serve. Evoking greatness from people describes the primary task of leadership as well as of leadership coaches. We stand ready, willing, and able to evoke the best from, through, and with the people we serve.

THE PROMISE AND PRACTICE OF COACHING

If ever there was a setting ripe for the new possibilities and energy that coaching conversations have to offer, it is the one we are living in now. Our world is inviting us to reinvent schooling and the learning that takes place in schools. It is time for a change in leadership practice that coaching can help bring about. That promise can only be realized, however, when leadership coaches develop strong partnerships with those they coach. Traditional "tell-and-sell" approaches to coaching interfere with adult learning, undermine the quality of relationships, limit the scope of conversation, and diminish the effectiveness of coaching. When it comes to adult learning, a different approach is required. That approach is what this book is all about.

Leadership coaching is individualized, job-embedded professional development. Coaching is one form of relationship-based professional development (RBPD).

These methods stand in contrast to large-group methods of professional development. While seemingly an efficient way to deliver information about new methods and approaches to a sizeable group of people at once, large-group methods have consistently fallen short in their ability to produce sustained changes in professional practice. The dimensions of RBPD fall along two continua—ask-tell and problems-possibilities—creating a two-by-two matrix, as depicted in Figure 1.1. When we ask about problems, we show up in the role of *analyst,* whereas when we give advice about how to solve those problems, we show up as a *consultant.* When we shift our focus from problems to the possibilities inherent in a situation or in the capabilities of the person we are working with, we move to the right side of the matrix. When we offer advice based on our own experiences and propensities, we may be in the role of a *mentor.* To serve in the role of a *coach,* however, is to move to the upper right-hand quadrant and to do more asking than telling and to focus more on possibilities than on problems. Notice that the circle representing each role extends beyond the boundaries of its quadrant. This indicates there are times when an analyst might inform about possibilities, a mentor might ask about problems, or a coach might talk about possibilities. The diagram is just a reminder that the primary job of a coach is asking rather than telling, with a focus on possibilities more than on problems.

The evocative approach aims to inspire motivation and movement without provoking resistance or power struggles. To do this, it honors both the autonomy needs of educational leaders and the educational standards of their schools. It is challenging but not impossible to do both. That's the tightrope evocative coaches seek to walk, and it happens only when they treat leaders as though they have the inherent creativity, intelligence, and tacit knowledge to figure out for themselves how to be

FIGURE 1.1   Relationship-Based Professional Development

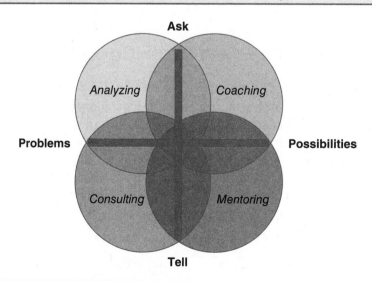

successful. Rather than taking a consultant approach, evocative coaches emphasize listening more than talking, asking more than telling, and reflecting more than commenting. Such coaching is not about giving advice, demonstrating techniques, solving problems, or offering constructive criticism. Although these occasionally become part of the process, they are neither the starting point nor the primary method we employ. We prefer to listen with empathy and to inquire appreciatively into the strengths of the person we are coaching. These inquiries open up clients to the prospect of change and engage coachees in their own unique performance-improvement processes.

Evocative coaching connects leaders to the best of what is and moves them to the best of what might be. In even the worst of circumstances with even the most problematic of schools or districts, evocative coaches LEAD (**l**isten—**e**mpathize—**a**ppreciate—**d**esign) to shake loose something new. Evocative coaches respect the individuality of clients and collaborate with them by exploring their stories, understanding their feelings, appreciating their strengths, and enhancing their designs. These four steps make up the dynamic process of evocative coaching conversations, enabling educational leaders to reconnect with their passion and move to increasing levels of personal and professional mastery. The process of evocative coaching can be viewed as a dance that builds self-efficacy through awareness, trust, and experimentation.

Evocative coaching develops growth-fostering relationships that challenge and support people along the journey of professional growth. Instead of taking over and directing traffic, evocative coaches assist educational leaders with clarifying and defining their own paths of development. It keeps the responsibility for professional growth with the coachee, exactly where it needs to be for sustained learning and performance improvement. We coach with the awareness that we will not always be there to support our coachees, so it is crucial our focus remain on building capacity so they can flourish on their own. Once we abandon the role of change agent, we can build trust and rapport and engage the leaders we coach in nonjudgmental conversations about their experiences, feelings, needs, ambitions, and goals. We can help them outgrow negative behaviors by working with positive data regarding their strengths, opportunities, aspirations, and resources. Doing so enables us to see them come alive, right before our very eyes, as they brainstorm new ideas and experiment with new approaches. When learning is a self-directed task, it becomes more enjoyable *and* productive.

It takes courage to start a conversation. But if we don't start talking to one another, nothing will change. Conversation is the way we discover how to transform our world, together.

—Meg Wheatley (2002, p. 31)

THE FIVE CONCERNS OF COACHING

Coaching becomes evocative when it taps into five animating factors of adult learning: consciousness, connection, competence, creativity, and contribution. Without attending to these five concerns, the promise of transformational change is unlikely to be realized. With attention to these concerns, educational leaders may rise to new heights of ambition and ability, discovering powerful new solutions to the persistent and complex challenges they often face.

CONCERN FOR *CONSCIOUSNESS*

Coaching becomes evocative when the coach's concern for consciousness generates increased self-awareness, self-knowledge, and self-monitoring on the part of the coachee. This lays the groundwork for all experiential learning. Mindfulness—nonjudgmental, attentive awareness of what is happening in the present moment—represents both the consciousness that makes conversations evocative and the consciousness generated by such conversations. When coaching conversations entail pressure, demands, and implicit finger-wagging, educational leaders take that consciousness into their efforts to improve performance. When coaching conversations entail empathy, requests, and curious "what-ifs," educational leaders become more willing and able to play with different variables and to make appropriate and meaningful innovations.

Understanding this, evocative coaches lean in to listen to stories, express empathy, ask questions, and cocreate experiments that increase mindfulness. By demonstrating an appreciative interest in the whole person, including the fullness of their experience, evocative coaches expand awareness to include what is happening in the moment, what needs are being stimulated, and what strategies or approaches are working better than others. Assisting educational leaders to attend to such matters facilitates natural learning. Paulo Freire (2000) called such facilitation the raising of a critical consciousness that engages learners in reading their world. The goal of such critical consciousness, according to Freire, is for people to become active agents in the creation of their own lives and the democratic ideal in society at large.

A clear and accurate appreciation of the present moment, without generalizations, exaggerations, or evaluative judgments, is critical to continuous skill and performance improvements. One must recognize what is really going on. Evocative coaches learn to listen for the observational core behind stories and then, through empathy and inquiry, make those dynamics known to the leader. It is not a matter of pointing them out but of getting coachees to recognize and understand those dynamics for themselves. As Zeus and Skiffington (2000) noted, "Coaching involves helping individuals access what they know. They may never have asked themselves the questions, but they have the answers. A coach assists, supports, and encourages individuals to find these answers" (p. 3).

As part of the self-awareness that grows from an evocative coaching relationship, educational leaders come to a greater consciousness of their readiness to change. When coachees are feeling ambivalent about how best to meet a leadership challenge, for example, evocative coaching can assist them to appreciate what that ambivalence is all about and what they can learn from it. When coachees express resistance or defeat, communicating either an "I won't" or "I can't" attitude, the adroit use of empathy and inquiry, rather than analysis and pressure, soon translates these attitudes into "I might," "I will," "I am," and "I still am" (Prochaska & Norcross, 2002).

Fostering greater awareness is a key work of evocative coaching. Effective coaching "helps clients to discover for themselves the new thoughts, beliefs, perceptions, emotions, and moods that strengthen their ability to take action and achieve what is important to them" (International Coach Federation, 2008b, p. 3). Masterful coaches assist clients to process in the present in order to "expand the client's awareness of how to experience thoughts and issues at the level of the mind, body, heart and/or spirit" (International Association of Coaching, 2009, p. 2).

CONCERN FOR *CONNECTION*

Coaching also becomes evocative when we establish a life-giving connection between ourselves and those we are coaching. As with consciousness, this connection spills over into the way leaders connect with themselves and with others in the educational environment. The carrot and stick may goad and prod people into action, but only life-giving, high-trust connections have the ability to inspire greatness. Such connections free clients to venture out and take on new challenges by virtue of the safety net they provide. When the connection is strong, the adventure of learning and performance improvement becomes an enjoyable game rather than a punishing task. Absent such connections, coaches and educational leaders inevitably fall short of accomplishing their mission to promote student success (Tschannen-Moran, 2014). With such connections, a zone of possibility opens for leaders and their schools and districts to accomplish the mission at hand in new and satisfying ways.

Human beings are hardwired for connection. Incentives are not required to generate the motivation for people to want to connect in productive ways with themselves and with others. Evocative coaches recognize the power of listening, empathy, and inquiry to establish connection and foster growth. Freire (2000) noted that "dialogue cannot be reduced to the act of one person's 'depositing' ideas in another, nor can it become a simple exchange of ideas to be 'consumed' by the discussants" (p. 77). It is rather an act of cocreation that comes from the connection itself. Dialogue, in Freire's sense of the word, is engaging and energizing, enrolling people in the search for the best in themselves and in their methods. That happens only when nobody is trying to win. When coaches are trying to win over educational leaders to their point of view or strategy of action, dialogue is disrupted. Evocative coaches set aside the desire to be right, seeking instead to establish the quality of connection that makes learning and growth possible.

CONCERN FOR *COMPETENCE*

Evocative coaches work from the belief that coachees are whole, creative, resourceful, resilient, and able to master the art and science of leadership, even though they may be out of touch with these abilities in the present moment. The concern for competence, then, is not to "make" educational leaders competent. That approach gives priority to the expert knowledge of the coach. The concern is rather to discover, recognize, and celebrate the competence these leaders already have. By appreciating that competence, both obvious and latent, evocative coaches prioritize the process of adult learning. Assisting leaders to clarify what they want and need, to identify and build upon their strengths, and to conduct no-fault learning experiments in the service of mutually agreed-upon goals is the key to assisting coachees to make quantum leaps forward in the identification of designs and strategies that work for them. The challenge for coaches is to suspend the desire to demonstrate our expertise. As well intentioned as it may be, the expert approach communicates judgment and undermines the confidence of leaders in their own abilities. Professional competence is not just a matter of knowing the right way to do something; it means adaptively applying skills to meet the changing needs of emerging situations.

There is no one universal path to competence in any profession, apart from a love of learning and a commitment to continuous performance improvement. Until and unless that passion is evoked, the process of coaching will likely revert to the telling of war stories and the giving of advice, and the competence of coachees will go both unrecognized and unfulfilled. Once that passion is evoked, however, coaching enables leaders to develop and better use their intrinsic competence for performance improvement. By paying attention to strengths, opportunities, aspirations, and resources, leaders find the motivation and self-efficacy for taking their competence to another level. Instead of a remediation of problems, evocative coaching generates an appreciation of possibilities. This shift, from a focus on incompetence to competence, changes both the tone and the outcomes of coaching.

CONCERN FOR *CREATIVITY*

In addition to paying attention to consciousness, connection, and competence, coaching must also unleash creativity if it is to be evocative. That calls for a light-hearted and playful approach to the coaching dynamic. Although the work of coaching is serious business, with a serious agenda—performance improvement—that does not make seriousness the method of choice when it comes to evocative coaching. Indeed, pressing too hard for and getting too attached to an outcome are sure-fire ways to cook up resistance and spoil both the experience and outcomes of coaching. Overly intense pressure can block creativity and get clients fixated on doing things "right" rather than on entertaining new interpretations and possibilities through brainstorming and exploring a wide variety of hypotheses. Although evidence-based methodologies are worth learning and practicing to see how they go and how they feel, true performance mastery emerges only when people creatively adapt and appropriate these methodologies for themselves.

Creativity starts with curiosity, a natural human trait that needs only to be unleashed and encouraged. Just as little children leverage their built-in curiosity to learn, adults also have a natural inclination to explore new frontiers, to test their limits, and to make just-in-time adjustments in the service of desired outcomes. Instead of trial and error, we frame it as trial and correction—win-learn rather than win-lose. Judgments of failure, both internal and external, block the creative impulse. Understanding this, evocative coaches use empathy and inquiry to turn the coaching dynamic into a playground where coaches and coachees alike can explore freely what they want on the way to performance improvement. Performance anxiety is replaced by positive energy as the conversational space is filled with humor, delight, and wonder. Whether things work well or not, evocative coaches respond with fascination and joy. No experience is so terrible as to have no redeeming aspects, nor is any experience so perfect as to have no improvable aspects. All experience is cherished for what it has to teach.

CONCERN FOR *CONTRIBUTION*

Most educational leaders entered the field because they wanted to make a contribution to the learning and well-being of students, families, and communities. However, that interest too often gets lost under the stresses and strains of life and work. The pressures of schooling, exacerbated in the era of data-driven accountability, can cause leaders to lose sight of the reason they became educators in the first place. Evocative coaches always communicate respect for that original inspiration. When the need for contribution is recognized, honored, and met, people gain the satisfaction that comes from connecting the dots between everyday realities and transcendent aspirations.

That is the powerful gift evocative coaches give to overwhelmed and discouraged educational leaders. By honoring the contribution of these leaders, evocative coaches awaken their passion. When the need for contribution is dismissed, minimized, ridiculed, or caught in the crossfire of conflicting interests, leadership becomes a chore and simply surviving to retirement becomes the goal. Evocative coaches turn the tables on this dynamic by their own certainty that a meaningful contribution can yet be made.

THE DYNAMIC DANCE
OF EVOCATIVE COACHING

To understand why we have come to call this approach to coaching *evocative*, it helps to consider the root meanings of the word. It comes from the Latin *ēvocāre*, meaning to call out and to give voice. This captures both the power and the promise of a coaching process that respects and fully applies the insights of adult learning theory and positive psychology. Building on this root meaning, we define evocative coaching in this way:

> Evocative coaching is to call forth motivation and movement in people, through conversation and a way of being, so they achieve desired outcomes and enhance their quality of life.

When we *provoke* someone, we do something *to* them in a way that provokes a reaction. To *evoke*, on the other hand, means that we do something *with* someone that unleashes or calls forth his or her full potential in transformational shifts rather than mere incremental improvements. Instead of generating resistance, such coaching assists people to get to where they want to go by unleashing their innate cognitive, emotive, aspirational, and experiential processes. It enables people to find their voice, to answer their calling, and to impact the systems in which they live and work.

Evocative coaching is a person-centered, no-fault, strengths-based coaching model that departs in significant ways from what often goes on under the guise of mentoring or coaching. Rather than focusing on improving the performance of educational leaders through advice-giving, evocative coaches focus on how we can equip those leaders to improve their own performance. We ask and trust clients to take charge of their own learning and growth and are careful not to take too much responsibility ourselves. To do this, we make sure coachees are talking more than we are. We give coachees our full, undivided attention and accept them where they are right now, without making them wrong. Evocative coaching uses empathy and inquiry to appreciate stories and generate new designs. We enable coachees to appreciate the positive value of their own experiences and harness the strengths they have to meet challenges and overcome obstacles. We reframe difficulties and challenges as opportunities to learn, and invite our coachees to discover possibilities and find answers for themselves. We dialogue with our clients regarding their higher purpose and uncover their natural impulse to engage with those they lead and to collaborate with those followers to design and conduct appropriate learning experiments. We assist coachees to draw up a personal blueprint for professional mastery, inspiring and challenging them to go beyond what they would do alone. We support clients in brainstorming and trying new ways of doing things, and we assist them to build supportive environments and teams. We maintain an upbeat, energetic, and positive attitude and use humor to lighten the load when appropriate.

All this constitutes the distinctive elements of evocative coaching. As we shall see throughout the rest of this book, evocative coaching is a dynamic dance that can be choreographed with four steps: listen—empathize—appreciate—design. The first two steps, which assist educational leaders to appreciate the best of what is, turn naturally into the second two steps, which enable coachees to generate the best of what might be. The process then loops back for additional iterations, which are portrayed on a Möbius strip to reflect the dynamic and expansive interplay of these elements in the service of continual learning and growth (see Figure 1.2). The steps are easy to remember, albeit challenging to practice. Coaches are so accustomed to traditional "tell-and-sell" methods that they may find it hard to trust more evocative, client-centered approaches. Yet traditional methods have not produced desired results. To turn that around, it is time for a new vision, model, and framework for transforming schools, one leader and one conversation at a time. Person-centered, no-fault, strengths-based conversations are more likely to generate openness to change and less likely to generate resistance than traditional coach-centered, high-stakes, problem-focused conversations. We introduce each of four dance steps below.

LISTEN

Coaching begins when people share their stories. These stories reflect the sense people make of their experiences. They are never the experiences themselves; they are rather attempts to understand, value, and shape the experiences in ways that make sense and guide future actions. Because coaching works with the stories educational leaders tell to themselves and to others, it is possible to change everything in the twinkling of an eye. Tell a new story and we get a new experience. That is especially true when we begin to work with the attributions of cause and effect explicit and/or implicit in most stories. Coaches listen for those attributions because they illuminate a client's path of development. For example:

- What is the overarching theme? Does it lie more with threat or opportunity?

- Where is the locus of control? Does it lie more with the leader or on blaming others?

FIGURE 1.2   The Möbius Model

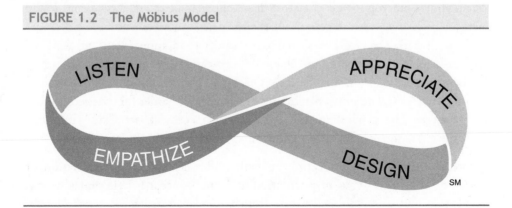

- How is the problem defined? Does it frame others as enemies or allies?

- What is happening with energy? Is it diminishing or increasing?

- What is happening with values? Are they being honored or compromised?

- How is the objective defined? Does it lie more with metrics or morale?

There is a panoply of attributions we can listen for and find. The secret is to listen mindfully, without judgment or haste, and then to ask new questions that explore the way things might be. How else can the story be told? What might have happened if different decisions had been made? How does the experience advance understandings of and aspirations for professional praxis? Reframing stories in this way, and exploring client stories with curiosity, is what we call *imaginative story listening*. It is an attempt to flesh out the details and meanings of stories in the service of client learning, growth, and change. It may be tempting to rush through stories to get to strategies, but that often generates unhappy results. Quick fixes rarely work, and if they work they rarely stick. Unappreciated stories tend to undermine behavioral change efforts. That's why evocative coaching starts with listening for stories.

Storytelling needs to be in the tool kit of the design thinker—in the sense not of a tidy beginning, middle, and end but of an ongoing, open-ended narrative that engages people and encourages them to carry it forward and write their own conclusions.

—Tim Brown (2009, p. 158)

EMPATHIZE

Most of the time, the stories educational leaders tell include a mix of empirical observations and subjective evaluations, including attributions about what is going on, what works and doesn't work, who is to blame, and how things might improve. When things are going well, the story has a more upbeat, generative, and joyful energy. When things are not going well, the story has a more downbeat and discouraged energy. Either way, coachees need to feel understood, appreciated, and accepted in order to release their energy and channel it in creative directions. Until and unless this happens, not much will come from coaching. The tension of negative evaluations will likely escalate into a distracting din, making it harder for coachees to find a way forward. That is why empathy represents such a critical part of story listening. Empathy clears the palette, inviting new interpretations and ideas to emerge.

Authentic empathy is a respectful, no-fault understanding and appreciation of someone's experience. It is an orientation and practice that fosters radically new change possibilities by shifting the focus from particular strategies to universal needs.

People tell stories to make meaning of their experiences, attempting to describe and account for things that happen through their narratives. Often, however, we misattribute our feelings to particular strategies rather than to what is happening with the underlying needs. As a result, people get caught up in a self-defeating cycle of interpretations, judgments, criticisms, blame, and diagnoses (Rosenberg, 2003, pp. 52–54). This cycle is counterproductive to both the coaching dynamic and to performance improvement. Evocative coaches learn to work with the distinction between strategies and needs in order to facilitate the movement and flow of both the coaching conversation and the developmental progress of clients. To do that, coaches learn to make use of the Nonviolent Communication model developed by Rosenberg (2003) and others over the past 50 years. Upon hearing a story, coaches notice and reflect the client's feelings and needs in ways that release tension, facilitate calm, and expand awareness. Expressing empathy and connecting with clients on this level is the second step in the dynamic dance of evocative coaching.

APPRECIATE

Once educational leaders have told their stories and explored the richness of those stories, and once they have received empathy for their feelings and needs, the flow of evocative coaching turns naturally to inquiry and design. Educational leaders come to understand themselves in new ways and become open to the consideration and observation of new possibilities. They eagerly want to notice what works and to learn how to make things work better. The first two steps of evocative coaching are designed to broker that eagerness. Once there, the next two steps are designed to translate that eagerness into action. That happens best when we inquire into a client's strengths, opportunities, aspirations, and resources rather than into their weaknesses, deficiencies, requirements, and avoidances.

Coaching does not become evocative as long as coaching conversations revolve around how educational leaders can fix their problems. This is not to say that coachees have no problems, but that it is easier to outgrow problems when leaders focus on strengths, opportunities, aspirations, and resources rather than on weaknesses, deficiencies, requirements, and avoidances. Both adult learning theories and positive psychology support this approach. Research indicates that appreciative, strengths-based inquiries are more effective and empowering than analytic, deficits-based ones (Fredrickson, 2009). Positive inquiries also represent a much more enjoyable way to learn and provide yet another way to reframe stories and engage in story listening. It is wonderfully reorienting and empowering to ask open-ended, strengths-based questions such as the following:

- What is working with your approach? What else is working? What else?

- What talents and abilities are serving you well? What else?

- What fills you with energy and hope? What else?

- What enables you to do as well as you are doing? What else?

- What is the positive intent of your actions? What else?

- What would success look like? What else?

The more aware clients are of their problems, deficits, and limitations, the less likely they are to imagine and pursue new possibilities. The point of asking "What else?" on multiple occasions is to evoke other ways of telling the story. Strengths-based questions remind coachees that stories of hardship, frustration, and failure do not represent the whole picture. Appreciative, strengths-based inquiries turn that around. They remind coachees they have what it takes to learn what they need to know. With the knowledge that in every situation something is always working, no matter how bleak or discouraging things may appear, coaches can be courageous in their inquiries as to high points worth celebrating. Such inquiries elevate the focus, self-efficacy, resourcefulness, and wherewithal of educational leaders.

Along with appreciating educational leaders' strengths and opportunities, evocative coaches also inquire into the aspirations coachees hold. Aspirations power change. Assisting educational leaders to visualize where they want to lead their school or district increases self-efficacy and motivation. Coachees become engaged with their visions, open to new possibilities, and eager to try new approaches. Such questions beckon clients forward. Asking educational leaders what and how they want to learn, rather than telling them what to do, enables them to discover and design that learning for themselves through observation and exploration.

DESIGN

When the stories educational leaders tell are received and reframed through listening, expressing empathy, and appreciative inquiry, ideas bubble up and coachees become inspired to design ways to turn their aspirations into actions and their opportunities into realities. Little to no instruction or incentives are required to get this going. Instead, once educational leaders become detached from both the fear of failure and the illusion as to how bad and impossible things are, they become fearless in the self-directed pursuit of that which will enable them to learn and grow. We forward the action by designing learning experiments to test the hypotheses that leaders hold about themselves and their organizations. In this way, they attend to both the process and impact of their actions. By assisting clients to become confident and optimistic about their ability to conduct learning experiments, coaches become catalysts for growth and change. The old adage, "Where there is a will there is a way," can be flipped to reveal an important insight into the power of self-efficacy: "Where there is a way there is a will." As clients see a way forward for improving their skills and performance in their schools and districts, motivation and movement naturally follow.

Brainstorming is an essential part of design thinking. This process involves generating many new ideas as to how to do things better without regard to their desirability, feasibility, or value. Sharing in the process of generating new ideas—taking turns with the coachee as one idea morphs into another—can open up the process even further. Some central questions to brainstorm around are "What could I pay attention to that would improve my performance in this situation?" "How could I build on what's worked in the past in some new ways?" and "What untapped resources do we have available that might help in this situation?" Such questions foster learning that is both self-directed and enjoyable. By getting educational leaders to identify what's important, coaches nudge them to make new choices and to try new behaviors with a minimum of resistance. The nonjudgmental generation and exploration of possibilities can quiet negative self-talk and free up creative energy. Evocative coaches assist educational leaders to review the options generated through brainstorming, choose the most interesting and doable ones, and field-test their ideas through learning experiments that are challenging, yet not overwhelming. We can play with different possibilities, pick the ones that appear intrinsically interesting and valuable, design experiments, and align resources to make those experiments more fruitful.

The key in the design phase is for coaches to avoid bringing out judgmental frames as to how things are to be done "right" or even "better." We are not the experts telling educational leaders what to do. We are the cocreators with coachees of experimental designs that may or may not work out as expected. Either outcome represents success as long as the experiments are conducted, data are collected, learning is captured, and results are incorporated into future experiments. Skill and performance improvements are continuous, iterative, personalized, and evolutionary. What works for one person, in one place, at one time, may not work for another. Coaches and clients, therefore, design experiments that coachees find interesting, doable, and relevant to the challenges they face.

In her new role as director of special education, Maureen was having difficulty with a behaviorist who could be very assertive in department and IEP meetings. She was finding herself being reactive to his input and felt like she was being thrown off her goal to facilitate open communication. So we designed an experiment in which she tried giving him greater input outside of the meetings. She would e-mail him and ask for agenda items before the meetings and talk to him about his perspective on issues that would be coming up. She found that the meetings ran much more smoothly, with broader participation by others. When another issue came up later in the year, she asked me, "Can we do another experiment?"

—Linda, Leadership Coach

WHY EVOCATIVE COACHING WORKS

Evocative coaching works because it applies the principles of adult learning theory and positive psychology. It not only supports self-directed learning, it also draws upon the increasing evidence of the impact of positive relationships, images, energy, and emotions in fostering positive actions (Cooperrider, 2000; Fredrickson, 2009). By respecting the underlying interests and abilities of educational leaders, empathizing with them, appreciating their experiences, and building on their strengths, evocative coaching enables people to achieve better results than they would on their own or with the use of more traditional methods.

As children most of us were taught through a combination of two processes: instruction and incentives. Parents and teachers told us what to do and how to do it correctly. They may have also offered incentives, such as rewards, compliments, punishments, and reprimands to get us to do the work and master the domain. Although it is not uncommon to use these same processes with adults, especially when it comes to training and knowledge transfer, educational and psychological research documents the limitations of this approach. Adults seek to figure things out for themselves, for their own reasons, in their own way, on their own schedule, and with their own resources. For coaching with adults to be effective, it needs to take these and other adult-specific factors into consideration. Timothy Gallwey (2000), an early leader in the modern coaching movement, called for a limit to the use of instruction and incentives in coaching due to their oftentimes debilitating impact on the internal dynamics that optimize skill development and performance improvement. Ironically, he noted, the more important the stakes (i.e., external requirements and reinforcements), the more instruction distracts people from their own natural learning style. Gallwey's insights build upon a century of research and practice in adult education and learning theory (Knowles, Holton, & Swanson, 2005), from which the following characteristics of adult learners have come into focus:

- Adults are autonomous and self-directed.

- Adult learning builds on a wide variety of previous experiences, knowledge, mental models, self-direction, interests, resources, and competencies.

- Adults want to know the relevance of the content to be learned to their goals and roles before they will invest the attention and effort needed for new learning.

- Adults are focused on solutions. Instead of being interested in knowledge for its own sake, adult learning seeks immediate application and problem solving.

- Adult learning needs to be facilitated rather than directed. Adults want to be treated as equals and shown respect both for what they know and how they prefer to learn.

- Adults need specific, behavioral feedback that is free of evaluative or judgmental opinions.

These characteristics of adult learners explain why instructions and incentives often interfere with performance. Although it is tempting to tell people how to do things better, this can undermine motivation, provoke resistance, usurp responsibility, rupture relationships, discourage risk-taking, limit imagination, and restrict results. Such methods may "work" in the short run, if "work" is understood as compliance, but they seldom work in the long run, if "work" is understood as mastery. Instruction may undermine autonomy and self-direction. It builds more on the instructor's experience than the client's. Incentives set up a dynamic of enforcement rather than support. In short, the use of instructions and incentives violates much of what has been learned about how adults learn.

People don't resist change; they resist being changed.

—Irving Borwick (1969, p. 20)

While educators were studying and developing adult learning theories, psychologists were seeking to understand and improve the dynamics of growth-fostering relationships. The traditions that evocative coaching rests most directly on include humanistic psychology, positive psychology, and social-cognitive theory. Drawing upon these traditions, the following recognitions undergird evocative coaching:

- People are inherently creative and capable.

- The human brain is hardwired to enjoy novelty and growth, which explains the inherent joy of learning.

- Learning takes place when people actively take responsibility for constructing meaning from their experience, either confirming or changing what they already know.

- The meanings people construct determine the actions they take.

- Every person is unique, and yet all people have the same universal needs.

- Empathy, mutuality, and connection make people more cooperative and open people up to change.

- The more people know about their values, strengths, resources, and abilities, the stronger their motivation and the more effective their changes will be.

These recognitions explain why evocative coaching represents such a promising model for generating performance improvements in educational leaders. By assisting coachees to explore their experience with empathy and inquiry, evocative coaching produces freedom, increases positivity, stimulates curiosity, elevates self-efficacy, and leverages latent competencies in the service of desired outcomes. Such coaching does not try to change clients or to persuade them to do things the "right" way. Rather, evocative coaches dance with educational leaders as they consider their options and invite them to become fully engaged in the process of discovering their own unique strategies for doing better.

You cannot teach a person anything. You can only help him find it within himself.

—Galileo

Key Points in This Chapter

1. Coaching becomes evocative when it taps into the five animating concerns of coaching: consciousness, connection, competence, creativity, and contribution.

2. Coaching is one form of relationship-based professional development. RBPD can be arrayed along two continua—the ask-tell continuum and the problems-possibilities continuum—forming a four-quadrant model of analyzing, consulting, mentoring, and coaching.

3. Evocative coaching is to call forth motivation and movement in people, through conversation and a way of being, so they achieve desired outcomes and enhance their quality of life.

4. Person-centered, no-fault, strengths-based conversations are more likely to generate openness to change and less likely to generate resistance than traditional coach-centered, high-stakes, problem-focused conversations.

5. The flow of LEAD (listen—empathize—appreciate—design) is understood as a dynamic dance between coach and coachee in which the coach attends to and is responsive to signals about the coachee's willingness and readiness for change.

6. Given its foundation in adult learning theory and positive psychology, and its demonstrated success when it comes to skills and performance improvement, evocative coaching holds great promise as it sets the stage for high-quality professional learning experiences.

Questions for Reflection and Discussion

1. What makes learning enjoyable for you? Why is it valuable to incorporate fun into the coaching process?

2. What is the best learning experience you have ever had as adult? What made that experience so wonderful? How has that impacted the ways you work with others?

3. What principles of adult learning theory are most relevant to your own experience of learning as an adult? How are those principles different, if at all, from the pedagogy of children?

4. What do you make of Irving Borwick's claim that "people don't resist change; they resist being changed"?

5. How does evocative coaching differ from your experience of traditional mentoring and coaching?

6. What happens to the coaching conversation when coaches get attached to an outcome? How can you release attachment and engage curiosity?

7. Call to mind a particular educational leader you know or have worked with. How might evocative coaching enable that leader to achieve performance improvement in ways that other approaches have not?

Coaching Presence

Before describing the "how to" of evocative coaching, expressing the dynamic dance of listening, empathizing, appreciating, and designing, we turn first to our intentions and way of being in coaching: the "what for?" and the "who is?" of the process. That is because evocative coaching cannot be reduced to a tool or technique. Without the right intention and presence, coaches fail to evoke greatness and educational leaders fail to realize their own and their organizations' full potential, no matter what approaches or strategies are used. Ironically, the more coaches want to help, the less dynamic and effective they may be because the coach-as-helper metaphor shifts the dynamic of coaching away from its evocative stance. It places responsibility for change primarily with the coach rather than with the coachee, where it belongs. What is needed is a new metaphor for coaching presence: the mindful coach.

In the professional realm, we often try to jostle others into compliance by using requirements and incentives. Evocative coaches take a different stance—a benevolent presence in order to generate growth and development. If we do not authentically care about the leaders we are coaching, if we think of them as defective, uncooperative, or uncoachable, we are likely to stir up resentment and resistance, the twin enemies of change. If this happens, none of the tools and techniques in this book or any other coaching book will do much good. Benevolence is a hallmark of trust and a central tenet of evocative coaching. When coaches listen deeply for the needs of educational leaders, without judgment or intimidation, and when they themselves show up with a mindful awareness of all that is possible in the coaching moment, coaches can generate amazing transformations in relatively short periods of time.

Relational authenticity in coaching is about a quality of presence that contributes power-fully to flourishing in connection. The coach's emotional presence is an important source of information for coachees and a resource for growth in the coaching relationship.

—Adapted from Judith Jordan (2004, p. 67)

EVOCATIVE COACHING AS A WAY OF BEING

Our definition of evocative coaching as calling forth motivation and movement in people through conversation and a way of being so they achieve desired outcomes and enhance their quality of life highlights two key dimensions of how coaching supports growth and change: what coaches do (having conversations) and who coaches are (a way of being with people). Failure to exhibit full coaching presence with the people we are assisting undermines the potential of coaching conversations, regardless of their frequency or length. If coachees are failing to engage and progress, it has more to do with the nature of coaching presence than the utilization of specific coaching techniques. Evocative coaches master both. The disposition of the coach matters greatly when it comes to client outcomes. As we prepare for a coaching session, it is essential that we ensure that our way of being—our energy in that moment—aligns with our intention to be quite helpful to the person we are coaching.

One universal trait of coaching presence is the dance between intention and attention in the present moment. Although the presence of a masterful coach may appear effortless, it does not happen by accident. It takes clear intention and plenty of guided practice. Evocative coaches prepare mentally and emotionally to be fully present and attentive before every coaching conversation. We do not multitask or rush through them. We do not show up with a predetermined agenda, such as to deliver expert advice, teach a new technique, or correct the mistakes of a struggling educational leader. All such intentions interfere with the work of evocative coaching. It is only through positive connection, presence, and engagement that adult learning gets stimulated. With this understanding, evocative coaches pay close attention during coaching conversations to the energetic dynamics of the coaching space. Evocative coaches take note when things begin to spiral downward, when negatives preoccupy the conversation, and when agitation and anxiety threaten to overpower the moment. Without a shred of judgment or fear, evocative coaches calm things down and call out new awareness. We receive conversational challenges as gifts, without being intimidated, so as to unwrap and explore their potential for growth and change. We find positive ways to be with educational leaders in order to generate new possibilities. All this comes from the heart of coaching presence.

Presence is a state of awareness, in the moment, characterized by the felt experience of timelessness, connectedness, and a larger truth.

—Doug Silsbee (2008, p. 21)

The International Coach Federation (ICF), a leading association dedicated to the advancement of professional coaching, identifies coaching presence as a core coaching competency. The ICF defines coaching presence as the "ability to be fully conscious and create a spontaneous relationship with the client, employing a style that is open, flexible, and confident" (International Coach Federation, 2008b, p. 2). To this end, the ICF indicates that professional coaches are present and flexible during the coaching process, "dancing" in the moment. They are open to not knowing and taking risks. They access their own intuition and trust their inner knowing and gut feelings. They see many ways to work with the client and choose in the moment what is most effective. A coach uses humor effectively to create lightness and energy and confidently shifts perspectives and experiments with new possibilities for action. Finally, a coach demonstrates confidence in working with strong emotions, can self-manage, and can avoid being overpowered by or enmeshed in the emotions of the coachee.

Whether coaching or not, evocative coaches radiate a steady, confident energy toward others. Evocative coaches also embody a full-trust relationship to life itself. "Don't just do something, stand there!" is a Buddhist saying that expresses this understanding. It is not up to us to solve every problem and put out every fire; it is up to us to trust that life has a way of working out. From this vantage point, we are available to participate in the process of transformation rather than be consumed with making things happen. Coaches combine urgency on behalf of students with patience on behalf of educational leaders by learning from the future as it emerges (Scharmer, 2007). Modeling this presence and trust, evocative coaches generate the self-efficacy needed for educational leaders to move forward successfully with their vision and goals.

THE MINDFUL COACH

Much has been written of the role of mindfulness in coaching and leadership. Mindfulness is the intentional cultivation of nonjudgmental focused attention and awareness in the present moment (Kabat-Zinn, 2012). Silsbee (2008) described the role of mindfulness in coaching this way: "A mindful choice is to focus our full attention on what we're doing rather than getting distracted by unrelated matters. As coaches, it is up to us to train our minds to recognize distractions when they pull at us, and to bring our attention back to our clients and the work at hand" (p. 47). By practicing mindfulness and showing up mindfully for our coaching sessions with clients, we enable coachees to learn, grow, and develop beyond what they might otherwise have imagined possible.

Understanding this dynamic, evocative coaches get ready for mindful listening in the minutes prior to the start of every coaching session. A coach's ritual of preparation is important to the course of a coaching session. The most important moment of a coaching session is often the one just before it begins, because in that moment the coach has the opportunity to adopt a mindful stance—to ready himself or herself to be fully present with the coachee and what is alive in the coachee in that particular moment. To make sure that we are in the right frame of mind before a coaching conversation begins, we take time to pause and gather our thoughts. Using the word STOP as an acronym can serve as a simple reminder of the importance of taking that moment.

Stop.

Take a breath.

Observe, acknowledge, and allow what's here.

Proceed.

—Brown and Olson (2015, p. 36)

That STOP in the minutes just before the start of a coaching session enables evocative coaches to clear their minds, set their intentions, and get into the coaching frame of mind. No tool or technique will prove effective if we are not fully present. It can also be helpful to mentally rehearse what we know of the client's experience (reviewing notes, memories, and communications) and to frame the questions we will ask in advance so we are ready to listen well.

Being comfortable with silence is an important part of mindful coaching presence. Moments of silence in a coaching session convey comfort, respect, and spaciousness for the client's experience. Feelings, needs, and desires can take a while to surface and become clear. Silence makes space for this to happen. Comfort with silence can be supported by an ongoing practice of contemplation or cultivating other mindful moments throughout the day.

To some extent, mindfulness reflects how we care for and carry ourselves. There are many strategies that we can use to cultivate mindfulness. These are but a few that are a good place to start.

Strategies to Cultivate Mindfulness

- Close your eyes and take three deep, slow breaths. Notice your breath as it moves in and out. Breathing in and out through the nose is more calming and centering than mouth breathing because it stimulates and soothes the vagus nerve, the main pathway of the rest-and-recover nervous system.

- Stretch and savor the feeling of stretching.

- Set a timer for one minute. Close your eyes and become aware of your breathing. Become aware of the places where your body touches and is supported by your chair and the floor. Become aware of the sounds in your environment.

- As you walk to meet with your coachee, choose to walk mindfully. Notice your feet striking the ground. Notice the movement of your limbs. Notice the weight of anything you might be carrying.

- Set aside your papers; turn away from your computer, tablet, or phone; and look out the window, noting whatever physical or emotional sensations come up in response.

- Say out loud any of the following statements, letting their message sink in:
  - I am grateful for this opportunity to connect and make a difference.
  - I intend to evoke trust, rapport, and positive energy.
  - I have an opportunity to make a pivotal contribution.
  - I am open to and curious about what will unfold.

- Ask yourself any of the following questions:
  - Where am I?
  - What is going on around me?
  - What do I notice that is unexpected or surprising?
  - What am I thinking about?
  - What am I feeling?
  - How can I enhance my experience of coaching?

- Smile as you recall your coaching client's signature strengths and contributions.

- Do whatever other activities bring you into the present moment and prepare you for coaching. (Adapted from Moore, Tschannen-Moran, & Jackson, 2015)

Whichever rituals work, the key is to practice these activities routinely in advance of coaching sessions and at other times throughout the day. Starting and ending each day with rituals of silent reflection, meditation, appreciation, and/or respiration are great patterns for coaches to adopt and follow. Simple actions throughout the day, like turning aside from electronics and stepping back from work to find a quiet place, looking out the window, or going for a walk, are also helpful habits to develop and practice on a routine basis. Regardless of their duration, such breaks give coaches time to connect with mindfulness. Even small timeouts can make a big difference. The key is for coaches not only to understand the value of mindfulness but also to experience that value through daily visits to the eye of the storm. The richer our experience with mindfulness, the more impact it will have on our coaching presence.

Using your five senses in mindfulness practice helps to get you into the present moment. When you pin your awareness to exactly what is happening in the present moment via your five senses, you get out of your head. Your thoughts slow or stop, and that feels calming. Being fully present, that elusive sixth sense is welcomed in. You hear a laugh that sounds like a cry, that sounds like yearning; you see a smile that is tinged with regret; you notice a posture that looks brave and confident but sense insecurity and hopelessness in the tiny slump of the shoulder; or hear a catch in the throat and understand that with a little support you can encourage someone to find their voice. You sense the fear or the longing or the confusion as well as the clarity when it arrives. In this way, coaching presence expands beyond the five senses.

—Donni, Special Education Consultant

FOSTERING TRUST AND RAPPORT

Without a solid foundation of trust and rapport, no coaching alliance can generate a productive and fulfilling change process. It is the key to the success not only of individual clients but also of the schools and districts they lead. The dynamic of one generative coaching relationship can be contagious. It can make everyone more sensitive to the many ways in which trust matters. Establishing such an alliance can be especially challenging when we have been assigned to coach struggling leaders. They already know, or think they know, why we are there: to make them do things they do not want to do in ways they do not want to do them. They start to worry that working with a coach is a remedial punishment rather than an exciting opportunity. As a result, their defenses may go up and their openness to change may go down. In such settings, the trustworthy presence of an evocative coach becomes all the more important.

Trust has paradoxically been likened to both a lubricant and a glue. It creates conditions for the social cohesiveness necessary to a high-functioning organization, and it also facilitates smooth functioning and the ease and efficiency of getting things done (Tschannen-Moran, 2014). More than two decades of research on the impact of trust on the work of schools supports why the person-centered, no-fault, strengths-based approach of evocative coaching is so important. We define trust as the "willingness to be vulnerable to another based on the confidence that the other is benevolent, honest, open, reliable, and competent" (Tschannen-Moran, 2014, p. 19–20). Trust is a matter of feeling at ease in a situation of interdependence in which important outcomes depend upon the contribution of others. To work effectively together, coaches and clients are necessarily open and vulnerable with one another, which makes trust essential. Evocative coaches understand the importance of these five qualities and make use of them in every interaction with a client.

BENEVOLENCE

Perhaps the most essential ingredient in establishing trust and rapport in a coaching relationship is a sense of caring or benevolence. Coaches who hope to earn the trust of educational leaders need to demonstrate goodwill and genuine concern for the well-being of their coachees. In a coaching relationship characterized by benevolence, there is a sense of caring not just about the immediate outcome of the coaching project but also about the leader as a person and about the coaching relationship. Coaches show consideration and sensitivity for clients' feelings and needs. Benevolence enlivens the coaching relationship with a sense of warmth, which generates full engagement. It is a contagious quality of being that invigorates conversations, relationships, and circumstances. When people warm up to each other, their energy elevates, new ideas emerge, and new possibilities are generated.

Evocative coaching requires a judgment-free environment. Safety and a strong sense of support, which are preconditions for success in all coaching sessions, are especially important when clients are challenged to stretch to the limits of their abilities. Establishing such an environment enables clients to be open and authentic so that important things can be said and considered. The caring or benevolence required in trust has also been described as "unconditional positive regard" (Rogers, 1989, p. 62), or as being completely accepting toward another person without reservations. Without such empathic support and understanding, the coaching alliance will be weak and unsuccessful. Judgment, criticism, and contempt—spoken or unspoken—do not motivate or support behavior change. It is not our place as coaches to point out educational leaders' shortcomings and teach them a better way. Rather, we are called to champion their strengths and invite them to figure out a better way. When we believe in coachees and hold them in positive regard—regardless of what they do or do not accomplish—we establish a relationship that can bolster self-efficacy and confidence.

HONESTY

Honesty is not only the best policy, it is the *only* policy when it comes to coaching. Through straightforward inquiries and honest reflections, evocative coaches build authentic and meaningful relationships. Evocative coaches have a genuine and humble way of stepping up to the plate and making conversations real. We boldly and yet gently express our observations and distinctive reflections without sounding critical or judgmental because we steep ourselves in compassion, empathy, and appreciation. We have a fearless, conversational prowess that shakes things loose and stirs things up without blaming, violating, or demeaning people. Respectful and genuine interactions with our coachees can promote the change they seek.

Honesty concerns a person's integrity and authenticity. Integrity is the perceived match between the values people express in words and those they express through action. When a person says one thing but does another, trust is compromised. In an effort to please or to avoid conflict, coaches will sometimes be tempted to be less than completely honest and up-front with clients. We may also be tempted to promise things we cannot fully deliver in a timely fashion. The revelation of such apparent dishonesties may be more damaging to trust than lapses in other facets of trust because it is read as an indictment of the coach's character. Once a coach has been caught in a lie and the client has lost faith in the word of the coach, trust can be difficult to reestablish because the communication process itself is now suspect.

Perhaps the most challenging way of being for many coaches involves the courage required for authenticity. The word *courage* may conjure up images of conflict and tough talk. But being courageous is about naming what is there in order to increase client awareness, create connection, and generate movement. Approaching coachees with courage and authenticity may be challenging at first. As long as we stay with accurate observations, free from evaluations, and honestly reflect a judgment-free understanding of what we are experiencing and seeing, we enable clients to gain new awareness and understanding of who they are and what they are facing. As a result, coachees can muster the courage to more fully meet their needs. By shining a light on what "wants to be said" by noticing carefully what is actually happening, coaches can move coachees forward in dynamic and powerful ways.

OPENNESS

Openness is a process by which people make themselves vulnerable to others by sharing information, influence, and control. Creating the conditions in which coachees openly share stories, feelings, needs, and ideas is essential for the coaching relationship to be successful. In taking the initiative to extend trust by engaging in acts of openness, evocative coaches can induce the same dynamic in coachees. When coaches exchange thoughts and ideas freely with clients, coachees are more likely to become open and willing to share their thoughts, feelings, and ideas with their coach. This initiates an upward spiral of trust in the coaching relationship. Personal disclosure on the part of the coach is appropriate and valuable when it serves the best interests of the client and the coaching program. It becomes counterproductive, however, when the conversation ends up revolving around the feelings and needs of the coach rather than the coachee. As coaches, we must carefully discern if and when to share who we are, how we came to our coaching role, what our victories and struggles have been, and what we know and do not know about educational leadership.

Some clients may initially be intimidated or uncomfortable about personal disclosure. To allay those fears, evocative coaches establish from the very beginning the safety of the coaching space as well as the parameters of coaching confidentiality. It is important to assure clients that we respect their right to privacy and that no information will be shared with others without the prior permission or knowledge of the coachee. We are fundamentally prudent in the protection of those rights within the limits of institutional regulations and the law. As a general rule, we commit to not sharing concerns with a supervisor unless we perceive that something illegal or unethical is going on, in which case we share those concerns with the client before making them known to the supervisor. Such clarifications represent the ethical foundation of coaching, and the coach should make this clear both orally and in writing.

RELIABILITY

For coaches to garner trust, we must demonstrate consistency in our behaviors so coachees are confident they can count on us in their time of need. In a situation of interdependence, when something is required from another person, reliability implies you can depend on the person to do what is expected without investing energy worrying whether they will come through or in making mental provisions as to how to manage the situation in case the person lets you down. Trust is compromised by broken promises. That is why evocative coaches are careful to monitor and select their words carefully, both during coaching sessions and in communications between sessions. Some promises, such as being on time, ready, and available for coaching appointments, are unspoken parts of the coaching agreement. Other promises, such as sending coachees information, are offered in the course of conversation. If the coach fails to follow through on promises, has trouble managing his or her time, gets distracted easily, or otherwise demonstrates a lack of reliability, trust will be damaged. Clients may conclude that their coach is a nice person and means well, and even that he or she is very capable and helpful, but nonetheless withhold the trust that is essential for coaching to be successful. Therefore, evocative coaches seek always to underpromise and overdeliver on promises.

COMPETENCE

When it comes to building trust, evocative coaches demonstrate change management expertise, which means we set aside our leadership expertise in order to facilitate the natural process of discovery learning in our clients. In this sense, coaching competence means giving less advice so educational leaders can figure out their own ways of working more effectively. It means slowing down, paying full attention, and asking good questions. If coaches are in a hurry to get down to business or to tell clients what they ought to do, trust and rapport will be compromised. As a result, progress will be impeded or blocked altogether. Evocative coaches demonstrate competence by slowing down to listen well. The press for results does not trick us into hurrying through the coaching process. Discovery learning requires that we slow down. It is not possible to do these things in a hurry. They take time and patience. We have to be quiet to hear what people are saying and, perhaps, to hear what they do not yet know how to express. By listening well, evocative coaches empower people to become more deeply aware of and connected to what they are trying to say. That is the very point at which learning becomes accelerated. In the hectic world of schools, we often think we have no time for such powerful listening. We may think it will save time to just tell people what to do and how to do it, but this may well end up taking more time because these solutions seldom stick. Evocative coaches get results more quickly precisely because of how we connect with clients using a calm, confident energy that generates willingness, openness, and excitement. We cannot be good listeners when we feel impatient and rushed. We cannot discover new wisdom and truth when our agenda takes us through life at warp speed.

In addition to slowing down, evocative coaches also pay full attention. Trust and rapport are not built through multitasking. We cannot pay full attention when we have other things on our mind. Trying to do two things at once may cause us to lose strands of the conversation and may degrade the quality of our inquiries and reflections. When coaches are distracted, whether physically, intellectually, emotionally, or spiritually, the coaching relationship suffers. Clients can tell when coaches are not 100% present because our energy becomes less focused and engaging. They may accept this low level of focus and engagement since it is so common in modern culture. It is up to the coach, therefore, to take the conversation to a higher level by paying full attention.

In conclusion, trust and rapport are essential elements of the coaching relationship. Trust is not earned once and for all. It is earned, or lost, during every moment of every coaching conversation. Without trust, the client's energy will be invested in self-protection or in assessing the available recourses in case of disappointment or betrayal. To free these energies for the coaching process, the coach needs to embody benevolence, honesty, openness, reliability, and competence in each and every coaching encounter.

In January of my first year as a regional director, the superintendent asked me to coach Caroline, the principal of a school that was on a downward spiral. He let me know that she was ready to quit immediately and said, "If you can at least get her to stay until the end of the year, I would be very grateful." When I arrived at the school, Caroline was waiting for me. She said, "Since you didn't send an agenda in advance, I have written down a list of things I want to talk with you about." I said, "I would love to hear all of it, but first let's just walk around the school together." As we walked, I could see that there was a lot that needed to be done, and I could sense in myself the desire to plunge right in to try to fix it. But I had to quiet that sense of urgency and remind myself of the importance of building a relationship first. I knew I could tell her what to do, but it wouldn't make any difference. Lots of people had been telling her what to do. As I invited her to share her story and the story of the school with me, and I extended empathy in terms of acknowledging her many conflicting feeling and needs, she began to trust me more and more. She let down her guard and we were able to work together to come up with some very effective strategies. She not only stayed for the remainder of the year but she went on to have a career as a very effective administrator.

—Jolie, Regional Director

HOLDING THE COACHING SPACE

To be successful, evocative coaches pay special attention to the quality of the dynamics between coach and client. Coachees resonate in response to the way the coach comes across. It is the coach's job to hold open the interpersonal space in which the work of coaching takes place. A key element in that space is the flow of energy and emotion between the coach and client. When we are connected in life-giving ways, the dynamics become those of calm assurance, playfulness, and openness to new possibilities.

One of the tasks of the coach is to create a safe and creative change space. *This involves a place that invites clients to feel safe enough to explore and disclose, and a creative place for brainstorming, playing around with ideas and options, experimenting, and taking risks.*

—L. Michael Hall and Michelle Duval (2004, p. 255)

CALM ASSURANCE

Evocative coaches exude a sense of calm assurance because we come from a framework of deep appreciation for the present moment. We respect the learning process that is unique to every client. Some clients immediately seize new opportunities, while others play with possibilities for much longer. Either way, evocative coaches respect the learning processes of our clients, conveying patience rather than urgency for change. It comes down to awakening and attending to what clients want, need, and feel comfortable with. Extending calm assurance is about assisting coachees to respond to life's experiences without catastrophizing, regardless of the situation. We learn to set aside those critical inner voices that interfere with feeling at peace with ourselves, the world, and our work.

Calm assurance is about steadfastly acknowledging a person's capacities, characteristics, and strengths for change. The mantra "My certainty is greater than your doubt!" expresses the framework in which evocative coaches hold the coaching space. This positive tone builds self-efficacy and fosters motivation for change. When educational leaders know that coaches believe in their capacity to achieve desired outcomes, they are more likely to get out of their own way and try new strategies. Such an endorsement enables coachees not only to get excited about the possibilities generated through the coaching conversation but also to move forward with one or more of them.

PLAYFULNESS

Although coaching is serious business with serious goals in which people are seriously invested, the coaching conversation itself need not have a serious tone. In fact, a consistently serious tone may cause coachees to dread their coaching sessions and consequently fail to thrive. Playfulness ignites our energy for and engagement with life. Both humor and curiosity underlie playfulness. The more we can get coachees to laugh and see the lighter side of their challenges and opportunities, the more they will open themselves up to change. Without the ability to laugh, especially in the face of life's ironies, incongruities, and adversities, one would seldom find the energy for exploration. Young children laugh many times per day; adults much less frequently. Laughter can leave us feeling refreshed, relaxed, and rejuvenated. Evocative coaches know how to laugh and have fun, and we invite our clients to join in that fun.

Evocative coaches avoid joking about things that may make a client feel vulnerable, however. We use empathy to distinguish between those areas that are ripe for humor and those that may make coachees feel worse if treated too lightly. We make sure clients never think we are laughing *at* them. Laughing at ourselves, though, is fair game. Using humor and playfulness in coaching energizes the change process so that solutions expand in scope, sustainability, and effectiveness.

OPEN TO POSSIBILITY

People come to coaching not only to learn techniques but also for inspiration. Most people already know, or at least have a sense of, what they "should" be doing to improve their practice. They just do not know *how* to do it consistently, and they may not even be sure that they *want* to do it. Part of the coach's response-ability is to maintain an optimistic stance toward what is possible. By anticipating the best, evocative coaches create the conditions that bring out the best in people. In spite of life's obvious challenges, evocative coaches radiate openness to possibility in ways that generate conversations for change. It is almost impossible for coaches who are filled with optimism not to infuse that energy into coaching conversations. Coachees sense and come to share our emotional state (de Waal, 2009). When we demonstrate positivity and openness to possibility, motivation and movement are sure to follow. In their book, *The Art of Possibility*, Rosamund and Ben Zander (2000) draw attention to "shining eyes" as evidence of people dwelling in the realm of possibility. The opposite of openness to possibility is residing in what the Zanders call "the downward spiral," where it seems that we are facing insurmountable odds and future options look bleak. It is the coach's job to shore up coachees who are experiencing the downward spiral and train their attention on positive options.

Connie, the new assistant superintendent of instruction, said her goal was to bring the district together, to get everyone on the same page, and to get all of the arrows pointing in the same direction. That was the theme song of our work together. To cut costs, the school district had left the position of assistant superintendent of instruction unfilled for eight years. In the absence of leadership over the instructional program, everyone just did their own thing. There was no coordination, no conversation about how actions in one part of the organization might impact another. Connie was especially frustrated with her relationship with the superintendent, Frank. She couldn't get Frank to consult her, and she felt like she spent all her time cleaning up the messes he'd made that could have been avoided if he'd talked to her before he acted. In our coaching, we worked on shifting the focus to the things that she could control instead of those she couldn't. When I asked her, "What do people around here really appreciate about you?" she came up with about ten things. Then I asked, "How could we give energy to these ten things and not give energy to the situation with Frank?" One idea we talked about was how she could expand her circle of influence by empowering others. She identified two people in her department, and we brainstormed strategies of how she could coach them to help her get more of the arrows aligned. As she watched these two people flourish, her own sense of satisfaction and enjoyment at work grew.

—Lindsay, Leadership Coach

CONVEYING COACHING PRESENCE

Coaching presence is conveyed in many ways, including body language, facial expressions, eye contact, intonation, word choice, phrasing, and pacing. When coaching presence is conveyed artfully, coaches and clients lean into each other with full engagement. This leaning in can be seen in the eyes and heard in the voice as one thing leads spontaneously to another. If one participant or the other is leaning out or pulling away, then something isn't working. It is time for the coach to try a different approach. Evocative coaches use all modalities at their disposal, including somatic and vocal shifts. Sometimes we move our bodies or use our voices to build excitement with stimulating optimism and energy. At other times, we move our bodies and use our voices to calm things down with soothing energy. Either way, coaching presence is conveyed not only by what we say and do in the moment but also by how we say and do it. We can help put our coachees at ease when we match their body language, tone, and rhythm, as in a dance. We do not copy their body language exactly, as this can be annoying and disconcerting, but we are in tune with it.

Although our metaphors and descriptions of coaching presence may sound superhuman, everyone understands that coaches are, in fact, humans who sometimes experience impatience with the rate of change or irritation at some of the attitudes or behaviors of the educational leaders we are coaching. This may be especially true if we focus on the educational experiences and outcomes of the students placed in the leaders' care. In these instances, the coach can step back from the coaching encounter, take a deep breath, grieve these negative emotions, and then reengage in ways that are *charge neutral*. Charge neutral means that our body language, words, and voice tone carry neither a negative nor an inauthentic positive tone. It is to communicate in a manner that is both even and direct.

When coaching conversations begin, we do not initiate them by focusing attention on reviewing homework from the last session; there will be time enough for that later. First, we seek to read, understand, and connect with the presenting energy of the person we are coaching. That is how we reestablish trust and rapport each and every session.

CREATIVE ENERGY CHECK-IN

Nowhere is coaching presence more important than at the outset of a coaching conversation. To get clients to open up, coaches have to come alongside them in terms of energy, emotion, pacing, and understanding. We have to connect as human beings. If we get out in front of them or behind them, coachees will feel pulled or pushed to do what we want. When that happens, especially at the outset of a coaching conversation, we fail to establish rapport and lose effectiveness. To avoid seeming in a hurry to get down to business, we begin each and every encounter with a brief check-in as to how educational leaders are feeling in that moment.

By using one or more opening questions, we communicate authentic compassion for and engagement with the educational leader as person. In so doing, we elevate positivity and readiness to engage. Asking "How are you?" or "What's up?" are common ways of doing that, but they may simply yield a perfunctory answer, such as "Fine" or "OK." There are far more evocative and creative ways to communicate a genuine interest in and respect for whatever may be stirring inside a coachee as the conversation commences. After setting things up by saying something like, "Before we get started, I'd like to ask . . ." coaches might ask, for example:

- If your energy right now was a weather condition, how would you describe it?
- What song could be the theme song for your day today?
- What color might capture how you feel right now?
- What object in your school reflects how you are feeling right now?
- What three adjectives might describe how you're feeling right now?
- How would you describe your energy right now, on a scale of 0 to 10?
- What's especially present for you in this moment?

The reason for setting up the initial check-in by saying, "Before we get started," is to give the client permission to talk about whatever is showing up for him or her in the moment, both personally and professionally. It expresses caring for the personhood of the coachee even as it recognizes the work of coaching that is yet to come in the conversation. By asking first how coachees are feeling in the moment rather than by immediately asking about or commenting on how things are going in their work or with their homework from the last coaching session, coaches gain insight into leaders' presenting emotional energy. If you don't ask, they may not share how they are showing up for coaching. By doing a brief initial check-in, through empathy and inquiry coaches can match whatever energy clients bring to the conversation.

COACHING PRESENCE IN
LATERAL AND VERTICAL RELATIONSHIPS

When a coach is internal to the organization and occupies a position higher in the organizational hierarchy than the coachee, evocative coaching can be more challenging. If the coach is in a position to both evaluate and coach the client, establishing trust and rapport will take particular attention. There is no way for coaching to be evocative if clients are intimidated or afraid in the relationship. To foster coaching presence while also holding a supervisory or evaluative role, it is important to be transparent about our responsibilities to the school system, to taxpayers, and to parents in monitoring whether educational leaders are doing what they are paid to do. It is also important to be open about the criteria on which they will be judged, the evaluation tool to be used, and how and when the evaluation will take place. It is also important to articulate how the intention and ground rules change when the evaluation process is complete and the coaching begins. Once these dynamics are out on the table, it is helpful to check in on how the client is feeling periodically, to empathize with his or her needs, and to acknowledge the challenges of being "under the microscope." Once such a human connection is made, greater openness becomes possible.

It may be easier to take a nonjudgmental, low-threat, and collaborative stance in the absence of the power dynamics created when one is in a supervisory position over the coachee. When coaches are not in the position to use coercive authority to "make" coachees do as they are told, their presence as learning partners can flower more easily. However, with transparency and the tools of evocative coaching, engagement and growth are possible even in relationships in which the coach plays a dual role of both supervisor and coach. One of the biggest challenges supervisors and evaluators face when it comes to coaching is bracketing their own power in the relationship. We may think we are just voicing an opinion, brainstorming an idea, or making an observation, but our coachees may hear our words as mandates or judgments to which they will be held accountable. In these situations, the coachee may come to view the coach as an adversary rather than as an ally. It is nonetheless possible to host engaging and productive conversations under such conditions.

It is important when coaching from an internal position within an organization to keep the conversation focused on the strengths and aspirations coachees can leverage for learning rather than on the weaknesses they have to fix and problems they have to solve. This appreciative approach is a fundamental part of the evocative coaching model. Such an orientation lowers the threat level, opens up clients to the coaching process, and elevates their readiness to change. It enables clients to have the energy, creativity, and confidence to develop successful designs for skills and performance improvement.

People do better when they are not governed, constricted, and tightened up by fear.

—Rosamund and Benjamin Zander (2000)

Mentoring relationships may share some of the same challenges in terms of introducing a power differential into the coaching relationship. There is an expectation that mentors hold and will share their greater professional knowledge with the novices. Their advice may be quite welcome, but it can also interfere with the developing self-efficacy of new leaders and may limit their creativity. Once the mentor puts an idea on the table, the novice may assume that idea is the only "correct" way to handle the situation. Where the mentor takes too much responsibility for the learning and growth of the novice, the novice may become passive and take too little initiative for her or his ongoing professional learning. Mentors can use the evocative coaching model to avoid these dynamics and to engage coachees more fully in designing their own learning and development plans.

Peer coaching and collaborative study groups minimize the power differential, but they may suffer from problems with confidentiality and a lack of coach training if care is not taken when they are established. Studying the evocative coaching model with others is one way to stimulate thinking and conversation about how to be with one another in strengths-based coaching relationships.

The First Coaching Session

Although everything we have just written applies to initiating every single evocative coaching session, the initial session with any client deserves special comment because it represents the first, fateful impression of our presence and energy, of who we are and how we work, and of what our agenda is with that coachee. It is important to start off the coaching relationship on the right foot. Through the way we initiate the first coaching session, coachees will decide whether or not we can become trustworthy partners in their professional development. The conversation will most likely include an open yet brief disclosure of our background, our intentions, and how we work with people, as well as discussion of our passion for coaching, learning, and supporting the work of educators. "What more do you want to know about me?" is a great way to end an introduction and to invite questions that build rapport.

It is important to clarify expectations around the understanding that evocative coaches do not come in as experts to tell educational leaders how to do things right; they come in as partners to ask questions and cocreate designs. We are not "answer people," we are "question people." We are not showing up to observe and evaluate clients, to identify and fix their problems, or to tell them what to do. We are facilitating discovery that will enable them to reach their goals and develop themselves professionally. If educational leaders think we have the answers and are there to solve their problems, then they can sit back and relax. They do not have to work very hard or take full responsibility for their situations. In setting up the relationship, then, evocative coaches communicate the desire to avoid such counterproductive dynamics. We express our intention to engage with coachees as professionals who are already doing many things right and who have the ability to learn how to do even more things right. Most clients welcome this frame and quickly warm up to such a coaching relationship, to the many questions we ask, and to the creative approaches we take over time. We may on occasion make suggestions or share advice, particularly during brainstorming, but that is not our primary role. Our primary role is to help clients find their own answers and achieve exceptional results, even in the face of challenges. If clients still seem especially wary or troubled, we reflect those feelings and needs with a stated desire to understand them fully, to accept them right where they are, and to work with them only in ways that they will enjoy and appreciate.

Once we have a beginning sense of trust and rapport, it is time to introduce the coachee to how evocative coaching works. This is best done by as quickly as possible extending a story invitation that will get the coachee talking about his or her experiences as an educational leader in positive ways. That sets the tone for all that follows, including the discovery of strengths, the framing of aspirations, the assessment of opportunities and resources, and engagement in design thinking. In other words, the best way to explain coaching is to coach. Once we have coachees talking in this way, we have successfully initiated the evocative coaching relationship and conversation.

Key Points in This Chapter

1. Absent an evocative way of being, no tool or technique will work.

2. The most important moment of a coaching session is often the one just before it begins because in that moment the coach has the opportunity to adopt a mindful stance—to ready himself or herself to be fully present with the coachee and what is alive in the coachee in that particular moment.

3. Without a solid foundation of trust and rapport, no coaching alliance can generate a productive and fulfilling change process.

4. A key element in the coaching space is the flow of energy and emotion between the coach and client. When we are connected in life-giving ways, the dynamics become those of calm assurance, playfulness, and openness to new possibilities.

5. Coaching presence is conveyed in many ways, including body language, facial expressions, eye contact, intonation, word choice, phrasing, and pacing.

6. We use creative energy check-ins to communicate a genuine interest in and respect for whatever may be stirring inside a coachee as the conversation commences.

7. When a coach is internal to the organization and occupies a position that is higher in the organizational hierarchy than the coachee, coaching evocatively can be more challenging but is nonetheless possible.

8. Evocative coaches do not come in as experts to tell educational leaders how to do things right; they come in as partners to ask questions and co-create designs. We are not "answer people," we are "question people."

9. Evocative coaches see clients as whole human beings who can figure out for themselves how to be more successful once they find supportive environments and encouraging relationships.

Questions for Reflection and Discussion

1. What dimensions of coaching presence resonate with your experience? How do these dimensions promote mutuality and involvement?

2. How do you convey coaching presence in your everyday interactions with others, even when you are not coaching?

3. What helps you to get into a coaching frame of mind before a coaching session? What practices assist you to adopt a calm, open, and playful stance before a coaching session?

4. How do you nurture your sense of calm assurance during a coaching session and how do you convey that to the person you are coaching?

5. How open are you to possibility? What would support you in cultivating greater optimism and gratitude?

6. What's the difference between being nice and being authentic? How can a coach share perceptions and hunches without blaming or shaming the coachee?

7. Who could you listen to, with your undivided attention, for at least 10 minutes today?

8. What helps you to bracket the pressures of your position in order to attend to the quality of your presence?

Loop I:
The No-Fault Turn

FIGURE I.1 Möbius Strip

Möbius strips are fascinating creations with an ancient history. Although named after the German mathematician and theoretical astronomer August Ferdinand Möbius (1790–1868), who was one of two people to discover its unique characteristics in 1858 (the other being Johann Listing, another German mathematician), variations on the design date back more than 4,000 years to the early alchemists of ancient Alexandria, Egypt. The design has fascinated people throughout time. A Möbius strip is a two-dimensional object in three-dimensional space. It has only one side and an edge. To create one, take a strip of paper and give one end a half-twist before attaching it to the other end. Now trace the center seam with a pencil and you will end up back where you started, having covered the entire surface. Cut along that seam and the Möbius strip does something else that is unexpected. Cut the strip along a line just one quarter of the way across the width of the strip and it turns out differently again!

Those mysterious properties are exactly what drew us to the Möbius strip as a model for the evocative coaching process. It reflects the human quest for continuity and infinity within the bounds of space and time. When coaches and coachees meet, it appears that two separate people, with two separate perspectives, are talking and working together. In actuality, they are sharing one experience. Evocative coaching facilitates an interconnected and intertwined mode of existence. We want to bring something new into being, but we can do this only through relationship. The coach is not in relationship without the client, and the client is not in relationship without the coach. Together, they form one relationship with one experience, looking to create new possibilities. So we start with the no-fault turn, where relationships can emerge and flourish. Once the no-fault turn has begun to work its magic, we can trace that line around the Möbius strip to explore new territory through appreciation and design. And then we come back to listening and empathy, at which point a new round of the dynamic dance of evocative coaching starts all over again.

The first two steps in the dynamic dance of evocative coaching, story listening and expressing empathy, represent the no-fault turn, the opening turn or loop of our Möbius strip model. Although they are presented individually as distinct steps, in reality they are inextricably intertwined and constantly cocreated. Coachees share their stories in conversation with coaches, revealing their understandings, energies, and emotions in the process. Coaches then respond with listening and empathy. Back and forth these two steps go, in iterative fashion, until they become generative. When clients feel heard in this way, it opens up both the potential and movement of the conversation. When story listening and expressing empathy are done fully and well, it naturally turns the conversation in the direction of appreciative inquiry and design thinking.

There's no way to rush through building the trust and rapport that expands awareness and facilitates the readiness for change. We just have to let it happen in its own good time. We take this approach because skill-building means little unless coachees are first open and receptive to what coaching has to offer. We also take this approach because we know that in the end educational leaders must always figure things out for themselves, even when they are implementing mandates from above. They are the ones who have to make things work, and no one can do it for them. By communicating our trust in our coachees' abilities, we bolster their motivation and increase the probability that the answers they come up with will actually work.

The no-fault turn pivots around the trustworthy presence of the coach and the quality of the coaching relationship. Although evocative coaches facilitate dialogue with many interesting, creative conversational techniques, how we engage with clients in the moment makes all the difference in the world. When our presence and connection are vital and life-giving, when our energy and orientation are respectful and caring, then coachees will turn in a positive direction in response to just about any approach. In the absence of such vitality and respect, however, no technique can be expected to generate these results. By setting and sustaining the intention to understand and respond without judgment, blame, or coercion to the experiences and emotions of coachees, evocative coaches start their clients on the path to self-discovery and self-directed learning. Our presence invites a bond that can prove to be transformational.

Research points to four ways to build high-quality connections. The first is respectful engagement. Be present, attentive, and affirming. The second is to support what the other person is doing. Do what you can to help her succeed. The third is trust. Believe you can depend on this person to meet your expectations, and let it show. The fourth way is play. Allow time simply to goof off, with no particular outcomes in mind.

—Barbara Fredrickson (2009, p. 201)

If we want coachees to do the work of designing new strategies for performance improvement, then we must eliminate the fear of failure from the equation. Rather than failure, we frame outcomes that are less satisfying than we had hoped for as fascinating experiences that coachees can learn from and build on once they feel safe enough to try again. If we want educational leaders to risk considering new perspectives and trying new things, then we must listen to their stories and respond with empathy, regardless of how things work out. We never communicate a sense of impatience or ridicule. Instead we communicate a sense of ease, understanding, and discernment.

In every experience coachees have authentic feelings and legitimate needs. The no-fault turn brings those into the foreground so they can be worked and played with in the crucible of coaching. After having experiences that generate emotions, the most common way that people process those experiences is to look for the causes and decide what they mean. This typically involves making assumptions, evaluations, and attributions. In the process, we ascribe credit or blame to people and events, pigeonholing their significance in familiar terms. We function, in other words, in a fault zone that can shift with the destructive force of an earthquake. The no-fault turn changes all that. By creating a safe place where clients and coaches can work and play together, the first loop of evocative coaching puts both the relationship and the conversation on solid ground. Educational leaders become willing to talk candidly about their experiences and emotions. Instead of hiding their mistakes, pretending to know things they don't, stretching the truth, and jockeying for position, they let down their defenses and engage their curiosity. Instead of framing their experiences and emotions as problems to be solved, they come to see them as possibilities to be explored and embraced. Who else? How else? What else? A no-fault zone is a possibility zone. Once educational leaders feel heard, accepted, and understood, they turn away from their attachment to what is wrong and toward the possibility of discovering what is right. That is the energy coaches seek to facilitate through the first turn of evocative coaching.

As coach, my responsibility (is) to maintain a nonjudgmental focus, provide appropriate opportunity for natural learning, and stay out of the way.

—Tim Gallwey (2000, p. 11)

CHAPTER 3

Listening for Stories

The Story of Principal A and Principal B

Once upon a time, on a bright morning in early summer, Antoinette and Brad, both assistant principals at the time, got a call from the superintendent letting them know they had each been selected to be the principal of a Title I elementary school in the district. Both were thrilled to be taking this next step in their careers and to have the opportunity to make an even larger difference in the lives of underserved children. They were also told they would be assigned a coach to assist them to be successful in their new role. The coach, Cindy, met with Antoinette and Brad separately twice over the summer as they prepared for the upcoming school year. At these meetings, Cindy began by inviting them to share their stories of what had brought them to this point and what this opportunity meant to them. Cindy learned that Antoinette's passion was fueled by having been a child from a disadvantaged background herself. Because of this, she was determined to give every student the best chance possible for success in life. Brad had been deeply committed to providing meaningful learning experiences to low-income students ever since he'd worked with disadvantaged children during his student teaching. As Cindy invited Antoinette and Brad to share their stories, she also encouraged them to be curious about the stories of the teachers in their new schools and the history and culture of the schools themselves. She emphasized the importance of building relationships and developing trust before making changes.

Antoinette had studied brain research on the importance of the environment on learning, and she had a clear vision of the kind of orderly, serious learning environment she wanted to cultivate in her school. She was dismayed by the noise and chaos of students

(Continued)

45

(Continued)

on the playground before school and the challenge of settling them down once they entered the building. So she decreed that the students who arrived at school early could sit and read on the playground, but they were not to play on the equipment or run and shout. This caused grumbling among the teachers, who had not been consulted in this decision. Antoinette also wanted to emphasize the importance of respect and was bothered that the secretary, who had been at the school since its opening over two decades before, was referred to by her first name not only by parents but even by students. In the culture Antoinette had grown up in, it was considered a sign of disrespect for a child to call an adult by his or her first name, so she insisted that the secretary be called by her surname by parents and students. Parents rolled their eyes as they used the more formal greeting. As planning began for the annual Halloween parade, Antoinette grew increasingly ill at ease about the disruption to instruction this would cause. Finally, two days before the event, she canceled the parade. This provoked even more grumbling and eye rolling from teachers and parents.

Meanwhile, Brad had spent the fall getting to know his teachers and the history and traditions of the school. As he became aware of the challenges the teachers faced, such as missing or broken equipment and materials, he did what he could to remedy the situation as quickly as possible. He asked teachers about their aspirations for teaching and granted permission and resources to support their creativity whenever and however he could. When the end of October drew near, he was also uncomfortable about the loss of instructional time due to the Halloween parade and party, but he listened to his teachers and what they valued about the celebration. He allowed the celebration to go on as it always had that year, but he suggested they begin conversation about at least moving it to the end of the day the next year so it might be less disruptive to instruction.

At the end of the year, Brad got another call from the superintendent, this time to let him know that his school had been honored as a high-performing Title I school by the state and that he and a team of his teachers would be asked to attend the state Title I schools conference to receive their award. A year later, his school was designated a state-wide School of Distinction. Antoinette had a less happy meeting with the superintendent that spring, and she was informed she would be reassigned the following year to teaching in the adult night school. Antoinette was distraught and tearfully protested, "But this is *my* school. I was only doing what was the right thing for kids!" The superintendent explained that the school board members were tired of the stream of complaints they had received about her leadership. The main complaint, he explained, was that "she just didn't listen."

There are key lessons to be learned about the importance of listening in the tale of Principal A and Principal B. First, there are striking parallels in their stories. Both had compelling personal narratives about what brought them into education and to educational leadership. Both had earned the confidence of their superintendent during their time as assistant principals, and they were each given a challenging Title I school for their first principalship. Both had high hopes for turning their schools around. There are also important points of divergence. While Antoinette nodded in agreement when her coach encouraged her to build relationships and learn the story of her school before making substantive changes, her urgency to enforce the changes she saw as essential to meeting students' needs led her to proceed without input from teachers or parents. This generated discord and set up a power struggle that ultimately undermined her high hopes for the school.

Brad, on the other hand, appreciated the time his coach spent listening to his story and understood how important it would be for him to listen to the stories of the teachers he sought to lead. He also was genuinely curious as to the history of the school and where the traditions and rituals that were a part of school life had originated. Although there were certainly aspects of the school he readily saw were in need of change, he took the longer but more robust path, initiating a process to articulate a shared vision among the teachers and parents. He then worked to build the capacity of the teachers to be true partners in the transformation of the school into the kind of learning environment they had collectively envisioned. His efforts ultimately paid off and the school showed measurable progress in its outcomes for students. Antoinette, however, failed to genuinely listen to the stories of the teachers in her school and to understand the history of the school itself, thus ultimately writing a story with an unhappy ending for herself and her school.

The stories educational leaders bring to coaching conversations are at the heart of the enterprise. We need to invite them to explore their own stories as well as the stories of the schools or districts that they lead. For a coach who has been trained to listen well, these stories provide crucial information about the educational leader's values, feelings, needs, experiences, and thinking. They reveal who educational leaders are as human beings and what they think is going on in their world. Stories represent the currency of evocative coaching. They not only represent a down payment on the changes coachees want to make, they also represent the principal and interest that accrue over the course of the coaching relationship. Getting educational leaders to tell their stories and to explore different facets of those stories are the opening moves of any coaching conversation. Listening well is a critical skill for both coaches and leaders alike. It is the starting point for the evocative coaching model.

Great works of fiction and humble everyday stories both can open our imaginative eye. When good stories are shared, evocative images arise in the interaction between teller and listener. Such poetic language stirs and stretches our imagination of what might be true.

—Danielle Zandee (2008)

THE POWER OF STORY

In the last chapter we described how coaching presence includes careful attention to the dynamics of the coaching relationship. Evocative coaches are more concerned about the person than about the project. In this we take our lead from a key insight of quantum physics: *"Relationships are more fundamental than things"* (Senge et al., 2004, p. 193). If we fail to get the relationship right, then few things are possible. If we do get the relationship right, then all sorts of things become possible.

But what does it take to get the relationship right? First and foremost it requires coaches to practice listening to people's stories. People need to be heard before they can be helped, and stories carry the heart of what they want others to know. Stories have that kind of power because they are among the most ancient forms of human communication. Long before written languages were developed, people were telling stories accompanied by the use of gestures, pictures, music, and dance. After the sun would set, the long hours of darkness drew families and tribal groups together around fires where they would naturally review, rehearse, and recreate the days of their lives. Stories help us make sense of experience in ways that integrate emotion and meaning, facilitating movement, direction, and purpose. Stories have evocative power. Over time, our brains evolved to pay attention to the structure and meaning of stories in special ways (Haven, 2007). They are our first and still our most memorable and meaningful of mental constructions. The use of mnemonic devices by attaching a story, no matter how silly, is a useful tool to help people remember lists or facts. Once a list becomes attached to a story, such as "**E**very **G**ood **B**oy **D**oes **F**ine" for the lines of the treble clef, it becomes locked in our brains.

The default activity of our brains and minds seems to be telling stories, especially ones to do with people. The great advantage of this is the human capacity to "live" in the past and future as well as in the present.

—David Rock & Linda Page (2009, p. 107)

As cognitive neuroscientists unlock the mysteries of the human brain, we've come to see just how stories function in the brain as people make sense of experience. Our brains are literally hardwired to attend to and glean meaning from stories. For all its analytic powers, the left side of the brain is too small a canvas on which to paint a compelling picture. It takes engaging the right side of the brain to create the stories that explain our past, explore our present, and envision our future. Stories are a specific type of narrative account of a real or imagined event or events that feature characters who face challenges, overcome obstacles, and achieve important goals (Haven, 2007). Although stories have plots, the primary focus and reason for telling stories are the characters. Haven highlights five core elements of stories, listed here.

The Five Core Elements of Stories

1. **Character.** You need a viewpoint character to see who is doing the action and to gauge the relevance of this story to your own life. To do that, you need perspective and sufficient detail about the character to interpret his or her emotional state, beliefs, and attitudes. From these we can activate our "character" banks of prior knowledge and experience as well as our neural story maps to create meaning and relevance. Often, the characters in our stories become caricatures that make people out to be villains, victims, victors, or vindicators.

2. **Intent.** You need to know what story characters are after and why. Intent is composed of two key elements: the goal and the motive. What the character seeks—the goal—defines the story's outcome or *resolution*. Why that goal is important to the character constitutes the motive. Goal and motive reveal the point and purpose of a story and of every scene and event in it. Actions matter to the extent that they are related to the goal: a meaningful and fulfilled life.

3. **Actions.** As the story unfolds, you need to see what characters *do* to achieve their goals. You will assess the characters' beliefs, attitudes, and values by comparing their actions to banks of expected or "normal" behavior. Actions are the plot. In a story, you want to see those events—and only those events—that relate to a character's efforts to reach a goal because stories exist to explain and illuminate characters. Actions are embedded within a morally significant context that reveals a character's nature, and characters are held responsible for their actions.

4. **Struggles.** Struggles are an essential part of every story. "The cat sat on the mat" is not a story. But add a small change—"the cat sat on the dog's mat"—and you may have the beginning of a story. Struggles break with expected behavior. Struggles are actions characters take in the face of risk and danger. Actions make no sense and elicit no interest unless we see that they represent an attempt to reach an important goal. However, there are obstacles that block a character from reaching a goal. These obstacles may be conflicts, which are blockages created by other characters or entities in the story, or problems, which are blockages not created by a character. Obstacles may either be internal, such as a fight against oneself, or external, created by something outside the character. To establish context and relevance, we need to know that something is at stake. We need to be aware of the risk a character will have to face, and we need to see the character act and make decisions in the face of those obstacles and that risk or danger.

(Continued)

(Continued)

5. **Details.** Details—especially sensory details—about the character, settings, actions, events, and objects that drift through a story create the mental imagery that you use to envision the story and connect it to your own experiences. Details set the scene and provide a sense of authenticity. They also facilitate memory. Without details, stories are abstract and more difficult for hearers to connect with on an emotional level.

When coaches listen to stories, we listen for and assist our clients to explore these five core elements. Stories represent the raw materials that coaches and coachees have to work with together. They reveal what clients are dealing with, how they are feeling, where they want to go, and how they might get there. Daniel Pink (2005) claimed, "We are our stories. We compress years of experience, thought, and emotion into a few compact narratives that we convey to others and tell to ourselves" (p. 113). Although clients may express opinions or conclusions about these matters, their stories may reveal other dimensions. By noticing what stories are being told, and by getting people to work through the core elements of their stories, coaches have the opportunity to generate the insightful "aha" moments that lead to new possibilities.

Each story has three levels: the situation, the search, and the shift (Drake, 2008). Each level—the beginning, middle, and end of the story—presents an opportunity for coaches to engage in story listening. The situation gives us the context for the story and a reason for caring about what happens to the primary character(s). The search gives us the quest of the character(s) to deal with the situation and put life back in balance, as well as the underlying assumptions, mental models, and cultural forces that come into play. The shift gives us what happens to the primary character(s) internally and externally as things are understood, resolved, and appropriated. As coachees tell their stories, all three levels inevitably come into play. Drake (2008) summarized the role of story in coaching as follows:

> The stories that clients share in coaching conversations shed light on their efforts to reclaim, retain and/or reframe their larger narratives about who they are and who they want to be in the world. These stories generally reflect the inherent tensions between their drive for continuity (and stability) and their yearning for discontinuity (and change). At the same time, these same stories contain clues for what will resolve this tension and, thereby, lead to a new story about themselves, their lives and/ or others who matter to them. It is incumbent on coaches to have the pedagogical and practical tools to work with these stories in ways that are both honouring and transformative. (p. 67)

Telling stories is a powerful way for people to make sense of experience. When those stories are received by an attentive and caring coach with the wisdom to see their potential for personal and professional transformation, they become catalysts for change. When people tell a new story, they experience a new reality. Through telling and exploring their stories, people feel heard and discover new alternatives. By extending this invitation in the coaching space, coaches create the conditions for educational leaders to draw connections between the various elements of their stories and to entertain the possibility of telling a new story. In this way, through deep listening, coaches facilitate motivation, movement, and change.

Evoking Coachable Stories

It is not hard to evoke stories from coachees at the start of a coaching session. Indeed, they typically pour forth when we create a safe space and ask the right questions. Whether they be trivial or transcendent, tragic or triumphant, such stories paint a picture of what the client's experiences look, sound, and feel like from the inside out. People may feel especially vulnerable when telling stories about their own experiences because these stories expose what is happening in their world from their point of view. They reveal much about their understandings, feelings, needs, and commitments. Such stories are gifts to be received with care.

Although a safe environment is necessary for evoking stories, it is not sufficient for evoking coachable stories. A safe environment without the right questions will often induce clients to do little more than ramble, grumble, or gossip. Although telling unfocused, disassociated, or idle tales may release steam and feel good, it does not typically generate the kind of stories and energy we are looking for in coaching. That is why evocative coaches pay attention not only to setting the stage but also to crafting the script—asking questions that trigger stories related to client learning and growth. We want our coachees to tell stories that focus, empower, and engage their efforts to be the best they can be, and that takes a script that calls for both connection and exploration.

This is a recurrent theme in evocative coaching. We pay attention to feelings to navigate our way through the coaching conversation. When emotions are neglected or ignored, they confine the realm of the possible. When they are recognized and respected, they expand that realm. Evocative coaches appreciate how emotions generate motion, both in the coaching conversation itself, as coachees open themselves up to new possibilities, and in the coachees' work contexts, as leaders experiment with those possibilities in real-world applications. Coachable stories will not be evoked until emotions are acknowledged and accepted.

Stories serve as windows into the architecture of [our] psyches and the longing of [our] souls as well as the platform from which to build and express new ways of being in the world.

—David Drake (2008, p. 52)

On occasion, the initial energy check-in will lead immediately to a coachable story. That is especially true when clients show up for coaching with a lot of emotional energy around an ongoing coaching project. Most of the time, however, the initial check-in will simply establish an emotional bond between the coachee and the coach. It serves as the gateway to one or more follow-up questions that ask specifically for developmental stories. There is no telling exactly which questions will be the most productive since that depends upon many variables, including the emotional state of the coachee and the intuitive inklings of the coach. One thing is clear, however: Coaches can do better than simply asking clients, "How did it go?" That question invites an outpouring of complaints, opinions, and anecdotes. Although filled with energy that coaches can respond to with empathy, those are not often the best stories for fostering personal and professional development. "How did you grow?" questions are more likely to evoke coachable stories. Assuming that trust and rapport have been established during the initial check-in, "How did you grow?" questions invite clients to tell stories about themselves in relation to their goals, actions, struggles, and accomplishments through a different lens. "How did you grow?" is an intrinsically positive frame through which clients can view even the toughest of experiences. Such stories set the mood and form the groundwork for all that will follow in terms of empathy, appreciation, and design.

One way to evoke these fruitful stories is for coaches to invite coachees to tell stories about times when they felt engaged in, excited about, or challenged by their work. Examples of such invitations include the following:

Prompts for Evoking Stories

- Tell me the story of how you came to be an educator.

- Tell me the story of how you came to lead this particular school or district.

- Tell me a story about a time when you handled a tough situation well.

- Tell me a story that illustrates how your core values came through in an important way.

- Tell me a story that illustrates what you love most about your work.

- Tell me a story about an experience as an educator that taught you a valuable lesson.

- Tell me a story about a time when you tried something new.

- Tell me a story that illustrates what helps you to be your very best.

When coaching educational leaders, it is also important to invite stories about their schools or districts that lead to the same kinds of fruitful insights.

- Tell me a story of a time when the school/district faced a significant challenge and was successful in meeting that challenge.

- Tell me the story of someone who is considered a hero in this school/district. What are the traits this community values in him or her?

- Tell me a story of a time when a change initiative went surprisingly well.

- Tell me a story about a time when this school/district celebrated an outstanding achievement.

- Tell me a story of a time when an important conflict divided the staff or the community and how the conflict was ultimately resolved.

- Tell me a story about a time when the school/district was deeply engaged with its community. What was the engagement about, who were the key actors, and how did it turn out?

- Tell me a story about someone who joined the school community and became a real leader.

Such invitations sparkle with evocative energy. They transport people to a very different place than rambling, grumbling, or gossiping. They shape the stories that are told and the possibilities that are considered. These are the coachable stories that promote openness to change. They elevate motivation and prepare people for a productive conversation regarding what comes next. By inviting coachees to remember and to reveal the potential-laden dimensions of their experience, coaches communicate respect for the clients' experience and confidence in their abilities to handle new experiences. Such respect and confidence are crucial to the learning dynamic. When these kinds of invitations become infused throughout the ecosystem of the school or district, they have the power to shift the entire system.

Notice that all of the sample "Tell me . . ." invitations are in the form of open-ended inquiries. Ideally, more than 50% of all questions in a coaching session will be open ended. Such questions put clients in the driver's seat of the coaching conversation as they explore the fullness of their experience. Too many closed-ended questions that invite short "sound-bite" answers shut down this dynamic. It is hard to generate a story when an inquiry can be answered with a simple yes or no. The two question words that tend to generate stories in coaching sessions are *what* and *how*. These words seek descriptions rather than reasons. They beg for longer, narrative answers.

Although *why* is also an open-ended question word, it does not tend to evoke coachable stories. Rather, it invites analysis and can easily provoke resistance by communicating judgment. For example, asking, "Why did you approach the conversation in that way?" may cause a coachee to shut down and/or respond defensively. *Why* questions can nevertheless be powerful when asked at the right time and in the right way. *Why* is best used to explore motivation after stories are told. For example, after hearing a story, coaches can connect coachees to the meaning of their stories by asking, "Why did you care so deeply about that particular event?" or "Why did that touch you in the way that it did?"

At the heart of any good story is a central narrative about the way an idea satisfies a need in some powerful way.

—Tim Brown (2009, p. 137)

If clients are not opening up and telling their stories at the start of a coaching session, we have either set the wrong stage or asked the wrong questions. The stage is wrong if it is perceived to be an unsafe environment—if coachees sense they will be evaluated or judged on the basis of the stories they tell. It is also unsafe if clients sense coaches have a hidden agenda or do not have the time or interest to listen to their stories. For coaching to be evocative, we do not ask leading questions with an implied right answer, and we do not rush clients through the telling of their stories. We communicate a sense of spaciousness and a genuine desire to unearth and savor whatever the stories have to teach us.

Instead of asking clients to cut to the chase, evocative coaches invite coachees to tell their stories fully, teasing out the nuances and meanings that seem to be important to them. For all our interest in stories, however, evocative coaches do not force clients to share what they do not want to share or to reveal details they do not want to reveal. If clients appear reluctant to open up, if they can't come up with anything right away, if they appear to be avoiding a question, or if we do not think they are being totally honest, that usually says more about the stage we have set, the questions asked, and the trust established than about the client's coachability. It is best, then, to reset the stage, ask new questions, and connect with the heart. Check in on how the coachee is feeling. Find a different path of development to explore. Hammering away in the same vein for an extended period of time is counterproductive when it is generating resistance rather than curiosity and openness to change. If it is important, you can circle back later, reframing questions to evoke coachable stories in a particular area of interest once trust and rapport have been reestablished.

At their best, "How did you grow?" questions trigger a wealth of material that clients and coaches alike learn from and enjoy sharing together. "What has challenged and excited you since the last time we met?" is the basic orientation. Once clients start telling those stories—remembering something that went well or sharing something that they learned—they often gain perspective and connect with their explicit as well as latent abilities to make things work. There may not yet be any notion of how that will happen, let alone any specific designs, but an opening presents itself to consider anew the possibilities for change. When that happens, the foundation for moving forward has been laid.

As much as we want educational leaders to get to that place of integration and readiness, pressing to make it happen is generally counterproductive. Jumping to conclusions, making assumptions, or putting words in clients' mouths can damage trust and rapport and set back our ability to engage with them in designing experiments and aligning environments. To initiate coaching, then, we respect how coachees show up, what they are ready to share, and when they are ready to go deeper. If we get that right, if we ask that first "How did you grow?" question at the right moment and in the right way, coachees will open up and share what is in their hearts. If we give them a chance to express themselves fully, they will often run with their stories in surprising and productive ways. Such client-driven conversations may represent a shift from traditional training and development activities, but they enable coachees to move forward positively by taking charge of their own personal and professional evolution.

Relationship building is a subtle, unconscious dance between two partners, hinging on each person's ability to send and accept bids for emotional connection.

—Jim Knight (2007, p. 24)

Educational leaders may need encouragement to elaborate the details and dimensions of their stories. Sometimes when we make a story invitation or, later in the session, when we ask an appreciative question, coachees will respond with a truncated version of some event, a factoid rather than a story. When that happens, it is our job to get them to elaborate. They may assume that we do not want to know about the details, as if they are unimportant or irrelevant. Evocative coaches learn how to ask for details in ways that make sense. "Tell me more" is one of our favorite responses to elicit elaboration. Look for details as to what was done and what kind of effect it had on people. Ask about what led up to and grew out of an experience.

On the other hand, just as there are clients who are reluctant to share the details of stories, there are others who can't stop talking about them. These people are verbal processors and can easily take up an entire coaching session with their stories, never getting to the work of design thinking that is so crucial to calling forth motivation and movement. Elaboration is therefore a judgment call, like many things in coaching, as to when there is too much and when there is too little. Either way, coaches can move the conversation forward through speaking up with distinctive empathy reflections that show we understand and respect the coachee's feelings and needs. Most people who talk too much or too little do not feel understood. In dealing with them, navigating with empathy is the way to move things forward without coming across as either disrespectful or pushy. The longer we work with our clients, and the more trust and rapport we have, the easier it becomes to step in, tie off rambling conversations, and bring things back to center.

Story invitations are not limited to whatever design experiments coachees may have specifically agreed to work on in prior coaching sessions. A more general question, such as "Tell me a story about something that's gone well for you this week," enables coaches to connect clients with some positive energy even if their design efforts did not turn out as they had hoped. This raises the bar of the possible for the rest of the session. Clients should not, of course, be prevented from jumping right in to talk about their homework from the last session. But that is not how we phrase those first story invitations, and we do not rush to get there. We want coachees to elaborate on their stories of possibility and hope, wherever they may be found.

We must remember this simple truth: the human soul does not want to be fixed, it wants simply to be seen and heard.

—Parker Palmer (1998, p. 151)

ATTENTIVE LISTENING

The most powerful way to evoke coachable stories is to ask open-ended, positive-leaning, growth-oriented questions and then listen attentively. Attentive listening is one of the most important of all coaching skills. Multitasking is so rampant in the modern world that we have too often forgotten how to pay attention with both ears. We tend to listen with one ear as we frame what we want to say and mentally consider other things. When we listen halfheartedly we fail to experience, respond to, and grow from all that the other person has to share.

The first key to attentive listening, then, is to stop whatever else is going on, including the internal chatter and opinions about what "should" happen in a coaching session, and just listen. It is the coach's job to dance with coachees, not to drag them to a destination. Whatever may be going on with us as coaches, both personally and professionally, is consciously set aside in order to pay singular attention to the agendas of those we are coaching. It is a rare privilege to be listened to in this way. If we do nothing other than to listen attentively to clients' stories, we will have done a lot. There is evocative power in paying full attention in the present moment; such presence imbues ordinary and familiar details with new energy and radiance.

To listen attentively as coachees tell their stories means more than just clearing our mind, setting aside distractions, suspending judgment, and giving them our undivided attention. We also have to pay attention to what those stories are generating in the coaching space. Sometimes tears will flow, laughter will erupt, knees will jig, feelings will surface, and inklings will emerge. Once we understand that coaching is not about getting clients to do what we want them to do but about enabling them to figure out how they can serve their schools or districts better, we can attend to these and other such reactions without attachment to an outcome. The lack of attachment to an outcome, combined with careful attention to what is happening in the coaching space, transforms physiological and affective reactions into valuable grist for the coaching mill, giving us insights and intuitions that can assist us to better respond with empathy and appreciation.

In the normal course of affairs, people seldom have the undivided nonjudgmental attention of anyone, even for brief periods of time. Indeed, there may be no other relationship in a client's life where they are heard in the way they are heard by evocative coaches. That alone may account for why evocative coaching is powerful and refreshing enough to transform an entire school or school system. To have someone listen to you, with no agenda other than to listen, is a rare and beautiful thing. It can make a world of difference and a difference in the world. Listening attentively in this way requires coaches to listen quietly, calmly, openly, intuitively, and reflectively. It is what makes coaching evocative.

Listening is only powerful and effective if it is authentic. Authenticity means that you are listening because you are curious and you care, not just because you are supposed to. The issue, then, is this: Are you curious? Do you care?

—Douglas Stone, Bruce Patton, & Sheila Heen (1999, p. 168)

LISTEN QUIETLY

Listening requires coaches to shift into a relaxed and receptive stance. For that to happen effectively, it is vital that coaches become comfortable with silence.

Silence is an important part of every coaching conversation. As clients tell their stories, and as coaches respond with empathy and inquiry, clients will often pause to think, feel, or connect with their truth. It is essential for coaches to honor this silence, to be comfortable with pauses, to avoid interrupting, and to not intrude prematurely. It is a special gift to be with a client in silence, especially those clients who are introverted, because silence gives them time to organize their thoughts, feelings, and desires before translating them into words.

Once the ball is in the client's court, it is usually best to wait until the client hits it back. After asking a question, give her or him time to answer. Speaking again too quickly or rescuing clients from the discomfort of silence prevents them from making new connections, discoveries, and sense of their stories. Be prepared for the surprises of silence. Clients will often come up with additional details, new perspectives, alternative possibilities, and unexpected turns when given a chance to fully express themselves. Silence communicates both the coach's desire to hear what the coachee has to say and the coach's trust in the coachee's ability to handle the situation. It sends the empowering message, "I believe that you can figure this out by going deeper." Often, silence will lead to insights and directional shifts that coaches may never have anticipated.

After asking an evocative question, coaches should stop talking and wait for the client to respond fully. Honoring our natural proportions—in that we have two ears and one mouth—evocative coaches seek to listen at least twice as much as they talk during a coaching session. That receptivity is what validates emotions and invites stories. It may be difficult to do, especially when, as coaches, we are in a hurry or think of some value-added comment we want to make, but listening carefully, patiently, and deeply is essential to the work of coaching. Talking too much or too soon short-circuits the transformational power of clients' opening up.

> In evocative coaching sessions, educational leaders talk more of the time. To facilitate this, coaches take a WAIT and SEE attitude: **WAIT—W**hy am **I** talking? (Stevens, 2005, p. 161) and **SEE—S**top **e**xplaining **e**verything.

LISTEN CALMLY

A Swahili proverb, "Haraka, Haraka, haina Baraka," reminds us that "Hurry, hurry has no blessing." That is especially true when it comes to evocative coaching. Evocative coaching is based on a foundation of calm. We are not in a hurry to get anywhere. We value listening in its own right, not as a stepping-stone to something else. With the relentless pace of most schools and district offices, and the demands that come at leaders from many directions, it is hard to approach our client as if we had all the time in the world. That explains the value of those preparatory rituals. They may take only 60 seconds, but we won't do even that, slowing down and collecting ourselves before a coaching session, unless we understand how important such rituals are to the coaching process. The more rushed we are to get down to business—the more anxious we are to grill educational leaders on what happened and to tell them how to do it better—the more resistance we provoke.

If we do not have the time to listen attentively to clients, then it is not the right time to try to coach them at all. One reason for this is because of how agitated and reactive we become when we feel a sense of time pressure or time poverty. Little things irritate us that we might otherwise find fascinating. We may overrespond with an emotional charge in our voice that is counterproductive to the learning frame of evocative coaching. And we may end up talking too much. All this happens just by coaching in the absence of calm energy. To listen well, we have to listen calmly.

It's all about the time. We don't take the time to listen to their stories. You spend your whole life as a school leader with people asking, "Have you got a minute?" And the person asking wants you to fix it, whatever the problem is. Part of the job is in putting out fires, for sure, but your greatest contribution is not as a firefighter but in building the capacity of your people.

—Peter, Superintendent

LISTEN OPENLY

Attentive listening requires that we listen openly. We listen with genuine curiosity and an open mind because we are listening to understand the experience of another. We make no assumptions as we seek to appreciate a different point of view. In order to listen openly, evocative coaches suspend the judgments and bracket the opinions that surface in ordinary listening. Our job is not to filter and categorize what we are hearing as good or bad, right or wrong, but rather to understand the fullness and to appreciate the deep dimensions of the stories clients share with us. Evocative coaches can always find something to respect when it comes to educational leaders' stories, even when we disagree with their approach or attitude or we doubt the effort they invest in their work. When we listen openly, we establish the relationship on a very different basis. We grant that whatever the other person is trying to share, no matter how dissonant it may sound to our ears, is worthy of a respectful hearing and a considerate response. Legitimate needs are always at play in clients' stories. By suspending judgment and listening openly, we enable coachees to tell their stories fully, to hold them lightly, and to reveal details they might otherwise choose to leave out.

The posture of suspending judgment and listening openly is very different from harboring judgmental attitudes about educational leaders and biting our tongues. Listening openly takes place only when we authentically trust that wonderful things can always be found if we just know where and how to look. This can be especially difficult when we perceive educational leaders are doing objectionable things that do not facilitate student learning or a positive school climate. When coaches find ourselves in such situations, it is up to us to turn our attitudes around, engage our curiosity, avoid condemnation and ridicule, and sincerely go on a treasure hunt for a client's best qualities. That quest, in and of itself, regardless of what we find, can help to create a productive interpersonal space. Clients notice when we fail to take the bait of blaming and shaming them for doing things poorly. By holding clients in respect, we eliminate "the endless defensive crouch, which is, of course, the worst possible posture from which to learn" (Harry Spence, as quoted in Kegan & Lahey, 2009, p. 72). Listening openly has the power to transform situations and people because it fosters the possibility of discovering new ideas, new energy, and new life.

My first year as a principal, I was so excited, so gung ho to make a difference. When I got assigned to an underperforming school, I was just full of ideas for how to turn things around and to make it better for the students. But that spring, just after the transfer fair, my superintendent called me and let me know that over half of my teachers had put in for transfers to other schools. I was stunned. That was a really, really hard message to hear. It was clear that what I was doing wasn't working, but I had no idea of how to do it any differently. So at the next staff meeting, I called all of the teachers into the cafeteria and we put the chairs in a large circle. I said, "I want this to be a great school, and I don't know what I am doing wrong. So if you will tell me, I promise you that I will listen and I will do my very best to put what I learn into practice." They were reluctant at first, but one by one, they started sharing things that I had done that was making them so unhappy. And I really did change my tone and my approach after that. At the end of the year, I only lost a few of the teachers. That was confirmation that listening really matters to people so I'd better learn to do it!

—Elise, Head of Schools

LISTEN INTUITIVELY

The ability to get an intuitive sense of what lies behind someone else's experience is a fundamental skill of coaching. Stories generate reactions that are different from logical deductions or rational inferences. They are more like feelings or impressions that something might be the case. Paying attention to and using those impressions in coaching, therefore, means that we are listening simultaneously to the story and to what the story is bringing to the surface. The things that come up for coaches while listening to client stories, including physical sensations, visual images, charged feelings, spontaneous connections, and intuitive hunches, offer guidance as to what may be going on for the client. We dare not assume a one-to-one correspondence between what is coming up for us and what is going on with them, but we also dare not ignore what our intuition is saying.

Evocative coaches are not afraid to tune into the intuition channel, bringing imagination, inspiration, and integration into the coaching process. Those hallmarks of intuition assist coaches to better follow and guide what is going on in the service of desired developmental outcomes. Gallwey called this skill *transposing*. Put yourself in the shoes of the person you are coaching, he advised, "and ask yourself the following questions: 'What am I thinking? What am I feeling? What do I want?'" (Gallwey, 2000, p. 183). He wrote,

> [Transposing] allows the coach to have a richer picture of the three primary levels of the other person: thinking, feeling, and will. It is important, however, to remember that at best you are making educated guesses about how the other person thinks and feels. It is important to keep yourself open to feedback and new information, and to be willing to adjust your picture of the other person's reality. The purpose of transposing is not just to gain insight, but to be more effective in your communication. I find it helps me to anticipate how my message might be misinterpreted and to say it in a way that has a better chance of getting through. (2000, p. 185)

When we get this right, when we transpose someone accurately, fully, and compassionately, learning happens more quickly, easily, and enjoyably.

Albert Einstein called the intuitive or metaphoric mind a sacred gift. He added that the rational mind was a faithful servant. It is paradoxical that in the context of modern life we have begun to worship the servant and defile the divine.

Bob Samples (1976), *Metaphoric Mind:*
A Celebration of Creative Consciousness

LISTEN REFLECTIVELY

Evocative coaching conversations are unusual in that they are one sided and client focused. The point is to attend so well to a client's experience as to generate acceptance, appreciation, and authenticity. When coaches approach coachees from this stance, one of receptivity and possibility, clients will often figure out for themselves what they want to do differently and how best to move forward. They become interested in change rather than resistant to it. That is why evocative coaches spend so much time listening to the developmental stories of educational leaders. Such time is quality time. It is the seedbed out of which new shoots rise. It primes the pump for future plans and actions.

This stands in stark contrast to what might be called deflective listening. Here, instead of reflecting what we understand someone else to be saying, we deflect the conversation to what we want to be saying. Instead of listening to understand, we listen to evaluate, educate, and explain. We may even jump on bits and pieces of story logic with which we can argue and dispute. Such listening is driven by agenda. The wheels start turning as soon as we notice an opportunity to add value and make a point. Once we get into the mode of commenting on what someone has said, whether to acknowledge things we think they are doing well or to correct things we think they are doing poorly, we deflect the conversation to things *we* want to say, stories *we* want to tell, lessons *we* want to teach, and the sense *we* want to make of what is going on. Depending upon the assertiveness of the parties involved, conversations can become a competition for airtime rather than an opportunity for deep listening, discovery, and growth.

On Listening

When I ask you to listen to me, and you start giving advice,
you have not done what I asked.

When I ask you to listen to me, and you begin to tell me why I shouldn't feel that way,
you are trampling on my feelings.

When I ask you to listen to me and you feel you have to do something to solve my problems, you have failed me, strange as that may seem.

Listen!

All I asked was that you listen—Not talk or do . . . just hear me.

When you do something for me that I can and need to do for myself, you contribute to my fear and inadequacy.

I'm not helpless; maybe discouraged and faltering, but not helpless.

But when you accept as a simple fact that I do feel what I feel, no matter how irrational, then I can quit trying to convince you and can get about the business of understanding what's behind this irrational feeling.

And when that's clear, the answers are obvious and I don't need advice.
Irrational feelings make sense, when we understand what's behind them.

So, please listen and just hear me.

And if you want to talk, wait a minute for your turn,
and I'll listen to you.

—Ralph Roughton (1981)

Our job is not to comment on client stories but to develop them as if the coaching space were the reagent in a photographer's darkroom. The story goes into the solution and develops over time into a positive image. For that to happen, the solution—how coaches listen and respond—has to be the right mix of understanding, appreciation, and reflection. As coachees are telling their stories, coaches periodically check in with reflective summaries and paraphrasing in order to confirm we've heard what clients are trying to say. We offer our best guess as to what we hear them saying, feeling, needing, and wanting. Such reflections enable coachees to better understand, explore, and develop their own experience. By capturing not only the content of what educational leaders are saying but also the energy, commitments, and desires that lie behind that content, coaches invite them to go deeper in the search for meaning and movement in their story dynamics. By listening attentively, quietly, calmly, intuitively, and reflectively as our coachees tell their stories, we disarm resistance and evoke openness to change.

IMAGINATIVE STORY LISTENING

Once we have the gist of the story, it is time to use story listening to explore client stories in ways that expand the range of possibility. Clients do not always realize, however, that the stories they tell are not reports of the world as it is; they are rather recreations of the world. The map is not the territory. No story is ever "the truth, the whole truth, and nothing but the truth." It is rather a slice of the truth told from a certain vantage point, and the story that gets told creates impressions, parameters, and possibilities for coaches to work with through story listening. Joseph Jaworski (1998) captured the power of stories when he wrote,

> As I considered the importance of language and how human beings interact with the world, it struck me that in many ways the development of language was like the discovery of fire—it was such an incredible primordial force. I had always thought that we used language to *describe* the world—now I was seeing that this is not the case. To the contrary, it is through language that we *create* the world, because it is nothing until we describe it. And when we describe it, we create distinctions that govern our actions. To put it another way, we do not describe the world we see, but we see the world we describe. (p. 178)

Both the stories we tell ourselves and the stories we tell others not only determine the sense we make of the past but also create the way we experience the future. How we describe a situation—how we characterize the actors, intents, actions, struggles, and outcomes—determines how that situation is for us. We should therefore be both careful and intentional regarding the stories we tell. If we tell a story as a just-so story, explaining how a situation came to be, then our experience is circumscribed accordingly. Such stories may explain how the leopard got its spots, for example, but they do not invite the leopard to change its spots. If we tell the story as a maybe-so story, portraying how a situation might be, then our experience opens up accordingly. Even as we tell one story, we recognize that other stories can be told. The work of coaching, then, is to listen to stories as maybe-so constructions and to invite our clients who tell those stories to do the same. We are looking for new angles from which to appreciate stories and design reality. The more vividly we do so, the more reality takes off.

Listening to stories in new ways can be transformational. Instead of being viewed as givens to be accepted with resignation, they are viewed as propositions to be explored with anticipation and curiosity, opening the door to new frameworks, understandings, and possibilities. It is a form of empathy to play with stories as sources of inspiration and possibility, to imagine new scenarios and interpretations of experience. We invite coachees to play imaginatively with stories through exploring vantage points, pivot points, and lesson points. The limits of our stories are the limits of our world.

Those who do not have power over the story that dominates their lives, the power to retell it, rethink it, deconstruct it, joke about it, and change it as times change, truly are powerless, because they cannot think new thoughts.

—Salman Rushdie (1993)

EXPLORING DIFFERENT VANTAGE POINTS

We all know that each person in a story has a unique vantage point, but we often fail to do the work of transposing to understand, appreciate, and value those perspectives. Evocative coaches assist clients in doing this work as part of the coaching conversation. The first time clients tell a story, it comes primarily from their point of view. But most stories involve characters who are related to the client's path of development in both positive and negative ways. The more coachees can learn to see things from the vantage points of other characters, the more open they become to considering alternatives.

Asking clients to describe their experience from the vantage point of one of their characters, retelling the story from that point of view, is an effective, engaging, and fun way to try on a different perspective. So, for example, after a principal finishes telling the story of a heated exchange with a disgruntled parent, the coach might ask, "I wonder if you would be willing to tell the story as if you were that parent? Tell it in his voice and from his point of view, and speak to me as if I were you." Coaches can also interview clients while they are playing different roles to take them more deeply into the character's experience. Such transposing, retelling, and recreating often generate new understandings and possibilities for moving forward because of how the process engages the mirror neurons in the brain. To tell a story from different vantage points, also known as *perspective taking,* creates attunement, resonance, and shared intention. It changes the neural mechanisms of the brain in ways that facilitate the empathy and mindful awareness required to contemplate and construct new possibilities.

When Cheryl moved from a principalship to the central office as director of curriculum and instruction, she asked me to stay on as her coach. She was very task oriented and recognized that finding the time required for relationship building was a challenge for her. She was very direct in her communication, and her e-mails could be rather gruff at times. In the central office, she was not as bombarded with minute-to-minute demands, and she became more open to the idea of going slow (at first) to go fast (later). She got intrigued by the idea of leading by asking questions rather than doing all of the telling. Not long into the fall term, Paul, who had been promoted from assistant principal to principal in her old building after just one year as an assistant principal, handled a dicey situation in a way that really frustrated Cheryl. I queried her to explore what her frustration was about. Then I asked her, "If you were Paul, what would you be feeling and needing about now? What might have led him to act as he did?" That conversation really changed her; it opened her up to seeing situations from another person's perspective. When I asked her, "What do you see yourself doing really well this year that was harder for you last year?" she said, "I'm learning that I'm better at building relationships than I thought!"

—Denise, Leadership Coach

EXPLORING DIFFERENT PIVOT POINTS

Another creative and challenging approach when listening to coachee stories is to ask them to imagine how an experience might have turned out if one small factor had happened differently. When clients are willing to explore these critical junctures in their stories in the spirit of a "choose your own ending" novel, we call that *exploring the pivot points*. Clients may resist doing this since most people did what they did for their own good reasons. But when trust is high and judgment is low, clients may be willing to explore those junctions where things might have gone differently. What if they had chosen a different path or taken a different approach? What if they had understood the situation differently? What if one external element had been different or someone had reacted differently? Inviting clients to play with and retell their stories from such hypothetical stances, carrying the narrative forward as it might have gone rather than defending their position, opens up entirely new possibilities. It is important that the choice of the pivot point stays with the client to avoid the impression that the coach is pointing out, "Now, here's where you went wrong." When coachees are willing to play creatively with their experiences, they often shake loose attachment to decisions they made in the moment and generate engagement with alternatives they may want to try in the future. In so doing, they can discover new wisdom for improving their leadership skills.

EXPLORING DIFFERENT LESSON POINTS

Clients tell stories to make sense of their experiences and to glean lessons for moving forward. Stories can also serve as fables. The moral of the story is, in a sense, the reason for telling the story. Clients think they know what their story means. After playing with different vantage or pivot points, however, they may be ready and able to identify new lessons or takeaways. Those lessons were always there, embedded in the folds of the story, as it were, but clients may not have had the eyes to see them or the courage to look for them. All that changes in a safe space with evocative questions. "What else?" becomes an occasion for extracting new material and even an occasional stroke of insight. Asking what clients may have learned from exploring different vantage or pivot points invites educational leaders to go deeper and to see what else might be possible. The more articulate clients become about the many things they can learn from their experiences, the more open they will become to trying new things in the service of desired outcomes.

> When I have been listened to and when I have been heard, I am able to re-perceive my world in a new way and to go on. It is astonishing how elements that seem insoluble become soluble when someone listens, how confusions that seem irremediable turn into relatively clear flowing streams when one is heard. I have deeply appreciated the times that I have experienced this sensitive, empathic, concentrated listening. (Rogers, 1980, pp. 12–13)

Key Points in This Chapter

1. Once a connection is made through a creative energy check, coaches evoke "How did you grow?" stories from coachees in order to begin the exploration of how they see themselves and the worlds in which they work.

2. The point of story listening is to evoke a robust engagement with storytelling. The more clients understand their stories as explanations rather than as facts, the more they cultivate a willingness to change.

3. To evoke coachable stories, coaches ask open-ended, positive-leaning, growth-oriented questions and then listen attentively by listening quietly, calmly, openly, intuitively, and reflectively.

4. Retelling stories from different point of views (vantage points), hypothesizing as to what might have happened if different decisions had been made (pivot points), and constructing one or more morals of the story (lesson points) are all methods that expand the range and energy of clients as to the genesis and arc of their stories.

5. Having only one story to tell regarding what happened can become a self-fulfilling prophecy that confirms what people already know rather than inviting the consideration of what people might learn and how they might grow.

Questions for Reflection and Discussion

1. Who do you know who is a great listener? What makes them so? How does that listening make a difference?

2. What steps do you take to cultivate attentive listening in your life?

3. What helps you to be comfortable with silence? How can you best leverage silence for client learning and growth?

4. What are the benefits of reflecting what you hear your client saying, feeling, and wanting?

5. Tell one of your own stories in three different ways: change the vantage point, change the plot line, and change the moral of the story. What was that like? What did you learn?

6. How could you assist coachees to explore their stories in ways that generate new insights and innovations for moving forward? How can we make such explorations both fun and productive?

CHAPTER
4

Expressing Empathy

If schools are to become more life-giving places where students and educators alike learn and grow, then it is time to more fully put empathy into practice. Schools without empathy are schools without learning. There may be compliance and orderly conduct—there may even be measurable signs of achievement—but power- and fear-based organizations do not facilitate the connection, passion, openness, resilience, and initiative that real learning requires. Simply put, empathy facilitates communication, which facilitates change. In the absence of empathy, people are watching their backs, doing the minimum, defending their territory, digging in their heels, and resisting change. In the presence of empathy, people come to trust each other, to open up, to explore new possibilities, to share frustrations, and to embrace change.

When coachees feel understood, respected, trusted, empowered, and engaged by the ways their coach listens to and explores their stories, then new possibilities emerge. By receiving client stories with respect, appreciation, and understanding, especially the hard stories in which things do not go well and people do not feel good, we facilitate acceptance, expand awareness, create openness, and generate a readiness to change. This is especially true when educational leaders have a tale of woe to share about a seemingly unbridgeable gap between what they want and where they are currently. When clients are struggling, it is especially important that we connect with their feelings, needs, and desires in positive, supportive, and life-giving ways. The more a coachee feels "stuck" and unable to move, the more important it is for coaches to express empathy and appreciate the discomfort of immobility.

It behooves coaches to make empathy their way of being with educational leaders, both as an orientation and as a process for receiving and working through the stories leaders share about their experiences. Empathy points crop up at every turn. Handled adroitly, such moments can solidify the coaching relationship and advance the coaching process. Handled poorly, those moments can jeopardize everything.

> *When a coach empathetically listens to another person's ideas, thoughts, and concerns, the coach communicates that the other person's life is important and meaningful. This may be the most important service that a coach can provide.*
>
> —Jim Knight (2007, p. 43)

UNDERSTANDING EMPATHY

Empathy is more than the sympathetic ear of a caring friend. If empathy amounts to little more than agreeing with clients' approaches and commiserating with their predicaments, then we have not done much to shift either their internal frameworks or their behavioral dynamics. For clients to learn and grow through the process of coaching, we need a much more robust definition of what empathy is and of how it works. Empathy is "a respectful understanding of what others are experiencing" (Rosenberg, 2003, p. 91). It is the intention to "get with" where someone is coming from, and nothing else. Such empathy is more than a passive intention; it is an active skill that takes energy and practice to master. Empathy uses both emotional and cognitive awareness to connect with and give voice to what clients are feeling, needing, and desiring. It calls on coaches to suspend judgment, analysis, comparisons, suggestions, and the motivation to fix things in favor of connecting with what is stirring in that person in the present moment. A coach who is empathetic is curious without being demanding, interested without being intrusive, compassionate without being condescending, and persistent without being impatient. When clients trust that their feelings and needs matter and that their stories are being heard and recognized respectfully by their coach, a zone of new possibilities is created.

Empathy is about understanding and respecting where a person is coming from. Empathy differs from both pity and sympathy, and understanding the distinctions is important for the mastery of evocative coaching. Pity means grieving someone's experience and his or her circumstances. We may pity a person who has lost a job, faced unfair discrimination, or become seriously ill. Such sorrow can lead to charitable actions, such as giving assistance or showing mercy. Although helpful, these actions, which often stem from viewing and relating to people as victims or casualties, do not empower people within the context of a coaching relationship. Empathy is not about feeling sorry for someone. That attitude can undermine the self-efficacy needed for constructive change. Coaching comes from the framework of believing in the coachee's ability to learn from and grow in any situation. Pitying runs counter to this framework, implying fateful resignation.

Empathy is also distinct from sympathy. Sympathy involves identifying with someone's experience on an emotional level. The feelings of one person spread to another in emotional contagion. We feel another's pain or joy. Sympathizing with someone who feels angry, for example, means that we get angry on that person's behalf. If he or she is sad, sadness wells up in us as well. That is because emotions are intrinsically contagious. Although this dynamic is shared by virtually all animals (de Waal, 2009) and utilizes some of the same faculties as empathy, it doesn't engage the faculties of consciousness required for emotional processing and transformation. Empathy requires a conscious treasuring of emotions as the gateway to learning, growth, and change. While expressing pity and sympathy can be helpful at times, this does not have the transformational power of empathy. When we are empathetic, we say, in effect, "I respect your pain," or "I celebrate your joy." To do so, we recognize the felt sense of the emotion and appreciate what it has to teach us, no matter how difficult, painful, or confusing it may be. This requires us to cultivate empathy and to speak its language.

LEADING WITH HEART

Empathy is first and foremost a language of the heart. Although empathy proceeds from an intellectual framework—that respectful understanding is the doorway to growth and change—it must be embodied to become effective and durable. People can tell when empathy is not authentic. Empathy is not a professional mask that we put on for coaching sessions; empathy is a heartfelt orientation that we consistently come from as a way of being. Evocative coaches cannot be one way in coaching sessions and a different way in other settings. In every situation, we seek to understand people's motives and strategies for meeting their needs.

To say that empathy is a heartfelt orientation is not just a euphemism for sincerity. There are many references throughout history to the heart as the locus of a special form of intelligence rooted in the body. Blaise Pascal's assertion that "the heart has its reasons which reason does not know" underscores our experience that the heart and head are not always in sync. The mind does not consent to an idea until the heart internalizes that idea on a cellular level. Empathy is a case in point. It may sound like a good idea to accept people right where they are and just the way they are, but what happens when we encounter someone who doesn't work hard, who doesn't follow directions, who doesn't play nice, or who gossips about other people? That is when empathy has to bubble up from the heart; otherwise the head is likely to find all kinds of reasons for abandoning empathy in favor of more judgmental or coercive approaches.

The heart is variously described as a source of integrity, courage, generosity, celebration, compassion, mourning, and love. Others cast the heart as the repository of meaning and purpose. Such descriptions, it turns out, may be more than just metaphors. A growing body of scientific research suggests that the heart is a particularly rich locus of muscles and nerves that has its own distinct parts to play in memory and motivation. Paul Pearsall (1998), a pioneer in the field of energy cardiology, drew a distinction between the intelligence of the brain and the intelligence of the heart, suggesting the heart has an orientation around empathy, ease, and egalitarianism, while the brain is more naturally self-protective, territorial, busy, pessimistic, restless, and phobic. The brain, Pearsall noted, "compulsively sticks to the task of trying to win 'the human race'" (p. 25). The heart, on the other hand, yearns to make heartfelt connections. Those who seek to cultivate empathy in their dealings with self and others would do well, then, to adopt practices that contribute to and flow from positive heart energy.

THE LANGUAGE OF COMPASSION

When Marshall Rosenberg (2003) was a young boy growing up in Detroit, he became deeply troubled by the violence he saw around him. He made it his life's work to try to understand the underlying causes of violence and how it was that some people could manage to remain compassionate even under trying circumstances. At first, he conceived of violence as a form of mental illness, and he studied to become a clinical psychologist to try to learn how this disorder could be cured. But as he studied, he began to see the crucial role language plays and how the use of words could be the difference between inflicting pain and connecting with compassion. He came to believe that bringing more peace to the world would require making changes to our language structures. He called this language Nonviolent Communication (NVC), using the word *nonviolence* "to refer to our natural state of compassion when violence has subsided from the heart" (p. 2). This process is also referred to as compassionate communication.

The method works with four important distinctions. To express empathy we are encouraged to make observations rather than evaluations, to reflect feelings rather than thoughts, to reflect needs rather than strategies, and to make requests rather than demands. Gaining facility in the use of these distinctions can assist coaches with communicating in ways that foster empathy. Thus, evocative coaches *speak distinctly* when it comes to their empathy reflections with coachees. In common parlance, speaking distinctly has the connotation of speaking cleanly, clearly, and without muddying the waters with extraneous information. In the context of the NVC distinctions, it also means that we speak with a conscious and mindful awareness of the NVC model. Although the model is depicted as a set of steps with a focus on the language we use, it is more an orientation toward ourselves and others that seeks to foster greater understanding and harmony. This orientation can be expressed even in silence, without ever saying a word.

The model, as depicted in Figure 4.1, starts when we become aware of an emotional response in ourselves or another person (Rosenberg, 2003). This awareness leads to a choice regarding our intentions in the situation: Will we connect or correct?

We can proceed to engage in playing the game of "Who's right?" or we can explore the realm of possibility. Fortunately, even if we initially choose the game of "Who's right?" the choice of connection remains open to us at any point.

FIGURE 4.1   Compassionate Communication Model

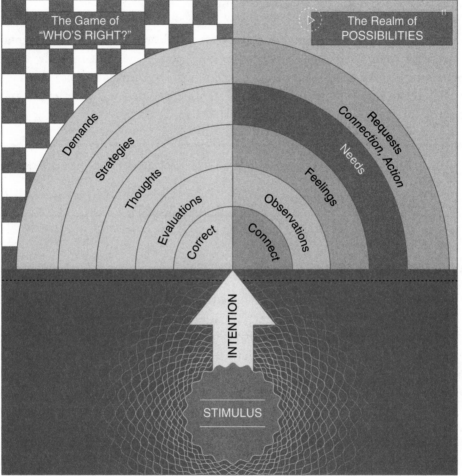

STIMULATING EMOTIONS

As clients share their stories during their energy check-in or the "How did you grow?" and experiential learning stories, coaches are alert to the emotions they reveal. These are access points for empathy that are useful whether coachees are telling their stories for the first time in the first person or whether they are retelling their stories from the vantage point of different characters, decisions, or lessons learned. Emotions are biochemical reactions released throughout our bodies in response to specific triggers that alter our physical state. Emotions are instinctive.

They are programmed into the deep recesses of the brain as patterns of stimulus and response. This flood of chemicals is unleashed in an instant, in less than a half-second, as we become aware of the stimulus. The effects can be seen in facial expressions and through body language, such as a clenched jaw or hands, flushed cheeks, raised eyebrows or a furrowing of the brow, widening or narrowing of the eyes, and/or leaning in or leaning away. Emotions grab our attention. Feelings arise later as we begin to integrate the emotion, think about it, and absorb and make sense of what has happened. Feelings are the cognitive interpretations of what is going on when an emotional response is unleashed. They are the mental associations and labels that we put to emotions, and they result from the brain perceiving and assigning meaning to the emotional response in the body. Feelings are subjective and are influenced by cultural influences, personal experiences, and beliefs.

Emotions play out in the theater of the body. Feelings play out in the theater of the mind.

—Antonio Damasio (2010)

PLAYING THE GAME OF "WHO'S RIGHT?"

Faced with a situation that has stimulated an array of negative emotions, and faced with the choice to connect or correct, we are likely to tee up a game of "Who's right?" We want to let those who have provoked whatever unhappiness we are experiencing know just how wrong they are and enlighten them as to the correct path they should have taken. Playing this game interferes with our ability to extend empathy to those we perceive as the cause of our distress. The game of "Who's right?" has four moves: evaluations, thoughts, strategies, and demands. We'll explore each in turn.

Evaluations. The opening move in the game of "Who's right?" is evaluation. Our clients may come to us filled with criticism, judgment, or blame, or with a diagnosis of their "opponent." Thinking of someone as an opponent in the first place is part of what sets the stage for these assessments. Clients may label those who have upset them as wrong, stupid, lazy, inept, rude, incompetent, ineffective, disorganized, or any number of other negative descriptors. Or they may diagnose them as hyper, paranoid, schizophrenic, depressed, or just plain crazy. They may also conjure up "enemy images" and make indictments as to the character of individuals. Such labels and diagnoses tend to interfere with the ability to encounter the other person with compassion. They make it hard for clients to transpose the characters in their stories, to view them as fully capable human beings, or to contemplate the possibility of real change.

Our clients may also play the game of "Who's right?" from the loser's frame, judging themselves harshly and holding up others as being right (i.e., smart, brave, successful, cool, or good). They may share stories in which they hold themselves accountable for negative things that have happened. They may be weighed down with feelings of guilt and shame. This is where empathy, as opposed to sympathy, can offer a powerful way forward. It is not helpful for us to join them in the suffering that comes with such harsh self-criticism. We can remain calm and open to possibility because we know that there is an alternative to the game of "Who's right?"

Thoughts. Although the ability to think and to reason is at the heart of the educational enterprise, there are times when thoughts interfere with the ability to develop an empathetic connection with those we coach and those our clients lead. These thoughts have to do with making moralistic judgments of others based on notions of right and wrong and how we think another person *should* behave. These opinions may be based on ethics and moral principles, policies, standards, norms, cultural traditions, upbringing, or ideas of good manners and proper etiquette. We are not suggesting that we or our clients abandon these principles and standards but merely that we become aware of the ways these thoughts can interfere with the ability to extend genuine empathy to others.

Another thought pattern that is destructive to compassion is the notion that some people get what they deserve. Marshall Rosenberg (2003) called *deserve* the most violent word in the English language. When bad things happen to people we think are doing wrong, we may smile or even gloat, taking pleasure in their misfortune. This is antithetical to the energy of compassion. We may also think that we deserve good things based on our good intentions and actions. A sense of entitlement is equally damaging to the energy of compassion. Other thoughts that interfere with compassion are a denial of responsibility. We may think that another person made us feel the way we do. We may shout, "You make me so angry!" In so doing, we confuse stimulus with cause. Another person's actions may have been what stimulated an emotional response in us, but it is our thoughts that are the cause of our feelings. Or we may deny responsibility for our actions, claiming, "I had no choice." It can be challenging to adopt a greater sense of responsibility for our feelings and the choices we make, but with that responsibility comes a more robust *ability to respond.*

Deliberately setting aside thoughts of should and shouldn't, good and bad, or right and wrong can open the space for compassion and connection even between people who previously considered themselves sworn enemies. Compassionate communication has been used effectively in situations of intergroup and international conflict, across racial and ethnic differences, in instances involving religious divisions, and to settle disputes between warring gangs. It taps ancient wisdom, as reflected in this poem by Rumi, a 13th century Sufi theologian and poet:

Out beyond ideas of wrongdoing and rightdoing,
there is a field.

I'll meet you there.

When the soul lies down in that grass
the world is too full to talk about.

—Rumi (2004, p. 36)

Rumi's field is not unlike the rich interpersonal space we hope to create with our coachees.

Strategies. Strategies are the behaviors that we engage in to meet our needs. They are the actions and struggles that form the backbone of story architecture. For example, stemming from the need to make a contribution, we might tell our client about our experience in a situation similar to her or his own and how we think the current dilemma should be handled, which may lead to resistance rather than the kind of a contribution we had hoped. The stories that our clients share with us about their experiences are all about their strategies, some of which work better than others at meeting needs. When Dr. Phil famously asks his clients, "So how's that working for ya?" he is inviting them to think strategically and to examine the effectiveness of their current behaviors. The point in compassionate communication of making a distinction between strategies and the underlying needs they are designed to meet is that without this awareness, our clients can become attached to a particular strategy and strive mightily to get others to conform to the part assigned to them. This can be a recipe for frustration. Once we assist clients to recognize the underlying need behind the strategy, they are freer to explore alternate paths to meeting that need. They can then have greater equanimity if someone in their world is not going along with the strategy they first had in mind.

Demands. One way our clients can diminish the chances of getting the cooperation and support they need is to approach the other person with a demanding attitude. Coaches use a short quip that goes "You insist, I resist!" to remind us of how easily a person's autonomy needs can be provoked by the insistence of another. The difference between a request and a demand is not in how politely or sweetly we phrase what we want but in our openness to having the other person say no. According to Rosenberg,

> Our requests are received as demands when others believe they will be blamed or punished if they do not comply. When people hear a demand, they see only two options: submission or rebellion. Either way, the person

requesting is perceived as coercive, and the listener's capacity to respond compassionately to the request is diminished. (2003, p. 79)

If our client is prepared to extend an empathic understanding of what prevents someone from doing what has been asked, he or she has made a request, not a demand.

When our client or someone the client is engaged with is playing any of the myriad versions of the game of "Who's right?" it is what Rosenberg (2003) called "a tragic expression of an unmet need" (p. 16) because it diminishes rather than enhances the likelihood the person's needs will be met. It more often leads to stubborn stand-offs and frustration than to cooperation and creative problem solving. Whenever coaches recognize their clients are caught up in playing the game of "Who's right?" they are being handed an important access point for empathy. By the time people have been playing this game for a while, their level of frustration and need for empathy are likely to be high. When they tire of playing that game, we can assist them to revisit their initial reaction, to switch the intention to one of connection rather than correction. In connection, they are invited to marshal genuine curiosity to explore their own and the other person's feelings and underlying needs. In doing so, they lay the groundwork for a productive process of negotiation in the interest of getting everyone's needs met. They will then have entered the realm of possibility.

The Four D's of Disconnection

DIAGNOSE, judge, label, criticize
e.g., "The problem with you is that . . ."

DESERVE
e.g., "She deserved what she got." "I don't deserve this."

DENY responsibility for one's actions and feelings
e.g., "You made me angry . . ." "I had no choice."

DEMAND
e.g., "You should (have to, must, ought to, are supposed to) . . ." "You can't do that."

—Raj Gill, Lucy Leu, and Judi Morin (2009)

EXPLORING THE REALM OF POSSIBILITY

To change from playing the game of "Who's right?" to exploring the realm of possibility is as simple and as challenging as changing our intention to one of connection.

Although coaches can make use of the four distinctions in reflecting coachee experiences and reframing coachee stories, we do not correct coachees or instruct them as to how *they* should speak in light of these distinctions. Instead, we invite coachees into the realm of possibility simply by reflecting our understanding of what they are saying with the language of observations, feelings, needs, and requests, without repeating their evaluations, thoughts, strategies, and demands. We call these *distinctive reflections*. In so doing, we awaken coachees to the possibilities latent within them and within their stories. We honor their process, respect their autonomy, and evoke their readiness to change. Each distinction will be considered in turn.

Making Observations. The first way to reframe coachee stories is itself a form of story listening: We reflect those details that can be detected by the five senses (sight, hearing, taste, smell, and touch) without including any derogatory or laudatory remarks or overtones. It is more difficult than it sounds to simply reflect those details that could be recorded on a video camera. Our goal in coaching is to cleanly describe the situations coachees tell us about, reflecting just the actions or outcomes that can be observed. We do not want to communicate in a way that implies rightness or wrongness. What was actually seen and heard? If the coachee's story doesn't provide those details, we can ask for clarification.

This is quite different from evaluating client performance. When expressing empathy, we do not critique coachee decisions, strategies, and outcomes as being good or bad, right or wrong, correct or incorrect, better or worse. Such evaluations may have their place but not as part of evocative coaching conversations. To stave off the tendency to praise, criticize, judge, interpret, moralize, generalize, catastrophize, exaggerate, or assume is not a typical way of conversing. In order to speak distinctly, it is important to edit out our own evaluative assessments. Our job as coaches is not to evaluate whether coachees are doing well or poorly; our job is to communicate an understanding of what coachees are doing and what needs they are attempting to serve so they can make new choices if they are so inclined.

Making observations without evaluations is the highest form of human intelligence.

—Jiddu Krishnamurti

Guessing at Feelings. The second way to reframe client stories is to venture a guess regarding the feelings they may be experiencing without including their thoughts about causal attributions and evaluative assessments. Reflecting a coachee's thinking serves to codify and reinforce that thinking. It gives tacit consent to a coachee's conclusions and strategies. Reflecting a coachee's feelings is arresting in the most positive sense of the word. To be seen and heard on that level gets one's attention and evokes an emotional release that leads to trust, openness, and change. Learning how to make such reflections is an essential part of expressing empathy.

Sometimes it is easy to reflect a coachee's feelings because the coachee tells us those feelings directly. More often than not, however, feelings are mixed into their stories and garbled with a variety of positive and negative evaluative assessments. When that happens, coaches can either ask for clarification as to how clients are feeling or guess what might be alive in them. As simple as it seems to ask direct and open-ended questions about how our clients are feeling, that is not always the best way to explore, understand, and validate their experiences. For one thing, they may not be able to identify their feelings and needs. Coachees may struggle to find just the right words to articulate the emotional response that has erupted throughout their bodies. Offering an empathy guess or reflection, using a tone that conveys genuine interest, can communicate a clear intent to understand, appreciate, and value those feelings, no matter how difficult or troubling.

Empathy requires practitioners to maintain a stance of hypothesis, always checking with their clients to ascertain where they have accurately understood the essence of the client's experience.

—Dianne Stober (2006, p. 23)

There is real power in naming the emotions that have been stirred up for our clients. The list of feeling words depicted in Figure 4.2 can help coaches offer useful guesses. It can help clients become aware of what they are feeling and to receive the gift of being heard. Mark Twain quipped that the difference between the right word and the almost-right word is the difference between lightning and the lightning bug. Expressing empathy in this way invigorates clients when the right words are found. Even a guess that misses the mark can be useful because it often helps lead the client to the feeling words that *do* fit their experience.

The English language offers many convenient loopholes for disguising thoughts as feelings, one of which is simply starting a sentence with "I feel" but following those words with "that," "like," or a noun or pronoun that is not an emotion. Although grammatically correct, each of the following sentences expresses a thought or a judgment rather than a feeling: "I feel like a failure." "I feel that you should know better." "I feel she is being manipulative." These expressions convey an evaluative tone rather than a compassionate connection. They take us back to the playing the game of "Who's right?"

In compassionate communication, feelings are valued whether they are pleasant or unpleasant because they get our attention and invite us to consider what is happening in the realm of needs. An apt metaphor is the light on our dashboard that alerts us our car is getting low on fuel, accompanied by a "ding" that gets our attention

FIGURE 4.2 Feeling Words

FEELING WORDS

WHAT'S ALIVE IN YOU?

FEELINGS WHEN NEEDS ARE NOT BEING MET	FEELINGS WHEN NEEDS ARE BEING MET
HOSTILE Animosity, Antagonistic, Appalled, Aversion, Cold, Contempt, Disgusted, Dislike, Disdain, Hate, Horrified, Repulsed, Scorn, Surly, Vengeful, Vindictive	**EXHILARATED** Ecstatic, Elated, Enthralled, Exuberant, Giddy, Silly, Slaphappy
ANGRY Enraged, Furious, Incensed, Indignant, Irate, Livid, Mad, Outraged, Resentful, Ticked Off	**EXCITED** Alive, Amazed, Animated, Eager, Energetic, Enthusiastic, Invigorated, Lively, Passionate
ANNOYED Aggravated, Bitter, Cranky, Cross, Dismayed, Disgruntled, Displeased, Exasperated, Frustrated, Grouchy, Impatient, Irked, Irritated, Miffed, Peeved, Resentful, Sullen, Uptight	**INSPIRED** Amazed, Astonished, Awed, Dazzled, Radiant, Rapturous, Surprised, Thrilled, Uplifted, Wonder
UPSET Agitated, Alarmed, Discombobulated, Disconcerted, Disturbed, Disquieted, Perturbed, Rattled, Restless, Troubled, Turbulent, Turmoil, Uncomfortable, Uneasy, Unnerved, Unsettled	**JOYFUL** Amused, Buoyant, Delighted, Elated, Ecstatic, Glad, Gleeful, Happy, Jubilant, Merry, Mirthful, Overjoyed, Pleased, Radiant, Tickled
TENSE Antsy, Anxious, Bitter, Distressed, Distraught, Edgy, Fidgety, Frazzled, Irritable, Jittery, Nervous, Overwhelmed, Pressured, Restless, Stressed Out, Uneasy	**RELAXED** At Ease, Carefree, Comfortable, Open
AFRAID Apprehensive, Concerned, Dread, Fearful, Foreboding, Frightened, Hesitant, Mistrustful, Panicked, Petrified, Reserved, Scared, Sensitive, Shaky, Suspicious, Terrified, Timid, Trepidation, Unnerved, Wary, Worried, Unsteady	**CURIOUS** Adventurous, Alert, Interested, Intrigued, Inquisitive, Fascinated, Spellbound, Stimulated
VULNERABLE Cautious, Fragile, Guarded, Helpless, Insecure, Leery, Reluctant	**CONFIDENT** Empowered, Proud, Safe, Secure, Self-assured

FEELINGS WHEN NEEDS ARE NOT BEING MET	FEELINGS WHEN NEEDS ARE BEING MET
CONFUSED Ambivalent, Baffled, Bewildered, Dazed, Flustered, Hesitant, Lost, Mystified, Perplexed, Puzzled, Skeptical, Torn	**ENGAGED** Absorbed, Alert, Ardent, Curious, Engrossed, Enchanted, Entranced, Involved
EMBARRASSED Ashamed, Chagrined, Contrite, Disgraced, Guilty, Humiliated, Mortified, Remorse, Regretful, Self-conscious	**HOPEFUL** Expectant, Encouraged, Optimistic
LONGING Envious, Jealous, Nostalgic, Pining, Wistful, Yearning	**GRATEFUL** Appreciative, Moved, Thankful, Touched
TIRED Beat, Burned Out, Depleted, Exhausted, Fatigued, Lethargic, Listless, Sleepy, Weary, Worn Out	**REFRESHED** Energetic, Enlivened, Rejuvenated, Renewed, Rested, Restored, Revived
DISCONNECTED Alienated, Aloof, Apathetic, Bored, Cold, Detached, Disengaged, Disinterested, Distant, Distracted, Indifferent, Lethargic, Listless, Lonely, Numb, Removed, Uninterested, Withdrawn	**AFFECTIONATE** Closeness, Compassionate, Friendly, Loving, Openhearted, Sympathetic, Tender, Trusting, Warm
SAD Blue, Depressed, Dejected, Despair, Despondent, Disappointed, Discouraged, Disheartened, Downcast, Downhearted, Forlorn, Gloomy, Grief, Heavy-hearted, Hopeless, Melancholy, Sorrow, Unhappy	**PEACEFUL** Blissful, Calm, Centered, Clear-headed, Mellow, Quiet, Serene, Tranquil
SHOCKED Appalled, Disbelief, Dismay, Horrified, Mystified, Startled, Surprised	**RELIEVED** Complacent, Composed, Cool, Trusting
PAIN Agony, Anguished, Bereaved, Devastated, Heartbroken, Hurt, Miserable, Wretched	**CONTENT** Glad, Cheerful, Fulfilled, Satisfied

and gives us the opportunity to take action before we find ourselves stranded by the side of the road. Wonderful feelings provide a self-reinforcing feedback loop, saying, "Whatever you're doing, keep doing it because my needs are being met." In these situations, coachees may communicate contentment, happiness, delight, satisfaction, gratitude, energy, or calm. Empathy here takes the form of celebrating progress. Unpleasant feelings, such as anger, resentment, disappointment, confusion, dissatisfaction, worry, envy, embarrassment, or sadness, work as warning signals that bring attention to unmet needs.

I have never worked with a more negative group of teachers than the ones I encountered at Brookstone Middle School. They were just mean—mean to each other and mean to the kids. They seemed to take pleasure in embarrassing or harassing the students. They had burned through a whole series of administrators over several years. No one stayed for long. By midyear I could see the toll the stress was taking on Jessica, the first-year principal who had been assigned to the school. She was looking increasingly anguished. Her health was suffering and her family was suffering. She described the sense of dread that she experienced on Sunday evenings as she anticipated the work week. A shift happened in early February when the school was closed for three days because of snow. When I got to the school the next morning, I was feeling refreshed and rejuvenated from the unexpected days of rest. But as I looked around at the teachers, I noticed that they looked just exhausted. They were stiff, had sore muscles from shoveling snow, and were generally out of sorts. I wondered about that so I suggested to Jessica that we use the community of practice meetings that week to conduct paired interviews about their best moments in teaching and the core values that animated them. What we learned in those interviews was that most were managing heavy personal responsibilities. Many were career switchers who had come to teaching as a way to manage their responsibilities, either as single parents or as the sole means of financial support due to husbands being out of work, injured, or ill. Almost all of them were teaching out of a necessity, not out of a sense of calling. So it was hard to reignite a spark that had never been there in the first place. This gave Jessica a new sense of compassion for the teachers, and in our coaching we focused on finding more effective ways to engage with the teachers in light of their unmet needs. We designed a mini-experiment to find out what encouragement would look like for these teachers. She began to make inroads with a small group of teachers. I can't say that it turned things around immediately, but it began to shift things in a more positive direction.

—Mackenzie, School Improvement Coach

Guessing the Underlying Needs. What makes empathy possible is this essential insight: Human beings all share the same set of universal needs, and all human behavior is motivated by the attempt to meet those needs. Since the time of Maslow (1968), psychologists, economists, and other students of human behavior have sought to classify those needs and have created a wide variety of taxonomies. Although social scientists may not agree on the exact nature and number of human needs, they do largely agree that humans have needs, that needs must be met to sustain and enrich life, that needs motivate behavior, and that feelings are indicators as to whether or not needs are being met. When needs are being met, we feel good; when needs are not being met, we feel lousy.

Thus, a way to reframe coachee stories is to venture a guess regarding the underlying needs coachees may be trying to meet with their strategies. Strategies are always means to an end, and that end is the meeting of one or more universal human needs, as portrayed in Figure 4.3. We express empathy when we reflect those universal needs in ways that clearly distinguish them from the strategies coachees are using. Needs are essential; strategies are optional. Needs are universal; strategies are particular. Needs are beautiful; strategies are functional. If our clients don't understand the needs they are trying to meet, then their strategies may be inefficient or ineffective.

Needs serve the organism, and they do so by generating wants, desires, and strivings that motivate whatever behaviors are necessary for the maintenance of life and the promotion of well-being and growth.

—Ping Zhang (2007)

Such an understanding assists us to extend empathy to clients, even those with whom we disagree or of whose attitude or approach we disapprove, because their stories, statements, and behaviors can all be understood as strivings to meet legitimate human needs. Regardless of how ineffective the strategies, statements, and behaviors of clients may prove to be in terms of getting their needs met, the needs themselves are valid and authentic. Since we all share the same needs, empathy becomes possible. Noticing which needs have been stimulated and are either being met or unmet is a critical access point for empathy. Figure 4.3 presents an array of ten universal needs on a wheel diagram. The needs across from each other represent qualitatively different energies that may be in creative tension with one another. All of the needs are understood to be equally important and active throughout the human lifespan. None of us can meet all of these needs simultaneously, but when there is a healthy rhythm between them we experience vitality.

Ten Universal Needs

- Subsistence-Transcendence. The realities and possibilities of existence require us to meet certain basic needs to support physical survival. These include such things as sustenance (including air, water, food, and shelter from the elements); sensory stimulation; and health. The need for transcendence lies at the other end of the spectrum, but it is just as essential. It incorporates such things as a sense

(Continued)

(Continued)

of meaning and purpose, inspiration, wonder, creativity, and beauty. If we pay attention, we will notice that even little children evidence this need.

- **Safety-Challenge.** Children also make clear the need for both safety and challenge. On the one hand, they love to venture out, risk, discover, and test their limits. These challenges are all part of the trial-and-correction process that leads to growth and development. But they are also quick to run to a parent's side when they feel fear, confusion, anger, or pain. They need safety and protection. Throughout life, the competing needs for safety and challenge play out. Too much safety and we are likely to become bored. Too much challenge for too long and we are likely to feel stressed. Some personalities may be prone to seek greater challenge or greater safety, but we all need a measure of both.

- **Work-Rest.** It is perhaps no accident that a Hebrew creation story portrays God as working for six days to create the universe and then resting on the seventh. The needs for work and rest are universal. People can neither work constantly nor sit around doing nothing all the time. There is a rhythm to making life whole. People get into gear when they have reason to become active; they pull back and rest when they need to recover. Work incorporates such things as contribution, competence, productivity, and exercise. Rest includes relaxation, sleep, humor, play, mourning, and celebration.

- **Honesty-Empathy.** Empathy—understanding what is alive in another person—is not just a strategy for evocative coaching; it is also a universal human need. So, too, is honesty—sharing what is alive in me. Both of these dynamics are important and both take courage. It is not always easy to speak the truth. The same is true for hearing the truth. Honesty requires clarity, self-understanding, authenticity, integrity, and self-expression. Empathy requires openness, compassion, connection, acceptance, and love. Understanding the distinction between needs and strategies can facilitate both honesty and empathy by offering alternatives to guilt and shame as well as to enemy images.

- **Autonomy-Community.** By nature, human beings strive for autonomy and bristle when that autonomy is threatened. On the other hand, we are social animals, hardwired with instincts that lead us to seek connection with others. Autonomy incorporates such dynamics as choice, control, self-efficacy, power, independence, and freedom, whereas community includes a sense of belonging and a desire to matter, to be heard, and to be acknowledged, supported, and appreciated. These two opposing needs may be seen in creative tension between our capacity for self-regulation and being regulated by the norms, values, and goals of the larger system.

Universal human needs are often below the surface of awareness, but they are at the heart of life and consequently at the heart of our work as coaches. Establishing an empathic connection can help people to be more aware of and accepting of these needs. With this awareness, the range of constructive actions they can take expands. As coaches, we become aware of the generative value of connecting with the living energy of people's needs in a calm, safe, and judgment-free space. Regardless of how clients show up for a coaching conversation, having their needs acknowledged, understood, and appreciated will move the conversation forward.

FIGURE 4.3   Wheel of Needs

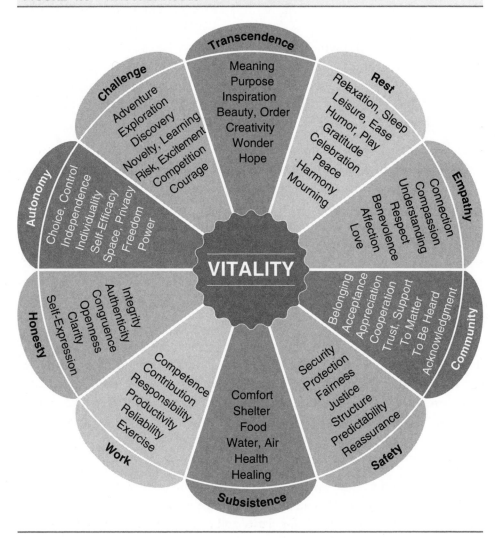

When I work with the wheel of needs with someone I am coaching, we shift from working shoulder to shoulder to crown to crown. We move beyond collaboration and become deeply engaged in acknowledging and honoring the needs that are alive for that person in that moment, in the midst of the situation they are facing. This is holy work.

—Donni, Special Education Consultant

By reflecting the universal needs that coachees are trying to meet, we express empathy and open the door to considering numerous alternative strategies to meeting those needs. We also release the frustration that arises when a particular strategy is blocked. When coachees confuse strategies with needs, they may become attached to a single course of action and thus less creative and open to new ideas, as well as more controlling and aggressive in how they engage with others. Evocative coaches shift that dynamic by putting the spotlight on needs.

When we understand the distinction between needs and strategies, we can hear complaints and criticisms with new ears. We can understand them as expressions of unmet needs and values (Rosenberg, 2003; Kegan & Lahey, 2009). Instead of responding with an impatient, "Oh, quit whining," we can instead get curious as to the need beneath the complaint. We can assist the one who is complaining to become more aware of his or her needs by offering a guess as to what need or needs may want attention. This clarity allows the complainer to consider a new strategy in service of that need. By guessing at the underlying needs beneath the complaints or criticisms, we can offer an empowering and open stance for looking at those needs.

Just as with the expression of feelings, the structure of the English language can allow us to use the language of needs when we are in fact expressing strategies to meet needs. Although the following sentences use the word *need* and are grammatically correct, they do not express universal needs: "I need you to stop talking and sit down." "You need to get to school on time." These are strategies for meeting universal needs; they do not represent the needs themselves.

Empathy is a powerful gift whether client needs are being met or not. When a coachee shares about a time when a meeting went particularly well, for example, an evocative coach might say, "It sounds like you're feeling a sense of satisfaction and contentment and that your needs for clarity and contribution were met. Does that hit the mark?" We want to savor their satisfaction, deepen their enthusiasm, and celebrate their progress. When a coachee makes negative comments about her or his abilities or situation, a coach might offer the following reflection and request: "I'm guessing that you're feeling hesitant and nervous because your needs for competence and control are not being met. Have I heard you correctly?" We want to understand their concern and appreciate their intention.

I have the list of feelings and needs taped to my desk, one set facing me and the other facing the other person. When someone comes to see me about a concern, we examine them together to see if we can get a deeper understanding of what is going on. It often leads to some very powerful insights.

—Alden, Leadership Coach

Causal Attributions. There are times when descriptions of how a client is feeling are tinged with a sense of judgment or criticism. There is an emotional charge that comes with ascribing blame. Words that are followed by an explicit or implicit "by you"—such as *attacked, belittled, criticized, intimidated, manipulated, pressured, provoked, put down, threatened,* or *tricked*—communicate a judgmental attribution. These kinds of feeling words are sometimes called *faux feelings* (or perhaps *foe feelings* because they conjure enemy images of the other person). They may sound like feelings but nevertheless imply that someone or something was the cause of a negative event or outcome. These words may indicate that the coachee has become fixated on a solution or strategy that often involves a desire to control someone else (an implicit "should").

Evocative coaches avoid reflecting causal attributions or evaluative assessments when expressing empathy. Such communications do not expand understanding, bolster motivation, or facilitate movement. They tend to turn coaching conversations into gossip and gripe sessions. When coachees give voice to causal attributions and evaluative assessments, which may come with intense emotional charges, coaches work to reflect the primary feelings and underlying needs without reflecting the judgmental thoughts. Figure 4.4 includes a list of causal attributions, along with some potential primary feelings and underlying needs associated with each. When our empathy guesses hit the mark, coachees may nod with understanding and expand their willingness to consider the underlying needs they are trying to meet. Reflecting the feelings that may be alive in a coachee as he or she tells a story rather than parroting the evaluative assessments that may cross the coachee's mind allows us to speak distinctly and to generate awareness and growth.

FIGURE 4.4   Reframing Causal Attributions

REFRAMING FAUX FEELINGS

Thoughts That My Feelings Are Caused "by You"

Causal Attributions	Possible Primary Feelings	Possible Underlying Needs
Attacked	Angry, Scared	Safety, Respect
Belittled	Indignant, Outraged, Distressed, Tense, Embarrassed	Respect, Autonomy, To Be Seen, Acknowledgement, Appreciation
Blamed	Indignant, Angry, Scared, Bewildered, Hurt	Fairness, Justice, Understanding
Betrayed	Outraged, Disappointed, Stunned, Hurt	Trust, Dependability, Honesty, Respect, Commitment, Clarity, Security
Boxed in	Angry, Frustrated, Scared, Anxious	Autonomy, Choice, Freedom, Self-Efficacy
Coerced	Angry, Frustrated, Scared, Anxious	Autonomy, Choice, Freedom, Self-Efficacy
Criticized	Irritated, Scared, Anxious, Humiliated, Embarrassed	Understanding, Acknowledgement, Recognition
Disrespected	Indignant, Frustrated, Embarrassed, Hurt	Respect, Trust, Acknowledgement
Distrusted	Frustrated, Sad, Hurt	Honesty, Authenticity, Integrity, Trust
Harassed	Angry, Aggravated, Exasperated, Pressured, Frightened	Respect, Consideration, Ease
Hassled	Irritated, Irked, Frustrated, Distressed	Autonomy, Ease, Calm, Space
Insulted	Angry, Incensed, Embarrassed	Respect, Consideration, Acknowledgement, Recognition
Interrupted	Resentful, Irritated, Hurt	Respect, Consideration, To Be Heard
Intimidated	Frightened, Scared, Vulnerable	Safety, Power, Self-Efficacy, Independence

Causal Attributions	Possible Primary Feelings	Possible Underlying Needs
Left out	Anxious, Lonely, Sad	Belonging, Community, Connection, To Be Seen
Manipulated	Angry, Resentful, Vulnerable, Sad	Autonomy, Consideration, Choice, Power
Misunderstood	Upset, Dismayed, Frustrated	Understanding, To Be Heard, Clarity
Overworked	Resentful, Angry, Frustrated, Tired	Respect, Consideration, Caring, Rest, Ease
Pressured	Resentful, Overwhelmed, Anxious	Relaxation, Ease, Clarity, Space, Consideration
Rejected	Angry, Defiant, Scared, Hurt	Belonging, Connection, Acknowledgement
Taken advantage of	Angry, Frustrated, Powerless	Autonomy, Power, Trust, Choice, Connection, Acknowledgement
Taken for granted	Angry, Disappointed, Hurt	Appreciation, Acknowledgement, Recognition, Consideration
Tricked	Furious, Indignant, Embarrassed	Integrity, Honesty, Trust
Unappreciated	Frustrated, Irritated, Sad, Hurt	Appreciation, Respect, Acknowledgement
Unsupported	Resentful, Sad, Hurt	Support, Understanding
Violated	Outraged, Agitated, Anxious, Sad	Safety, Trust, Space, Respect

One morning I got a got a call from Dan, a high school principal I'd been coaching as he transformed a very chaotic and even dangerous school to an orderly and productive school environment. I could tell he was upset the minute I heard his voice. He told me that he'd just learned that in order to manage a budget shortfall, the board had decided to discontinue its contract with a neighboring district to provide night school for disruptive and suspended students for the second semester and that those students would be back in his building starting Monday of the upcoming week. I just happened to have the

(Continued)

causal attributions chart open on my desk, so I quickly scanned down through it. My eye happened to land on the "taken advantage of" row, so I asked, "I'm wondering if you are feeling frustrated, angry, or powerless in this situation?" He said, "Boy, am I! I am really steamed that they would make this decision without even consulting me, and then on top of it, to give me so little time to plan for the change!" I probed further: "I'm guessing that your needs for autonomy, choice, and acknowledgement may have been stirred up in this turn of events." He paused and then said quietly, "Yes, yes they have." We went on to set up a time to map out a plan for how to cope with this new group of students. When he called back, he said how helpful it had been just to have that acknowledgment in moving past his fury and to move into a problem-solving mode.

—Diane, Leadership Coach

Making Requests. The final way to reframe coachee stories is to make requests, rather than demands, to confirm understandings and to explore possibilities. There are two kinds of requests coaches can make after reflecting observations, feelings, and needs: connection requests and action requests. For a connection request, coaches might immediately ask, "Would you be willing to tell me what you heard me say?" or "Is there more you would like me to know?" or "How do you feel when you hear me say that?" Such requests keep the focus of the conversation on the reframed elements rather than on the original story with its evaluations, thoughts, and strategies. It is essential for coaches to make such connection requests quickly so the client is not left hanging in a vulnerable space after their feelings and needs have been acknowledged.

Another kind of request, which we will work with extensively in the next two chapters, is an action request. Once feelings and underlying needs have been fully explored, coachees will be more open to new possibilities and will want to come away from a coaching session with some sense of what they might do differently in the future. Asking, for example, "What agreements would you be willing to make with regard to your work in the coming week?" is to frame the action as something coachees can do right now (make an agreement) that will facilitate their learning and growth. It is essential for coaches to make such requests without any sense of demand. If it is unacceptable for a coachee to say no and decline the request, then it is a demand disguised as a request, and the pretense of choice will damage trust. To jump right to an action request before making a connection request risks the possibility that the other person is still feeling judged and may therefore be reluctant to engage productively. Taking the time to make a connection request—to affirm both parties are ready to move forward—may increase the likelihood of negotiating a mutually satisfying solution strategy.

People are not machines. When their wants, emotions, and needs are not considered, their productivity decreases, as does their overall level of commitment.

—Jane Kise (2006, p. 162)

Expressing Gratitude. Evocative coaching assists coachees to be more successful in their personal and professional lives. When that happens, and when coachees show up for coaching with positive reports regarding their performance, learning, and/or enjoyment in their work, coaches have another access point for empathy and another opportunity for connection. Now, however, the energy of connection is more light-hearted and fun. Just because coachees are filled with positivity does not mean they have fully appreciated and savored what those emotions have to teach them. Instead of just quickly rushing in with a high-five and moving on, evocative coaches seek to enhance the benefits of positivity by enthusiastically reflecting the lively energy and the needs that have been met. By finding the right words to describe both the feelings involved and the underlying needs, coachees become more aware of what happened, why it is important to them, and how to cultivate those factors in the future.

As they understand how important awareness of progress is to the learning process, evocative coaches celebrate its evidence. Good work should be recognized or celebrated. We want to commend coachees for their progress, and we want to celebrate their capacity for continued growth. It is important that our praise and compliments are grounded in authenticity. If we want the coaching relationship to radiate the energy of possibility and hope, then coachees have to know not only that we believe in them but also that we see them as making progress toward their goals.

THE GOLDEN SIGH

When a coachee's need for empathy has been met—when the coach has listened well and communicated understanding in a way that the coachee appreciates—it often evokes what we refer to as a *golden sigh*. This release is sometimes accompanied by a slight nodding of the head, the signal of an opening to move on into inquiry. Whether or not there is an actual sigh or nod, this is a moment when the energy shifts toward a readiness to look forward rather than inward. If you are working with a coachee who is experiencing deep discouragement or who has felt unappreciated for a long time, it may take several sessions before these empathy needs will be met. However, it may happen very quickly. The key is to be attentive for the felt sense that something has shifted and a readiness to move on has emerged. When the need for empathy is met, the coachee will be ready to take steps to improve his or her situation and to move to a place of creative action. At this point, it is time to move the conversation forward with appreciative inquiry and design thinking.

If the golden sigh does not come, then one of two things may be happening: Either we are not speaking distinctly, perhaps reinforcing the client's evaluations, thoughts, strategies, and demands, or the coachee is just not at a moment in time when she or he can move on. Either way, it calls for coaches to change approaches. We must first look at our intention and our language. Are we truly trying to understand the coachee's experience or are we trying to change them? Whenever the coachee perceives that we have an agenda, it is likely to interfere with the coaching dynamic. Returning to the language of compassionate communication is one way to get back on track. If that doesn't work, then a shifted-focus reflection may be helpful (Miller & Rollnick, 2002, pp. 102–103). This amounts to changing the subject and shining the spotlight on some other area of coachee experience that may be more accessible and amenable to conversation in this moment. When coachees connect with these more positive dynamics, it can elevate the entire conversation and get them ready to return to those tougher areas where they feel stuck or otherwise conflicted about change. When coaches dance with coachees in this way, a shift in energy will eventually come—often more quickly than we might expect. At their core, coachees need to make sense of their experience and to contribute to their own learning and growth. They want to move on and be successful. Expressing empathy is key to helping that happen.

 Key Points in This Chapter

1. When coaches establish a no-fault zone, educational leaders can share and learn from their experiences.

2. As coachees tell their stories, evocative coaches express empathy, which is a respectful understanding of a coachee's feelings and needs. That differs from feeling sorry for them (pity) or getting swept up in their emotions (sympathy).

3. When emotions are provoked, it is not uncommon for coachees to engage in playing the game of "Who's right?" Evocative coaches respond by offering distinctive reflections, reflecting only observations, feelings, needs, and requests.

4. By offering our guesses as to clients' feelings and needs, we convey a respectful stance toward their experience whether our guesses are on target or not.

5. By connecting with coachees at the level of observations, feelings, and needs, coaches open a realm of possibility as coachees encounter new ways of understanding and processing their experience.

6. When clients get to the core of the matter, they release a golden sigh that indicates a readiness to move on.

Questions for Reflection and Discussion

1. What is the orientation of empathy? As a coach, how can you bring that orientation into the school or district settings in which you work?

2. What are your feelings and needs right now, as you think about expressing empathy with your clients?

3. What practices might assist you to cultivate empathy in your personal or professional life?

4. How might you enhance your skills at making distinctive reflections?

5. Recall a person you have recently dealt with who expressed a complaint. What do you suppose were the underlying unmet needs and values this person was experiencing?

6. Recall a time when you offered empathy to someone either in your professional or personal realm. What did that look like and where did that lead? What were the clues that the other person felt heard?

Loop II: The Strengths-Building Turn

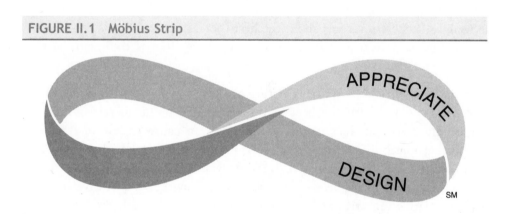

After coaches have established trust and rapport with educational leaders and those leaders have shared, explored, and received empathy for their stories, it is time for two more movements in the evocative coaching process: appreciate and design. Coaches listen to stories and express empathy not as ends in themselves but in order to facilitate client growth and change. When the first turn of evocative coaching has done its work generating the readiness embodied in the golden sigh, educational leaders are primed for a positive, action-oriented conversation. "Now what?" becomes the operative question. The new territory that coaches and educational leaders have to explore is the luminous realm of capacity, possibility, and fulfillment.

The strengths-building turn starts where the no-fault turn leaves off and shifts clients toward the future with a new sense of who they are and what they can do. We affirm the notion that all educational leaders are striving to meet legitimate universal needs, regardless of how ineffective or counterproductive their current strategies may be; thus we want to turn our inquiries to those things that make for openness, self-efficacy, trust, encouragement, and mobility. To do that, evocative coaches stay focused on strengths. Interviewing educational leaders regarding their strengths, opportunities, aspirations, and resources elevates self-efficacy, enhances motivation, and energizes action. It gets coachees in the mood for change as they come to see themselves in new, more positive lights. Extrapolating from the best of what is to the best of what might be takes inquiry to a whole new level. It engages the imagination and assists educational leaders to frame compelling aspirations of their best personal and professional selves. This awakens in them a sense of destiny, cause, and calling.

It may be customary and even appear logical to focus on a client's shortcomings and weaknesses in order to help her or him do better. That is generally the hope and intent of evaluation systems. But studies have demonstrated the relative ineffectiveness of focusing on and trying to fix weaknesses (Buckingham, 2007). To stay on the Möbius strip of evocative coaching and to stay connected in life-giving relationships, coaches assist clients to learn more about what they do well, to frame aspirations about the best they can be, and to design actions that will generate learning as to how to get there. That is the magic of the strengths-building turn.

There is no way to fully make that turn from the expert frame. Even when expertise is shared with the best of intentions—to build up rather than to tear people down—it does not have the power to cause educational leaders to claim responsibility for their own learning and growth. For that, coachees must discover and trust their own strengths, values, vitalities, and aspirations. That is the path to a coachees's self-efficacy and growth. So, evocative coaches use appreciative inquiries and vital observations to call forth those realities. They are always there, waiting to be found. They often get scuffed, marred, or obscured by the focus on what must be done, but they never get entirely lost. Evocative coaching awakens aspiration by focusing conversations on what wants to emerge. We seek to connect with educational leaders around their core purpose for being in education at all: the quest for contribution that makes a positive difference in the world.

Educational leaders are often working in high-stress conditions in which they may experience a sense of being overwhelmed and exhausted. It seems that what is needed is rest, but the antidote for exhaustion is not necessarily rest but *wholeheartedness*. Working wholeheartedly in education requires courage—a word which comes from the old French word *cuer*, meaning *heart*—as well as new understandings and approaches. It requires imaginative visualizations and creative flights of fancy of what people want as well as clear designs regarding how to get there. It is challenging but not impossible work. At their best, the designs shift entire systems into alignment with these positive visions.

THE LEARNING BRIEF

To make the transition from the no-fault turn to the strengths-building turn, it is helpful to sketch out a learning brief. The point of the brief is to clarify in broad strokes what coachees will work on and how coaches will seek to assist them. We seek to be neither too general nor too specific. The parameters of the learning brief answer questions such as the ones below.

SKETCHING A LEARNING BRIEF: WHAT WILL THE COACHEE WORK ON? HOW WILL THE COACH ASSIST?

- What is the learning focus?
  - What is the overarching focus of the coaching relationship?
  - What topic or subject area holds the most potential?
  - What is the learning focus of this particular coaching conversation?
  - What are the benchmarks for measuring progress?
  - What are the objectives to be realized?

- How will the coach and client work together?
  - What is the role of the coach?
  - What is expected of the client?
  - How will conversations take place?
  - Who will initiate what?
  - How will observations be arranged?
  - How long will the relationship last?

Evocative coaching is not just an engaging conversation; it is an engaging conversation with a clear focus that coaches and educational leaders agree to work on together. Clarifying objectives and benchmarks but leaving room for the unexpected to emerge gives substance to coaching conversations. The learning brief can address both long-term and near-term time frames. Getting clarity and consent regarding the goals of coaching will assist coaches to guide and structure the inquiry and design processes. It often helps to have these goals recorded either on paper or electronically so they can be reviewed and revised periodically throughout the coaching relationship.

Sometimes a learning focus will jump out immediately as clients begin to explore the possibilities with their coach. Often, however, coach and coachee will float different topics for consideration until one topic clearly rises to the surface as an area of interest. When that happens, it can be useful to summarize the understanding and then to ask the client how much energy, on a scale of 0 to 10, they have around that topic. If energy is low, there may be another topic worth pursuing, or it may be possible to invigorate the energy by discussing the coachee's energy rating. The learning focus is clarified at a much broader and higher level than the specific strategies that will come later in the strengths-building turn. It encompasses current conditions and organizational constraints as well as desired outcomes and benchmarks for measuring success.

Even when coaching is mandated around a clear issue of concern, it is still important for clients to feel at choice when it comes to the coaching. This can be done by asking educational leaders to identify the pieces they want assistance with and also other areas of interest that may improve their work. As coaches explore what and how the client would like to learn, it will quickly become evident whether or not the client is leaning forward to engage more fully or leaning away with a sense of wariness or disengagement. Clients cannot be coached against their will. If an educational leader does not want coaching, and if the coach's attempts at story listening and expressing empathy do not turn that around, then the coaching cannot go forward. We want educational leaders to work out of a sense of partnership. To that end, then, the relationship and the conversations must be experienced as desired and voluntary, even if they did not start out that way.

In addition to clarifying goals, the learning brief also clarifies basic expectations regarding the approach we take as evocative coaches and logistics such as how, when, where, and for how long coaching conversations will take place. It will clarify expectations about contact between the coach and coachee between formal coaching sessions. There may also be discussion about whether and how the coaching might include observations or shadowing experiences. The logistics should be clear and mutually agreed upon in order to maintain the trust needed for coaching to be effective.

Although an initial coaching session may clarify parameters for the entire coaching relationship, it is also important to clarify the focus of that particular coaching conversation on a session-by-session basis. If the learning brief negotiated during the first coaching session represents the macro level of the coaching project, then the brief for each subsequent coaching conversation represents the micro level of the coaching project. It clarifies where a coachee wants to go today. Having clarity about these elements is what distinguishes coaching from polite conversation or commiseration. We encourage clarity and consensus so people perceive coaching as a supportive and results-oriented relationship that adds real value to their professional lives.

A design brief that is too abstract risks leaving the [client] wandering around in a fog. One that starts from too narrow a set of constraints, however, almost guarantees that the outcome will be incremental and, most likely, mediocre.

—Tim Brown (2009, p. 24)

CHAPTER
5

Appreciative Inquiry

The third phase of the evocative coaching process shifts the focus of the conversation from the no-fault consideration of experiences and emotions to a forward-looking inquiry into what's next. The strengths-building turn kicks off with a process called appreciative inquiry (AI). AI is both a philosophy and an approach for motivating change that focuses on exploring and amplifying strengths. We seek to discover the best of what is going on in the present in order to build those dynamics into the best of what might be possible. We operate from the conviction that what we appreciate, appreciates. The benefits of appreciating the positive dimensions of life are plentiful. They include reminding educational leaders of their capabilities, generating optimism and positive energy, cultivating resilience, inducing wider search patterns, expanding novel and creative thoughts, creating more inclusive and flexible mindsets, and stimulating more of the behaviors that created previous success. The better clients feel about themselves, the stronger they feel about their capabilities, and the more passion they feel about their work, the more successful they will be in designing experiments that move them forward.

AI contrasts with traditional models of change that focus on weaknesses and gaps. Rather than inquiring into, analyzing, and fixing problems, evocative coaches target their inquiries to focus on strengths, opportunities, aspirations, and resources. In so doing, we assist educational leaders to reconnect with their joy and to realize their full potential. It is especially important for coaches to approach struggling educational leaders in this way, since they likely have deep unmet needs for competence, validation, and appreciation. Everyone, even a struggling leader, has shining moments. No situation is so bleak and barren as to be totally without beauty, promise, and merit. The secret is to find a vantage point from which these glimmering facets can be seen. Empathy starts that process by validating the unmet needs behind even the most unfortunate strategies. AI continues the process by shining a spotlight on what educational leaders can celebrate about the past, savor about the present, and aspire to in the future.

By celebrating what's right, we connect with our passion and find the energy to fix what's wrong.

—Dewitt Jones (2001)

This generative dynamic is what we as evocative coaches hope for as we begin to explore with educational leaders their inherent ambitions and present possibilities. Why am I here? What do I stand for? How will I contribute? By inquiring into the motivating passions and underlying values of educational leaders' personal and professional lives, coaches inspire clients to move beyond incremental improvements in technique to transformational shifts in attitude, orientation, and approach. When educational leaders are filled with passion for who they are and how they contribute—when they feel that passion in their bones—it moves them forward through the stages of change, elevates their understanding of the possible, increases their positive affect, and unlocks the door to greater self-efficacy. When freed from judgments and fear of reprisals, educational leaders can allow the coaching conversation to fully and honestly explore both the internal and external dynamics that make for educational excellence. Coachees will not discover new strategies until they tackle new questions. And they won't tackle new questions until they have new information to work with. Discovering strengths and observing vitalities are two productive ways to get that new information.

A world of questions is a world of possibility. The spirit of inquiry . . . opens our minds, connects us to each other, and shakes outmoded paradigms. [It invites] exploration, discovery, innovation, and cooperation. We have only to ask the right questions to begin.

—Marilee Adams (2004)

AI was initially developed as a research methodology for studying and understanding organizations by David Cooperrider (2000) and his colleagues at Case Western Reserve University. To their surprise, however, the process of inquiring into and studying the positive aspects of a system proved, in and of itself, to be transformational. Inquiry proved to be not only a prelude to action but a form of action. It enabled systems to change and to grow toward the highest aspirations of the organizational participants. AI is undergirded by five principles: the positive, constructionist, simultaneity, anticipatory, and poetic principles. The image of a pyramid illustrates how these principles are related to each other and work together to generate positive actions and outcomes (see Figure 5.1).

FIGURE 5.1   Five Principles of Appreciative Inquiry

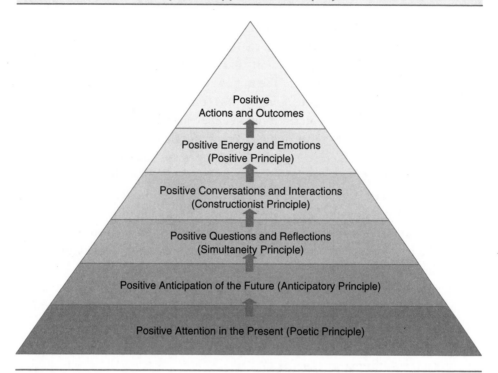

THE PRINCIPLES OF APPRECIATIVE INQUIRY

THE POSITIVE PRINCIPLE

Coaches hope our work with clients will result in positive actions and outcomes. Moreover, educational leaders hope their efforts with the people they lead will result in positive actions and outcomes. So how do we get that? The positive principle holds that positive actions and outcomes stem from the force generated by positive energy and emotions. Negative energy and emotions, associated with identifying, analyzing, and fixing or correcting weaknesses, generates friction that diminishes forward motion. At best, root-cause analyses of weaknesses correct the problems they seek to solve. At worst, they cause a downward spiral as people become more focused on what is wrong and who is to blame. Inquiring into and appreciating strengths is a way for people to set aside their negative internal voices and to envision and experiment with wholly new ways of understanding and doing things. Positive energy and emotions disrupt a downward spiral and build the inherent aspirations of people into a dynamic movement for transformational change. They broaden thinking, expand awareness, increase abilities, build resiliency, bolster initiative, offset negatives, generate new possibilities, and create an upward spiral of learning and growth (Frederickson, 2009). That is the kind of energy we want to unleash in educational leaders and the schools and systems they lead.

THE CONSTRUCTIONIST PRINCIPLE

If positive energy and emotions hold so much potential for good, how do we get that? The constructionist principle asserts that positive energy and emotions are constructed through positive conversations and interactions with other people. The constructionist principle makes clear the importance of the social context in creating the present moment and in changing future moments. Inner work and self-talk alone are not sufficient. New conversations generate new truths and new possibilities. People do not just make sense of their experiences through the stories they tell, they also create the reality in which they live. Stories are not just accounts of the world as people find it, they are also constructions and interpretations of the world as people understand it. If we focus our conversations on the things that are not working, then that is how the world will be for us: a tough and difficult place. If we focus our conversations on the things that *are* working, then we'll start to notice more of the best life has to offer. In this way, our stories can become wonderful, self-fulfilling prophecies. Zander and Zander (2000) suggest that "it's all invented anyway, so we might as well invent a story or framework of meaning that enhances our quality of life and the life of those around us" (p. 12). Coaching conversations can be viewed as an evocative way to invent life-enhancing stories and frameworks.

THE SIMULTANEITY PRINCIPLE

If positive conversations and interactions are able to create positive worlds, how do we get that? The simultaneity principle proceeds from the observation that conversations and interactions shift the instant we ask a new question. Asking, "What is the problem here?" tends to deplete the available energy and lead down a path of fault-finding, blame, and defensiveness. On the other hand, asking, "What is going well here?" tends to elicit positive energy, renewed hope, and creativity. The simultaneity principle views positive lines of inquiry and reflection as powerful ways to generate positive conversations and interactions. The energy lifts and the conversation lightens when people connect with and converse about positive things. Such questions have the ability to change things in the twinkling of an eye. They do not just begin a process that leads to a positive future, they simultaneously create a positive present by reorienting conversations and interactions around the stuff that enhances life. Our questions and reflections are fateful. "There are no 'neutral' questions," wrote Kelm (2005). "Inhabiting this spirit of wonder can transform our lives, and the unconditional positive question is one of the greatest tools we have to this end" (p. 54). When coaches ask strengths-based questions, we begin the process of reconstructing the worlds in which we live and work.

THE ANTICIPATORY PRINCIPLE

If positive questions and reflections are of such critical importance to the tenor and substance of our conversations, where do those come from? The anticipatory principle asserts that our future outlook impacts our present reality. Our questions and reflections flow from the things we anticipate happening in the future. If we are filled with dread and negative thoughts about the future, then it is hard to seek out, much less to celebrate, the positive. If we are filled with hope and aspiration, then things tilt in a positive direction. When equipped with a glimpse of what things look like at their very best, we become more creative, resourceful, and resilient in looking for ways to make it so. Positive anticipation of the future beckons us forward. The anticipatory principle asserts that it takes specific, positive images of the future in order to impact the dynamics of the present. Anticipating the realization of a larger vision, our inherent ambition (Gallwey, 2000) organizes the present moment. It enables us to outgrow, rather than to solve, our problems by getting us interested in what Carl Jung (1962) described as a "new and stronger life-tendency" (p. 92). The more concrete and real the images, the more yearning and movement they create. A vision is "a target that beckons" (Bennis & Nanus, 1985, p. 89). Thus, vision infuses the present with positive energy.

The greatest and most important problems of life are all in a certain sense insoluble. . . . They can never be solved, but only outgrown . . . once a higher and wider interest arises on the horizon.

—Carl Jung (1962, pp. 91–92)

THE POETIC PRINCIPLE

If positive anticipation of the future sets the stage for positive questions and reflections, how do we get that? Forming the base of the pyramid upon which all the other principles are built, the poetic principle connects intention with attention. That is what great poets do—they draw our attention to simple, ordinary things in a way that imbues them with meaning and purpose. The more we attend to the positive, life-giving dimensions of the present moment, the more positive will be our intentions for future moments. By seeing and attending to life's beauty, we become inspired. It is not that problems disappear. Rather, other things become more important. Becoming mindful of what adds richness, texture, depth, beauty, significance, and energy to life awakens us to life's magnificent potential. It is as though life becomes a work of great poetry, filled with hopeful meter and meaning as well as movement toward positive growth and change. That is because we get more of what we focus on. When we focus on problems, we get more problems. When we focus on possibilities, we get more possibilities. AI seeks to appreciate strengths. Thus, life's poetry resolves into a spiral of positive imagination.

SOAR: ILLUMINATING THE BEST OF WHAT IS AND WHAT MIGHT BE

It is the work of evocative coaching to look for those strengths and to arm clients with an understanding of what they are doing well. To do this, evocative coaches put the five principles of AI into action by engaging in a SOAR analysis with clients, inquiring into the leader's **s**trengths, **o**bservations, **a**spirations, and **r**esources to discover the best of what is and to imagine the best of what might be. SOAR fosters new realities, imbuing the entire coaching process with satisfaction, surprise, fun, wonder, joy, and deep relationship. Inquiring into their strengths, opportunities, aspirations, and resources invigorates coachees with can-do energy and readies them for design conversations yet to come.

It is easy for these positive dynamics to get lost in the continuous clamor of day-to-day deadlines and difficulties. For people to set aside fear and defensiveness, they require new information that reframes the situation and sets them on a different course. Positive, strengths-based data can do just that. When it comes to evocative coaching, we show up as partners in the search for whatever things are true, noble, reputable, authentic, compelling, gracious, beautiful, and praiseworthy. We trust that those things are always there, no matter how tough the situation, and we collaborate with our clients in the inquiry to find them.

The coach has the responsibility to, first, make sure the client is paying attention to what is positive—his or her strengths, what has worked well in the past, the upside of the problem. Second, the coach steadies the spotlight on the intended change, not by issuing orders but by asking questions.

—Rock and Page (2009, pp. 185–186)

Curiosity is an essential tool in the evocative coaching toolbox, and asking good questions is the essence of coaching. The right inquiries can reintroduce us to wonder, possibility, and connection—the prerequisites of change. The more coaches navigate by open-minded curiosity with regard to client strengths, opportunities, aspirations, and resources, the more coachees will discover about themselves, where they want to go, and how they want to get there. Curiosity on the part of coaches empowers clients to find their own answers, to be more resourceful, and to discover new possibilities for moving forward. By becoming curious as to the things educational leaders are doing well and want to do better, evocative coaches enable clients to become more curious about their own abilities and more willing to try new things. Coaching becomes a dance of self-discovery for educational leaders, enabling them to think differently about the learning focus and even to see themselves in new lights.

STRENGTHS

Inquiring into strengths lays the foundation for all that follows. The simultaneity principle makes clear that asking appreciative questions is transformational in its own right. Exploring life-giving stories, values, conditions, and wishes not only forms the basis for change, it simultaneously brings about the change we seek. It is important to not rush through the inquiry process in order to get to the design phase. By taking our time and savoring the experience of inquiry, we cultivate curiosity and encourage exploration. What are educational leaders successfully doing now that they can build on in designing a desired action or outcome? Evocative coaches inquire into and seek to appreciate a wide variety of inputs that educational leaders can build on to improve their skills and performance; these include stories of past successes, strength-based assessments, and observations of present activities. These are all explored in the sections that follow.

Once the data are collected, evocative coaches and coachees review the data together with appreciative eyes. No dataset is ever entirely positive, and it is tempting to mine the data with a fault-finding mentality. It is common for coaches to talk with educational leaders about their strengths *and* their weaknesses, their successes *and* their failures, their triumphs *and* their tragedies. Indeed, it seems so obvious and natural to talk about both sides of the coin that many people, including many coaches, have trouble imagining any other way to conduct a performance-oriented conversation. From this vantage point, it might seem necessary to make educational leaders face the music as to what they are doing wrong and must change. The notion that people grow only from having their mistakes observed, documented, and pointed out to them is overstated at best and counterproductive at worst. For all its apparent logic, a focus on shortcomings often fails to generate successful change. We notice a few positive things and then get to the heart of the matter: our recommendations as to what the leader should do differently. That doesn't work because the "Gotcha!" game puts clients into a defensive posture that diminishes creativity and resourcefulness and does little to facilitate higher-order learning and growth.

Recent research from the field of positive psychology suggests that identifying our weaknesses and working diligently to improve them is not the best way to promote learning, growth, and change (Buckingham, 2007). Identifying strengths and working to engage them—the broaden-and-build theory of positive emotions—has proven to be far more effective (Fredrickson, 2009). That is why evocative coaches and coachees instead approach data by asking, "What is working well here?" What can coachees build on and celebrate? When people are recognized and appreciated for what they do well, they open up, lean in, and get creative. They find the conversation enjoyable and engaging. Dialoguing with educational leaders in this way—with information gleaned from assessments and observations—assists them to know themselves and to move forward in the direction of their desired future.

Adopting an appreciative stance is not to pretend that everything is wonderful when it is obviously not. AI does, however, avoid inquiring into the root causes of what is wrong. It assumes that people will outgrow their problems the more they focus on their strengths. Coaches restrain their urge to talk with clients about what they are doing poorly and instead engage their curiosity to learn about what they are doing well. The more we stay in that positive frame—the more we dialogue with coachees about their strengths, opportunities, aspirations, and resources—the more they will come to believe in their abilities and the more progress they will make in their schools and districts. To avoid provoking defensiveness and resistance, evocative coaches focus our inquiries to discover where educational leaders shine, what's worked in other settings in the past, and what's working now, in this setting. What can we celebrate? The issues may be weighty, but the process of coaching can lighten the load in service of moving forward. This then sets the stage for the design thinking that follows.

It is especially important for coaches to inquire into strengths when the educational leaders they are coaching are discouraged or stuck. When coachees show up with complaints, hard-to-hear messages, and painful stories, evocative coaches respond first with empathy reflections and then with AI. Instead of dissecting the experience to figure out what went wrong, we look for ways to see the strengths that may be shining through. This appreciative approach is not meant to deny the existence of problems; it is rather meant to shift the spotlight away from the train wrecks and onto the positive aspects of experience. Evocative coaches proceed with the unshakable conviction that good things can always be found. No matter how bleak and barren the situation may appear, something is always working. By reconnecting clients with these experiences through appreciative inquiries, coaching evokes learning, growth, and change. Coachees begin to calm down, believe more in themselves, and generate new possibilities for moving forward. They discover the emotional and professional capital to dream new dreams and design new strategies for moving forward. Inquiring about the positive elements of client experiences, even when there are a lot of obvious negatives, is a way of reminding coachees we still believe in them and they have a lot to offer. Such implicit championing dramatically accelerates the behavior-change process.

Evocative coaches assist clients to value the best of every experience in order to generate the life-giving energy that facilitates change. By assisting coachees to stay focused on this quest, we enable them to reframe negative experiences in positive terms. Once people feel heard on this level, they open up to the consideration of what has worked in the past and what is working now. If a meeting or a presentation went even partially well, that is the moment we want to notice and nurture. "What happened there?" and "How can we get more of that?" is the drift of a conversation that has taken a positive turn. That is the drift evocative coaches work for in each and every conversation. To facilitate positive reframing of a difficult situation, coaches may ask one or more of the strengths-based questions below.

Sample Strength-Based Questions

- Tell me how you got through this and what's possible now.

- What did you try that worked, even if only partially?

- How did this experience make a positive contribution to your development?

- When did things start to go better and look up?

- What did you learn about yourself and your values today?

- What was the best thing you did in this situation, no matter how small?

- What values did you hold true to even though it was a tough situation?

- How did you manage to keep things from getting any worse?

- What did you learn about your followers?

- What was the best thing about this situation?

- What's the silver lining here?

Inquiries such as these represent the work of appreciative reframing, which is one of the three keys to successful and lasting behavior change. When coaches stay in that frame, coachees will eventually follow. By appreciating strengths, it is possible to quicken the interest of educational leaders in the life-affirming and life-giving dimensions of their own experiences. If clients can think of nothing positive to say in response to such inquiries, encourage them to go back further in time. Perhaps there was another tough situation that turned out better in the end. Remembering instances of successful perseverant effort in other areas, inside or outside of school, may get the conversation back on track. When multiple positive reframing efforts come up empty-handed, coachees may not be ready for the strengths-building turn. Going back to the no-fault turn is, then, the way to move forward.

I was asked to serve as part of a support team sent into work with a school system that was in its fourth year in district improvement status. What I quickly realized was that these people had seen a whole string of people coming through their doors, each with their own ideas of how to help. The problem was that nobody had listened, and nobody had thought that there were strengths there in the local community that were important to tap into. As a result, the educators in that district had gotten pretty good at deflecting all these efforts to "support" them.

—Andrea, School Support Team Member

Appreciative Interview Protocol. Evocative coaches use an array of tools to explore a wide variety of strengths in educational leaders. Through story listening we expand awareness and increase readiness to change as coachees self-report their experiences. AI practitioners have developed a generic, four-question appreciative interview protocol that coaches can use in coaching conversations to elevate energy and emotion. The protocol assists coachees to remember, connect with, and discover the things that are important to them and that they have done well.

1. **Best Experiences.** "Tell me about your best experience of leading a group of people to a positive outcome—a time when your contribution and way of being assisted the group to accomplish a significant challenge they might not have accomplished without your leadership. Who was involved? What challenges were you facing? What strengths, values, and capabilities allowed you to be successful in that situation? Describe the experience in detail."

2. **Core Values.** "Tell me about the things that matter most to you, that you value most deeply about yourself, your work, and your relationships. How are these expressed in your life and work?"

3. **Supporting Conditions.** "Recall a time when you worked or played in an environment where you were really at your best. What were the particular aspects of that context that brought out the best in you? Were there particular people, policies, or resources that seemed to matter most? How did you grow and what qualities emerged under those conditions?"

4. **Three Wishes.** "Tell me about your hopes and dreams for the future. If you had three wishes that would make this school/district a more vibrant and positive learning environment, what would they be?"

To explore the learning focus, evocative coaches adapt the generic appreciative interview protocol with specific questions about their client's stated learning focus. If educational leaders want to change how they lead meetings, for example, then coaches may evoke stories, values, conditions, and wishes related to times when leaders have changed their methods in the past. If leaders want to learn how to better handle a challenging encounter with a teacher or parent, then coaches may evoke stories, values, conditions, and wishes related to times when leaders have successfully handled similar situations in the past. The more closely we can target lines of inquiry to what educational leaders want to learn, the more effective we will be in building client motivation and self-efficacy around the design and implementation of new approaches for success. "When did you feel most comfortable and confident?" "What values did you express?" "What were the life-giving factors?" By asking educational leaders open-ended questions about the best of what is going on, we not only learn more about client frameworks and priorities, we also elevate client readiness and energy for change. The final question invites coachees to begin to explore their aspirations for themselves and their schools/districts in a playful way. Inquiries such as these both reveal and magnify client capacities, competencies, creativities, energies, and opportunities. They launch coaches and coachees into a spiral dynamic of meaning making, strength building, vitality boosting, and vision casting.

MaryAnn was a firecracker of a principal, very bold, and fearless in the face of conflict. She was the principal of a high-performing school in a wealthy district. She had been a teacher at that school for four years and assistant principal for two years before being named principal. So she thought she knew the teachers quite well. Her perception was that the school was high performing due to the high socioeconomic status (SES) of the students, not because of the quality of the teaching. From her perspective, the teachers had some pretty major changes to make in their teaching practices. The superintendent was encouraging principals to spend more time in classrooms, with a goal of visiting every classroom every day. When MaryAnn made classroom visits, she carried a clipboard and made notations about the degree to which teachers were implementing whatever initiative had been introduced during the previous professional development session. She would always leave a note on the teacher's desk with an observation and a question for reflection. When I visited MaryAnn's school and walked the classrooms with her, I noticed that when she entered the classrooms, the teachers seemed to flinch just a little and there would be a pause in the action as everyone became aware of her presence. I introduced MaryAnn to the appreciative inquiry generic interview tool, and she began to conduct paired interviews with teachers, taking one question each week for a month. The final question she asked was, "If you had three wishes that would make this school a more vibrant and positive learning environment, what would they be?" She took careful notes during each of these meetings. At our next coaching session, I asked how she had grown from her inquiry. I was taken aback when she burst into tears and cried, "I've been at this school for seven years and I don't know them at all!" She concluded that she needed to completely change her supervision of instruction. At the next faculty meeting she explained her new stance to her teachers. She took her list of look-fors off her clipboard and tore it up in front of her teachers. She said, choking back tears, "Part of my responsibility is to assess instruction and that is still in force, but my main job, and a much higher calling, is to make your three wishes come true." After that, when we walked classrooms together, I noticed that instruction proceeded uninterrupted by her visits, with perhaps a smile and a welcoming nod from the teacher.

—Mark, Leadership Coach

Appreciative Assessments. In addition to the use of AI interviews to explore how educational leaders view their experiences, evocative coaches can use many other tools for discovering and building on strengths. In addition to discovering strengths through appreciative interviews, many educational leaders also value a more objective look at strengths. Whether at the start of a coaching relationship or at a turning point, a healthy infusion of strengths-based data can come from taking an assessment and reviewing the results with an appreciative eye.

One self-assessment tool that lends itself naturally to a celebration of strengths is the Values-in-Action (VIA) Signature Strengths Questionnaire (Peterson & Seligman, 2004). The questionnaire can be taken online, free of charge, by going to VIA Institute in Character at http://www.viacharacter.org. After reacting to 240 statements, respondents receive a report of their 24 character strengths in rank order. The top five are identified as *signature strengths* since they are the ones that respondents tend to use most frequently, naturally, and easily. The 24th strength is not a weakness; it is a strength that one uses less readily. In the Peterson and Seligman taxonomy, the 24 character strengths are organized around six large categories called virtues that emerge consistently across history and culture as important in life and work. The VIA Signature Strengths Questionnaire can help educational leaders identify their virtues and character strengths that can be leveraged for motivation and movement. Coachees often find it quite affirming to discover and organize their strengths in this way. Posting an educational leader's top five signature strengths in a place where both the coachee and the coach can refer to them regularly, either in a low-tech way, such as inside a file folder, notebook, or desk drawer, or in more of a high-tech manner, such as developing a scrolling screen saver, can enable clients to tap into these strengths as they brainstorm ideas and design experiments to facilitate their learning and growth.

Coachees may have other personality assessments they would like to bring into the coaching conversations, such as their Myers-Brigg personality type (www.myersbriggs.org) or their Enneagram type (www.enneagraminstitute.com). These may be additional useful pieces of information that the client and coach can mine for strengths to draw upon in designing a way forward. Another way to assess leader strengths is for the leader to self-assess on each of the ten Professional Standards for Educational Leaders 2015 and the subskills linked to each (www.npbea.org). Educational leaders can calculate a mean score for the subscales of each of the ten standards and create a line or bar graph to display their relative strengths in each area. This may be a useful list to refer to when developing promising approaches to leadership challenges the coachee is facing.

I don't have to manage people, I just have to get them to see their higher self. I do that through coaching and building strong relationships. When we stop telling people what to do, their greatness can emerge.

—Daphane, Head of Schools

Observing Vitalities. Another key source of data on leader strengths is direct observation of the leader in action. When coaches focus on things educational leaders find inherently interesting and relevant to their experiences and effectiveness, and when coaches notice client strengths and vitalities, the process of collecting, analyzing, and reviewing data can raise awareness, stimulate thinking, and evoke change. Although some leadership coaching arrangements may be primarily via telephone, Skype, or FaceTime, other coaching settings afford coaches the opportunity for site visits and shadowing to observe educational leaders in action. In any case, the coach has the opportunity to make strengths-based observations of the coachee, although in the case of telephone coaching these may be based on descriptions of actions offered by the educational leaders themselves.

When making observations, evocative coaches focus a spotlight on what is happening in the present moment, especially on those things that demonstrate vitality, engagement, and connection. We stay focused on things that can be seen and heard. We look for body language, energy level, shining eyes, and smiling faces as educational leaders engage with those they lead. We look for evidence of competencies that coachees can celebrate and build on. Even struggling leaders will occasionally have such moments. By observing and appreciating those moments, they multiply in both quantity and quality to more fully meet the needs of the leader and their constituents alike. The more fully needs are met, the more vitality results. The more vitality results, the easier progress becomes.

Observing and dialoguing with educational leaders about their vital practices—the things they say and do that contribute noticeably to school and district vitality—expands their awareness of how their presence and techniques are landing. As a result of paying attention to the variables that matter, Gallwey (2000) noted that "self-interference decreases and performance inevitably improves" (p. 58). When people focus their attention on what is happening in the immediate environment, and when they are freed to respond adaptively without pressure or fear, they will naturally figure out ways to be more effective. When we inquire through an appreciative rather than an accusatory frame, when we look for strengths and vitalities rather than weaknesses and poor performances, we assist educational leaders to become ready, willing, and able to move forward in positive directions.

One critical variable worth observing, for example, is the difference in a subordinate's energy and body language when the subordinate approaches an exchange with the leader and as she or he departs. Did the subordinate approach the leader tentatively or with hesitation or seem to be uncertain or questioning? As the subordinate walked away, was there a spring in her or his step and did she or he walk with greater purpose or resolve? Stand a little straighter? Exchanges that leave subordinates feeling empowered and equipped to do their work add to the collective energy in the school or office. When multiplied over the dozens of exchanges the leader has in the course of a day, this contributes in significant ways to the energy and drive of the organization as a whole. Exchanges that diminish the subordinate's energy and resolve, when multiplied over dozens of interactions, can take the air out of the organization's tires.

Learning how to provide clear, specific feedback based on observations is an essential part of the coaching dance. When educational leaders know that their coaches see positive value in what they are doing and how they are interacting with their people, however fledgling their efforts, all manner of things become possible. Making clean observations without negative judgments expands awareness and evokes mobility, while criticism often provokes defensiveness, antagonism, and retrenchment. People may shut down and want to argue with a critique, even when it contains an element of truth. People open up and want to engage with observations, even when those observations contain challenging messages. Specific feedback is quite different, and much more arduous to provide, than general compliments. Although a compliment may be pleasant for the coachee to hear, it conveys very little substantive or useful information for the coachee. As evocative coaches, we are concerned with making vital observations that contribute to the learning and growth of the educational leaders we work with.

Excellence is not the opposite of failure, and you will learn little about excellence from studying failure. To learn about success you have to study success. Only successful examples can tell you what excellence looks like.

—Marcus Buckingham (2007, pp. 5–6)

OPPORTUNITIES

Once educational leaders have connected with the best of what is and have fully appreciated their strengths and vitalities, they naturally start sensing the opportunities for the best of what might be. Educational leaders and coaches are not limited to a strengths-based reconnaissance of the past and present. We can also inquire into and seek to appreciate the future. That is what Scharmer (2007) refers to as "learning from the future as it emerges" (p. 56) or "connecting with the Source of the highest future possibility and bringing into the now" (p. 163). That dynamic is not just about setting a goal to work toward; it is about imagining the best of what might be in ways that infuse the present with energy, guidance, and the wherewithal to move forward. Imagination, at its best, is a proleptic force that brings the future into the present moment and gets people to act as if the future is breaking in upon them. Such extrapolation is a vital part of the AI process.

Opportunities are expressions of what educational leaders would like to learn, explore, and do. Opportunities are filled with positive energy. The upshot of inquiry should be an enthusiastic response to the question, "Now what?" If there is no enthusiasm, then something is off, and coaches must adjust. If there is enthusiasm, then coaches can assist educational leaders to move forward by asking one or more of the following questions, which are designed to get them thinking about new opportunities. The selective use of these questions is an essential part of getting educational leaders ready for design conversations.

Sample Questions to Get Leaders Thinking About New Opportunities

- What opportunities do you see for yourself and your school/district in the coming year?

- What would you like to see more of in your school/district?

- What results do you think are most important?

- What new directions excite you right now?

- What are the best things that could happen in your school/district in the near future?

- What initiatives are working well and need to be strengthened and built upon?

- What new skills would you like to cultivate moving forward? What opportunities are there to gain those skills?

Were we to ask educational leaders these questions before discovering their strengths and observing vitalities, we might well get a rather limited and scripted response based on district goals and planning documents. By waiting to ask in the wake of a recognizance of strengths and vitalities, however, we get a much broader and more personalized response. Educational leaders begin to think for themselves as to how they could best expand the realm of the possible.

Such boldness can be encouraged by coaches through the questions we ask, as long as we do not ask them too soon. To a struggling educational leader caught in the grip of negative emotions or performance reviews, the invitation to frame new opportunities may sound empty, inauthentic, impossible, or even insulting. "Yeah, right, who are you kidding?" is more likely to be the reaction of such coachees than a free and willing engagement in the process of conceptualizing how their identity and behavior might change to support personal and professional mastery. That is why it is so important to validate educational leaders' experiences and to appreciate their strengths before asking them to extrapolate to the even more positive and constructive frame of opportunity. Discouraged and aggravated clients are not prone to aspire to new heights. They are not even prone to cook up small improvements in their life and work. Until they receive empathy for their negative emotions, and until they connect with positive emotions through appreciative inquiries into their strengths and vitalities, not much will take off in the way of vision casting. After their mood elevates, however, evocative coaches will find clients much more inclined to contemplate and work toward future opportunities.

I grew up in this community. My dad was the superintendent of schools. I went to high school here and, in this community, you are not really an insider unless you went to the high school. The schools are pretty happy places; the kids feel safe and comfortable and so do the teachers. But when I became a principal and began walking the classrooms with my coach, we noticed that the quality of instruction was really lacking in both rigor and engagement. My wife is a teacher in the district, and I figured that if I put pressure on teachers to change and she started hearing complaints from her colleagues, life could get pretty uncomfortable at home. So I assumed that I if I had any chance at all, any improvement efforts would have to focus on the younger teachers. But when my coach introduced me to this strengths-based method of change, I was astonished by how all the teachers got on board, even some who had only a few years left before retirement!

—Jacob, Middle School Principal

ASPIRATIONS

Aspirations capture who educational leaders are and want to be. They are expressions of identity and mastery. Framing aspirations is a visionary practice, calling on educational leaders to imagine both themselves and their schools and districts at their very best. Exploring, mapping, cultivating, and articulating aspirations fuels the evocative coaching process. Aspirations are visions that answer those larger questions in life and work regarding the contribution we make, the energy we muster, and the support we mobilize to realize our full potential and that of the schools and systems we lead. Unless people feel connected to a cause that is larger than themselves, they often do little more than muddle along as best they can. Educational leaders are lifted up to the full measure of their calling through evocative coaching conversations. They dare to dream the impossible dream and march to their own drummer when it comes to those questions of calling and vision. What do educational leaders really want? What resonates with their very being and calls out their very best? How do they imagine their future selves? What would make life more meaningful and productive? What aspirations do they hear calling out their name?

Evocative coaches encourage educational leaders to dream big and to articulate propositions regarding the best of what might be. It takes big dreams to stir hearts and move people to action. Such propositions have the most power to influence present attitudes and behavior when they are:

- Grounded: Building on the best of current reality

- Daring: Boldly stretching the status quo

- Desired: Reflecting what we want to move toward, not what we want to move away from

- Palpable: Sensing the future in the present, as if it was already happening

- Participatory: Involving all relevant stakeholders (Watkins, Mohr, & Kelly, 2011)

It becomes easier for educational leaders to talk about their intrinsic aspirations and spin them out for the future once they are connected to their strengths and vitalities. The better educational leaders feel about themselves and their work, the more they aspire to make themselves and that work even better. At their best, such aspirations go beyond yearning to the place of vision. Coachees come to see themselves and their work in new ways. The more coaches connect clients with images that are infused with the energy and emotion of possibility, the more these leaders move beyond imagining small tweaks in their performance to significant leaps forward that benefit themselves and the schools or districts they serve. Coaching this way elevates energy, improves mood, unleashes creativity, and bolsters both initiative and resilience. Capturing such aspirations in words and images, framed in the present tense as if they were already true, is an essential part of the evocative coaching dance.

Aspirational Images. Facilitating this future search requires a more creative approach to coaching than just talking about what educational leaders want or how they see the future. All talk and no play makes coaching a dull task. The poetic principle of AI encourages coaches to go beyond the limitations of analysis by utilizing images, metaphors, stories, and narratives to make dreams come alive. That is when educational leaders truly come into the fullness of their aspirations for change. Evocative coaches may therefore ask coachees to draw pictures, to use metaphors, to write poems, to create collages or vision boards, or to otherwise engage the right side of the brain in mindful creativity. By getting educational leaders to focus on what they want now, to feel how it sits in their bodies, and to flesh out the particulars with whatever creative modalities they might enjoy, evocative coaches enable educational leaders to become more articulate, confident, and creative in the possibilities they see for change. By engaging the heart and stirring the imagination through positive mental simulation, coaches enable coachees to generate both the willingness and the readiness to make dreams come true.

If you want to build a ship, don't drum up people to gather wood, give orders, and divide the work. Instead, teach them to yearn for the vast and endless sea.

—Antoine de Saint-Exupéry (1950)

Writing a Leadership Platform. Although framing aspirations is a visionary practice, with plenty of opportunity for right-brain engagement, the work is not complete until the left brain catches on and finds the words to describe what all those images, metaphors, stories, and narratives represent. However educational leaders get there, through whatever combination of creative right-brain and expressive left-brain activities, evocative coaching seeks to crystallize for those leaders a clear understanding and statement of their personal and professional aspirations—a leadership platform. In framing aspirations, we start with the need, give voice to the yearning stemming from the need, imagine its fulfillment, and frame its significance. Coaches can assist educational leaders to find the right words by inquiring appreciatively into values, outcomes, strengths, behaviors, motivators, and environments. All aspirations, however luminous, touch on these practical realities:

- Values: What are my principles? What do I stand for?
- Outcomes: What do I need? What do I want?
- Strengths: What am I good at? What makes me feel strong?
- Behaviors: What activities do I aspire to do consistently?
- Motivators: Why does this matter a lot to me right now?
- Environments: What support team and structures will facilitate success?

Clients should be encouraged to write down their aspirations and then to summarize them in a few memorable sentences. When asked, they should be able to easily and passionately share their aspirations with others. An example of an aspirational statement for educational leaders, written in the present tense as if it were already true, might sound something like this:

My presence and way of being with teachers, staff, students, and parents is life-affirming and inspires trust. I engage teachers' intellectual curiosity and ignite their imagination about the future we might build together. My teachers and staff members are confident that I value them as human beings more than I value the work we do together, although my enthusiasm for our work is contagious. It motivates all members of our school community to be extraordinary learners.

RESOURCES

To be effective, educational leaders must pay attention to the resources that are either available or can be marshaled to bring their aspirations for themselves and their schools or districts into being. There is a section on the experimental design template, which is part of the design-thinking process we will turn to in the next chapter, for supporting systems and resources. This section is not just a place for materials and equipment, it is a place where coachees can take note of all the necessary resources and supports, including systems, structures, money, supplies, physical arrangements, staffing, tools, and relationships, that can be used to bring their aspirations to fruition. The word *resources* most readily brings to mind financial resources, which can stir a scarcity mindset that leads to a constriction of creative potential. A broader search for the resources already at hand or that can be cultivated can help foster renewed hope that opportunities can be captured and aspirations reached.

The entire scope of the educational process may be impacted as the shifts made by one educational leader percolate into the larger school culture, leading that institution to more fully embody the vision of what Senge called a school that learns (Senge, 2006; Senge et al., 2000).

What Resources Do You Need to Realize Your Goals?

- **Financial Resources.** Coaching educational leaders to find creative solutions to the financial constraints posed by their environments can alleviate the stress they experience from seemingly chronic resource shortages. It may be that resources can be found by reallocating monies already in the budget or that new monies can be found through partnerships or grants. The work of the coach is to not allow the exploration of aspirations to be cut short by assumptions and fears about the lack of financial resources.

- **Human Resources.** Educational leaders interact with a multitude of people in both professional and personal settings. These networks of relationships are a

(Continued)

(Continued)

rich resource that can be tapped in bringing aspirations to life. Imagining how relationships might be cultivated or nurtured in service of the clients' aspirations can be a source of inspiration and encouragement.

- **Technology Resources.** Coaches work with educational leaders to assess the technological tools available and to find ways to marshal these tools to capitalize on leaders' strengths in service of their aspirations. These tools might also be built into the experiments designed during the next phase of the process.

- **Cultural Resources.** Organizational cultures are powerful forces that can either support or impede coachee aspirations. Cultural values and assumptions are given expression through norms and sanctions that guide behavior, rituals and ceremonies that point to what is important and valued by the organization, and traditions and stories of organizational history and heroes. Even the exercise of humor and play reveals important organizational values and assumptions. Coaches can assist clients to examine these cultural elements for ways they can be cultivated in service of client aspirations. As cultural values and assumptions are revealed and begin to shift, old assumptions and patterns of how things get done may give way to new understandings.

- **Material Resources.** Material resources that might support client aspirations include school equipment and supplies, school buildings and the meeting spaces within them, and the grounds around the schools. Considerations can be made as to how these resources are used and how they are allocated, arranged, and designed to support coachee aspirations. New sources of materials and resources may be found. New purchases may be made. The arrangement of furniture and equipment may be changed.

- **Recovery Resources.** If there is a single message that virtually every coach confronts in the course of our work with educational leaders, it is the message of being overloaded and overwhelmed. Educational leaders experience more demands today than ever before, and it shows in manifold ways, including increased health problems and reduced enthusiasm. This dynamic provides fertile material for empathy, but it also provides opportunities for coaches and their coachees to discover resources for recovery and renewal. Full engagement requires a rhythm of work and rest that educational leaders and coaches too often neglect. Paying attention to the rhythm of clients' lives lies at the heart of sustainable change.

SOARING INTO THE FUTURE

The SOAR process seeks to move educational leaders from an appreciative inquiry of the present and past to an appreciative inquiry into the future. The aspirations of educational leaders, both long term and short term, are part of how the future breaks into the present. Instead of coming at problems directly, focusing on what we want to eliminate and get rid of, aspirations come at them indirectly, through the lens of what we want to cultivate more of. The more educational leaders increase their awareness of how the future is emerging, the more they will move to a place of clarity and enthusiasm regarding their visions and goals. That is what we hope for out of the AI phase: a strong felt sense and a clear, compelling statement of what the future is calling educational leaders to be and do. By appreciating strengths and aspirations, coaches harvest positive energy and emotion; such reconnection provides the fuel for all that follows in terms of brainstorming and designing.

The question is not what you look at, but what you see.

—Henry David Thoreau

Key Points in This Chapter

1. The more coaches navigate by open-minded curiosity with regard to client strengths, opportunities, aspirations, and resources, the more coachees will discover about themselves, where they want to go, and how they want to get there.

2. Strengths-based inquiries not only get educational leaders ready for change, they are, in an important sense, change itself.

3. When evocative coaches engage in a SOAR analysis with clients, inquiring into the client's strengths, observations, aspirations, and resources to discover the best of what is and to imagine the best of what might be, it fosters new realities and invigorates the client with a can-do energy that readies him or her for the design conversations yet to come.

4. Evocative coaches assist educational leaders to explore their strengths through the use of appreciative interviews, assessments, and observations.

5. Opportunities are filled with positive energy; they are expressions of what educational leaders would like to learn, explore, and do.

6. Framing aspirations is a visionary practice, calling on educational leaders to imagine both themselves and their schools and districts at their very best.

7. To be effective, educational leaders must pay attention to the resources that are either available or can be marshaled to bring their aspirations for themselves and their schools or districts into being.

Questions for Reflection and Discussion

1. Why is it important to set the stage through story and empathy before evocative coaches invite educational leaders into inquiry and design?

2. What has been your best experience of building on strengths at work? How did you feel when those strengths were called upon and came out? What did that experience lead to?

3. How might you incorporate the four questions that constitute the appreciative interview protocol into an ongoing coaching relationship?

4. What does the VIA Character Strengths Questionnaire (http://www.viacharacter .org) reveal about your top five signature strengths? How might you use these when coaching?

5. When observing educational leaders in their schools, why is it important to avoid praising and criticizing their attitudes and actions? What can we do instead?

6. When educational leaders have difficult experiences, how can coaches assist them to reframe those experiences in positive terms?

Design Thinking

Once the work of the first three phases of evocative coaching is done, motivation and movement pick up steam. Coachees are in touch with themselves, their experiences, and their abilities. They have framed their aspirations and identified opportunities they now yearn to see realized. In short, educational leaders are inspired. At that point, then, one thing is necessary to complete a cycle of the evocative coaching process: design. "How do we make this happen?" is the operative question of the design phase. To give their opportunities traction and to move in the direction of their aspirations, educational leaders work with their coaches to brainstorm ways for moving forward, select the ideas they want to pursue, design strategies they feel confident about, experiment with new behavioral approaches, and integrate the learning into their daily practices. We want them to be creative in identifying possibilities, variables, ideas, and approaches they have not tried before.

Although design thinking is presented as the final phase of the evocative coaching process, in many respects evocative coaching is itself a design-thinking process. Design thinking involves three iterative, nonlinear steps—*inspiration, ideation,* and *implementation*—that are best thought of as a system of overlapping spaces. Design projects "loop back through these spaces more than once" as ideas are refined and new directions are explored (T. Brown, 2009, p. 16). Evocative coaching works in much the same way. Through the iterative, nonlinear use of story listening, empathy reflections, and AI, coaches inspire educational leaders with an awareness of what is happening in the present moment and an ambition to transform what might happen in future moments. Without *inspiration,* the work of *ideation* and *implementation* is just another chore. With *inspiration,* those concepts take off and soar. The word *inspiration* means both "stimulation of the mind or emotions to a high level of feeling or activity" and "something, such as a sudden creative act or idea, that is inspired" (American Heritage Dictionary, 2009). In other words, inspiration is both a process and an outcome.

Coaching becomes evocative when educational leaders find the inspiration to generate and implement ideas for change. Without listening to stories, offering empathy, and inquiring appreciatively, there is little hope for design. By dancing with educational leaders through the no-fault and strengths-building turns, coaches move educational leaders to innovate their designs into being. We inspire both eagerness and the ability to change. This invests ideas with emotional energy and moves people to action. With strong intrinsic motivation, high self-efficacy, positive energy, emotion, and images, educational leaders are ready to turn their opportunities into realities and their aspirations into actions. Nothing succeeds like success, so evocative coaches collaborate with educational leaders to design action strategies that generate quick wins in a fulfilling manner.

Investing the time and effort to develop realistic and inspiring designs is what gets people moving forward. It gets them excited about their capacity and vision for change while mapping out how to get started, which route to follow, and how to adapt in the face of adversity. It makes clear the destination by providing a path of development or the tools to get there. Through the design conversation, educational leaders come up with new, actionable ideas and commit to the ones they view as particularly doable, exciting, and impactful. They also devise ways to reengineer their teams, schools, and districts so as to better support those commitments. A key factor in assisting educational leaders to change their behaviors is building the behavioral and environmental infrastructure that will support and help them to realize their aspirations. Because the world is never static, designs must be continuously adapted to ever-changing, real-world conditions.

As in all phases of the evocative coaching model, the coach does not prescribe to clients what their designs should be. That posture is fraught with multiple dangers. It may generate resistance rather than openness, create a power-over rather than a power-with dynamic, and set up people for struggle and failure. Even when a client takes the advice, she or he is in the difficult and oftentimes awkward position of having to implement someone else's ideas. Coaching leads educational leaders through the process of discovering that they are capable of great things and then creates the space for compelling visions, desired outcomes, and transformational strategies to emerge.

The positive lens refers to . . . our capacity to construct better organizations and technologies through positive discourse. Joining a positive lens onto organizing with the transformative power of design thinking opens new horizons and uncovers previously overlooked possibilities for creating organizational and social well-being.

—Michel Avital & Richard Boland (2007, p. 3)

Designing SMARTER Experiments

No coaching conversation should end without some sense of what educational leaders will do differently in the days and weeks ahead. To get clients into the action phase of the evocative coaching model, coaches work with them to develop SMARTER experiments. These are distinguished from SMART *goals* because an experiment keeps the emphasis on learning and reduces the fear of failure. The notion of committing to and conducting an experiment conveys a very different energy than seeking to meet a goal. There's no way to fail at an experiment. Whether or not experiments work out as expected, they always provide valuable data that are intrinsically interesting and useful. From these we can design and build future experiments. By coaching clients to positively reframe unexpected outcomes as valuable learning experiences, we enable them to bounce back from setbacks. We want coachees to view their activities in the living laboratory of their schools and districts as win-learn rather than win-lose activities. This increases the fun and makes learning the intention of all new behaviors.

SMARTER experiments are **s**pecific, **m**easurable, **a**ttainable, **r**elevant, **t**ime bound, **e**valuated, and **r**efined. Experiments are *specific* about *how* and *when* educational leaders will do *what* and with *whom* to test their hypotheses and increase their level of success. Requirements as to materials and resources must also be specified. The more detailed the specifics, the easier it is to *measure* and understand the results of experiments. Did things work out as expected or not? To answer that question, coachees must be very clear as to what their experiments are designed to do. It is important for experiments to be perceived as *attainable*. Clients should feel confident in their ability to conduct an experiment, whether it represents an incremental step in the direction of a desired outcome or a bolder quantum leap. It is also important for experiments to be seen by coachees as *relevant* to their stated opportunities and aspirations. The change process will be hindered if they go through the motions of learning without seeing how those motions may contribute to their personal growth and professional development in their work. Setting a specific *time frame* for the experiments increases the likelihood that they will happen. Putting something on your schedule now increases the likelihood of success more than leaving an open time frame and hoping to get around to it eventually.

Once the experiment is underway, it is important to *evaluate* how the experiment is going and to reflect on what is being learned in order to *refine* it as necessary. SMARTER experiments leave clients with a clear sense of what they will do and what they hope to learn. There is never anything final about the designs that educational leaders and coaches cook up together for realizing aspirations and opportunities. Progress in living systems like schools and districts is never linear. Setbacks and surprises are inevitable. Experimental designs therefore require continuous learning, dialogue, and updating in order to be fulfilled and fulfilling.

The concept of conducting SMARTER experiments is a way of field testing ideas rather than implementing plans. Scientists call it the scientific method. Identify a puzzle. Develop a hypothesis. Collect data to test the hypothesis. If something works, great! Try it again to see if it works again. If something doesn't work, great! Modify the strategy or modify the hypothesis until something does work. But stick with the process until a discovery is made. In service of engaged learning, experiments typically involve the following:

- Hypothesis: An assertion that you want to test or explore

- Procedures: How the experiment will be conducted

- Materials: Things you will need to conduct the experiment

- Data Recording: How the observations will be recorded in real time

- Observations: What happens when the experiment is conducted

- Conclusions: What insights emerged as data were reviewed in relation to the hypothesis

Making use of an experimental design template can help coaches and their clients to develop SMARTER experiments. It can assist educational leaders to move successfully from ideas to action by adding procedural clarity to the design of their experiments. The experimental design template's primary function is to serve as a writing tool to capture the details of client experiments to ensure those details have been thought through before coachees conduct their experiments. The more carefully educational leaders think about, visualize, and write down their experimental design, the more likely it is they will take creative, innovative actions that will move them forward in their personal and professional mastery.

The experimental design template in Figure 6.1 captures an experimental design for Sylvia Cooper, an educational leader who became aware that her reputation as a micromanager was interfering with her success. Sylvia was the assistant superintendent of a district serving a diverse group of 60,000 students. The superintendent was well loved by the community, but he had never been an educator and thus left the oversight of the instructional program to Sylvia. Sylvia took seriously the enormity of that responsibility and had a great sense of urgency to improve the outcomes for the students of the district. Her coach, Monica, was aware that those who worked for Sylvia found her to be difficult. She was known to change the agenda for meetings or professional development sessions at the last minute, to turn a scheduled five-minute welcome at the start of an event into an hour-long lecture, and to start numerous initiatives at once without adequate planning or consideration for the time and resources it would take to implement them well. The spring before Sylvia began work with her coach, the district had conducted a trust survey. Sylvia was shocked and dismayed to discover she had received the lowest possible ratings on both honesty and openness.

The entire first year of their work together, Sylvia and Monica worked on greater transparency in decision making and greater alignment between words and actions. Throughout that year, Sylvia developed an abiding trust in Monica. That trust was put to the test in August when Sylvia prepared a video for all of the district teachers to open the school year. Sylvia and Monica watched it together, and Sylvia was eager for Monica's opinion. Instead of offering an opinion, however, Monica asked, "OK, let's watch it again together and you point out for me the places where empathy shows through." As Sylvia watched the video again, her mood shifted from triumphant to dismayed. As the video finished, she exclaimed, "There's none! There is no empathy there. I get it now. I see how I am being perceived." She decided to redo the whole video the next morning. In the new video, Sylvia shared from her heart why the work of the schools in the district mattered so much to her and related some of her own struggles and successes with getting through to hard-to-reach students. That stood out for the teachers, how she had made herself vulnerable for the first time, and it contributed to their growing trust in her. That year, Sylvia identified two areas she wanted to work on with her coach: (1) changing the way she was perceived as a micromanager by those she led, and (2) focusing on a small number of initiatives that would make a difference rather than on 20. Sylvia and her staff consolidated their initiatives under the acronym AIR[2]: **a**cademic vocabulary, **i**nformational texts, **r**igor, and **r**elationships.

Sylvia took that second R, relationships, to heart as she designed an experiment with Monica using the experimental design template. She summarized her hypothesis with an if-then claim: "If I consciously strive to be a trusting delegator, the capabilities of those I lead will increase and their contributions to the organization will be more significant and have a greater impact." She linked this claim to her core values, stating, "I want to lead a strong, cohesive, and collaborative team. I want to be a multiplier and not a diminisher." From there, she and Monica generated a list of potential strategies to test her hypothesis. Sylvia put forth some ideas, and Monica offered some variations on the themes Sylvia suggested when she seemed stuck. From the list of generated strategies, Sylvia selected four and then considered what kinds of supporting systems and resources she would need to enact her strategies. When Sylvia had described what she intended to do in her experiment, Monica asked her to rate on a scale of 0 to 10 how confident she felt that she would actually conduct the experiment. Sylvia answered, "Oh, for sure an 8, maybe even a 9! I'm going to do this for sure because this is important to me!" Then Monica asked her what kinds of data she would gather to assess what she had learned from the experiment. Sylvia thought for a minute and then said she would develop an anonymous survey with which to gather honest and specific feedback from her team and that she would ask for honest feedback from her coach as well.

Over the next several years, Sylvia's work with her team continued to improve. In response to a Gates Foundation survey of teachers in the district that found "voice and choice" as the lowest score on the climate measure, Sylvia led a leadership retreat devoted to enhancing the voice and choice of teachers. Teachers were invited to identify what professional development they needed to be successful with the AIR² initiative. They were then given choices as to how they would learn what they needed to learn, whether through reading, attending a webinar, working with a partner or a coach, or attending a workshop. A team of external evaluators who visited every school in the district noted dramatic improvements in the quality of instruction and a positive and productive climate in every building. When asked what she hoped her legacy in the district would be, Sylvia said that she sought to leave behind a strong team that had the capacity to carry on the good work they had begun together.

HYPOTHESIS

Most experiments start with a hypothesis, and these coaching experiments do too. The coach assists the client to frame her or his aspirations in terms of an if-then statement. For example, Sylvia's hypothesis stated, "If I consciously strive to be a trusting delegator, then the capabilities of those I lead will increase and their contributions to the organization will be more significant and have a greater impact." This may be challenging at first, and the coachee may need more support, but it helps to keep the focus on learning rather than on the accomplishment of a goal. The experiment may be either professional or personal because these two realms impact and interrelate with each other.

Experiments must be related to a larger, positive vision of who educational leaders are and where they want to go in the future. The second box of the experimental design template invites coachees to articulate the relevance of the experiment to their personal aspiration and/or to the professional standards that guide their practice. Experiments must also be grounded in the reality of what educational leaders know and have accomplished in the past. That is why evocative coaches spend so much time with story—empathy—inquiry. Those phases of the evocative coaching process pour the foundation for aspiring, brainstorming, and experimenting. They assist educational leaders to enhance not only their effectiveness but also their sense of meaning, learning, and joy in life.

In designing a way forward, it is important for a coach to be sensitive to a client's readiness for change. There are two kinds of experiments a client might choose: an awareness experiment or an action experiment. If coachees are in an early stage of change and not yet ready for action, it can be very useful to design an experiment addressing how they might learn more about the direction they are considering, such as selecting something they might read, research, or watch, or choosing someone they might meet with or observe.

FIGURE 6.1 Experimental Design Template

EXPERIMENTAL DESIGN TEMPLATE

Name: Sylvia Cooper	**Date:** Jan 30	**Focus:** _Professional_ _Personal_

State Hypothesis:

If I consciously strive to be a trusting delegator, then the capabilities of those I lead will increase and their contributions to the organization will be more significant and have a greater impact.

Describe Relevance to Personal Aspirations/Professional Standards:

I want to lead a strong, cohesive, and collaborative team. I want to be a multiplier and not a diminisher.

Strategies or Activities (Specific as to What, Where, and How):	**Supporting Systems & Resources:**	**Timeline:**
• Tell my team I am working on my micromanaging. • Give the team permission to check me, hold me accountable, and call me on it when I am perceived as micromanaging. • Clearly articulate in advance my expectations for team members' assignments with regard to meetings and training sessions to avoid the need to make last-minute changes. • Provide feedback that is timely, specific, and relevant.	Ideally, I need time and additional staff; however, since that is not available, I need to: • Look at the calendar in advance • Work with the team on thinking about the outcomes of decisions • Debrief at the end of meetings and events • Engage with team members in advance of meetings • Implement effective coaching strategies	February–June

Describe Data Collection and Reporting Techniques:

I will collect data regarding my progress from a survey that are more specific about my goals and behaviors and engage in honest dialogue with my team. In addition, I will get honest feedback from my coach.

Confidence Level (On a Scale of 0 to 10): 8–9	_Revise the strategy, systems, resources, and/or timeline until confidence is 7 or higher._

The first time I met with Carl, a high school principal at a school for students placed outside the regular high school program, he immediately escorted me into his office and closed the door. "We've had a rough week," he confided. "We had three kids with guns at school." He proceeded to tell a distressing tale of the challenges and difficulties he faced at the school. We met for over an hour, and I offered an empathetic ear. But the whole time we talked, it sounded like all hell was breaking loose just on the other side of the door. When his shoulders slumped and he let out a resigned sigh, I asked, "So what do you think we should do about this? Let's brainstorm some ideas." He began to throw out suggestions, and I had a few that I added as well. The longer the list of possible strategies grew, the more hopeful he seemed to become. He said finally, "This is really helpful! We should get the whole staff in on this!" So we designed a process of brainstorming with the whole staff. It turned out that there was an older gentleman on staff, Mr. Baker, who carried huge respect among the students and in the community as well. In working together with the staff to tap the insights into the students that Mr. Baker brought, a strong bond developed between Carl and Mr. Baker. The positive changes in the school climate and student behavior began almost overnight. It was like watching magic happen!

—Anne, School Improvement Coach

BRAINSTORMING DESIGN IDEAS

If coaching is about anything at all, it is about getting educational leaders to generate and try out new ideas to help them be more successful. If coaching fails to generate new ideas for moving forward, it fails to be evocative. Brainstorming design ideas is an essential part of how evocative coaching conversations move educational leaders forward in service of their opportunities and aspirations. Once opportunities have been identified and aspirations have been claimed, the next logical question is, how do we get there? Assisting coachees to brainstorm answers to that question is an important part of evocative coaching. Brainstorming is the rapid, playful generation of possibilities. It helps clients to think outside the box, come up with innovative ideas, and entertain notions they otherwise might not even consider. Brainstorming is a great way to break through bottlenecks and energize the design process.

Cluster diagrams can facilitate brainstorming because of how they show relationships between ideas. In addition, setting a minimum number of possibilities to generate ahead of time makes sure that the process does not stop prematurely. Six to ten is generally a good range. Setting a time limit to keep things moving rapidly can help get many ideas on the table in a short time. Coaches may also encourage clients to include

EVOKING GREATNESS

wild and crazy ideas because these may hold a kernel of a notion that opens thinking in a new direction. This is all part of what makes brainstorming evocative and fun.

Creative brainstorming is a good way to put lots of new ideas on the table without the coach coming across as the expert who prescribes what clients should do. Coaches can ask, "What else? What else? What else?" and the ideas just seem to pour out of the clients. Other times, however, clients have a hard time coming up with ideas. It is important to try to get coachees to put the first idea on the table so that they maintain ownership of their professional learning and growth and of the coaching process. A strategy we've borrowed from Hollywood screenwriters is to invite a client who is struggling to come up with even a single idea to come up with a really, really bad idea for going forward. This may break the tension and evoke a laugh before we move on to try to identify more productive approaches. Coaches and educational leaders can then take turns throwing out ideas without pausing to evaluate their relative merit or feasibility, putting forward possible approaches that build and bounce from one to another. This cocreative process assists coaches to step out of the expert role and assists coachees to step up to generating and playing with possibilities.

Coaches should be careful to not unduly influence educational leaders with our ideas, energy, and enthusiasm in the setting of strategies. When coaches are perceived to have a lot of expertise, coachees may ask them to provide answers and give directives. It may seem simpler to seek the advice of an expert about how to solve one's problems than to come up with solutions on one's own. Such didactic approaches, however, are fraught with hazards when it comes to facilitating adult learning and lasting behavior change. The coach takes on the primary responsibility for the client's learning and growth, setting up a dependency relationship that deprives the client of a mature sense of responsibility for her or his professional learning and growth. Regardless of how much research or data may stand behind us or how great our ideas may sound to our coachees, prescriptions for improvement generally will not translate into effective action. Even when they have asked for direction, coachees may harbor an undercurrent of resentment at an outside expert telling them what to do. Lack of ownership of an idea may prevent a client from staying with the idea long enough for it to become part of the behavioral repertoire. That is why evocative coaches redirect such requests—and even our own desire to add value to a design conversation—by proposing a brainstorming session in which clients and coaches work together to come up with an array of ideas. By creating multiple possibilities together in this way, educational leaders remain active and empowered in the search for more effective approaches, and coaches can float ideas that coachees might never come up with on their own or might otherwise resist without coming across as prescriptive.

There is a difference between brainstorming a strategy for moving forward and simply sharing information. When clients pose a procedural question, for instance, such as how to access certain data or file a particular report, if the coach knows the answer, she or he should just provide that information. The appearance of a cat-and-mouse game, in which the coach seems to be withholding information to see if a client will come up with it on his or her own, can generate frustration and diminish trust in the coach's intentions. Even expressing empathy at these points can be frustrating. As one client noted, "It is infuriating to receive empathy when what I need is information." Notwithstanding all that has been said about the limits of didactic approaches and expert advice, there are times to just tell educational leaders what they want to know.

The operational task is to generate and test multiple ideas for skill and performance improvements instead of getting wedded too quickly to a single course of action. Failing to brainstorm can squander the potential of the moment, either because no new possibilities are generated or because one possibility dominates the conversation before others are considered. Running with the first idea that comes up limits professional development and may even send clients in the wrong direction. As French philosopher Émile Chartier once quipped, "Nothing is as dangerous as an idea when it is the only one you have." Brainstorming can be both fun and productive, albeit challenging. To come up with so many creative possibilities in a relatively short period of time stretches the mind and the conversation beyond their normal limits. Such stretching capitalizes on and enhances a client's willingness to change.

When conversation between a coach and [a coachee] comes alive, ideas can bounce around like balls in a pinball machine, and people can start to communicate so well that it becomes difficult to see where one person's thoughts end and another's begin.

—Jim Knight (2007, p. 46)

PRIORITIZING AND CHOOSING

Once coaches and educational leaders have generated a large number of possibilities, it is time for them to prioritize the ideas, choose the ones they want to do something about, and design experiments that can assist the leaders to learn and grow. By developing and asking clients to choose from a universe of possibilities, the decision making remains in their hands, where it belongs. If the coach takes the lead in designing the experiment, the coach is taking responsibility for client learning and growth. Educational leaders always have choice in the experiments they design and conduct. Coaches should be sure clients understand that they may turn away at any point from any experiment.

To prioritize the ideas, we may ask the coachee to identify the three possibilities they find most interesting and promising. Each can be considered before settling upon the ones to develop further. To guide the selection process, coaches navigate with curiosity. Questions such as those listed below enable coaches and clients to explore and prioritize ideas together.

Questions to Prompt Exploration and Priority Setting

- Which ideas stand out as the best ideas? What attracts you to them? What makes them worth pursuing?

- Which ideas might have the greatest impact?

- Which ideas build on what you are already doing well?

- What strengths might you leverage to succeed with your chosen ideas?

- When have you tried something like this before?

Once coachees have explored those strategies they find the most intriguing or energizing, we invite them to pick those they want to work with in the days and weeks ahead. It is then time to get specific as to the *what, when, where,* and *how* of each of the strategies selected. These will be spelled out in the experimental design template with as much specificity as possible. The first part of the experiment might be an awareness experiment in which the educational leader engages in a literature search to discover evidence of the effectiveness of the potential initiatives and how they have been successfully implemented elsewhere. A robust dialogue between experience and the literature is central to choosing in the design-thinking model. Educational leaders might also be encouraged to identify backup strategies and be empowered to modify procedures as necessary and appropriate in the course of conducting the experiment.

Some actions are within reach during coaching conversations themselves. That's when the "Do it now!" principle comes into play. If educational leaders can take action on something immediately, such as putting something on their calendars, have them do it now. When progress is made in this way during coaching sessions, it elevates self-efficacy, energy, and mobility. Other actions can be mapped out using an abbreviated form of the experimental design template. Whatever form it takes, the key is to walk away from coaching conversations with a clear picture as to what clients will do, when, and with whom, captured in such a way as to facilitate commitment and accountability.

My job as a coach is to build the capacity of the leaders I coach. I could tell them in five minutes what they need to do, and it would be successful. But then they wouldn't know what to do the next time when I'm not there. I have to know that I haven't done my job if they can't do it on their own when I'm not there.

—Mike, Leadership Coach

SUPPORTING SYSTEMS AND RESOURCES

In designing SMARTER experiments, it is important to invite educational leaders to think through what would help them succeed with the strategies they have selected. It is seldom sufficient just to bolster their resolve and change their technique. Lasting change usually requires the alignment of environmental supports. Our design conversations with educational leaders regarding SMARTER experiments are therefore not complete until we pay specific attention to the laboratories in which those experiments are to be conducted. Physical scientists understand the integral connection between environments, researchers, and experiments. Many experiments simply cannot be conducted unless the right materials, equipment, human resources, financing, and other factors are in place. In the design phase, we not only assist clients to figure out what they will do on their own, we also assist them to think through how they might better align their environments to make their SMARTER experiments more satisfying and enlightening. If we assist educational leaders to think through these environmental dynamics, their experiments will be more successful and their self-efficacy will increase. The supporting systems and resources section of the experimental design template invites educational leaders to consider these environmental factors.

One process for playing with ideas is to use the ripples in a pond diagram. The analogy is of throwing a stone into a pond, watching the ripples expand, and noticing how they move outward (Watkins, Mohr, & Kelly, 2011, p. 251). This diagram works with three concentric circles in order to better understand and influence the environmental factors related to the experiment. The changes envisioned in the experiment are in the center circle. It is the pebble thrown into the pond, so to speak. The ripples that flow out from there invite coachees to consider various environmental factors, both human and systemic, that will influence and be influenced by their experiment.

The first ripple in the pond correlates to the people the experiment touches. Who will be impacted by this experiment most directly? Who will be impacted indirectly? Who might be called upon to help out? Who might resist the effort? Educational leaders can be asked to think of all the key stakeholders and put them on the diagram in the first ring. The second ring has to do with the organizational elements that may come into play. What resources and systems must be in place to conduct the experiment? What policies, procedures, materials, equipment, technologies, budgets, and other aspects of the system may be impacted by the experiment? Once all of the environmental factors have been identified and appreciated, clients are asked to consider how they might nudge or move those factors in a positive direction. They may be asked to consider what actions they can take as well as what requests they can make of others that will raise the likelihood their experiment will be successful. Be as specific as possible as to what the experiment requires and how the coachees will set up supporting conditions. If the timeline includes benchmarks or milestones to be reached before the next coaching session, make them explicit. Framing questions in terms of how educational leaders can align these many environmental elements to carry out their experiments supports the intention for behavioral change. Once those environments begin to shift, they support the design of new experiments.

EVALUATE: EVIDENCE OF SUCCESS

Experimental designs are not complete until clients decide how they want to collect, report, and reflect on their data. Because educational leaders design and conduct their own experiments, they also own the evaluation of those experiments. As with every aspect of the evocative coaching process, the more we support client autonomy and purpose, the more we generate motivation and mastery. How will the coachee observe, capture, and report on the results of the experiment? Will the coach be involved or will the coachee collect his or her own data? If the latter, how will this be accomplished? Will other people provide feedback? If so, how will that information be registered and reviewed? Data collection in real time can be done through concurrent note taking or the use of a log, recording with audio or visual equipment, inviting the coach or someone else to observe the experiment in action, and/or getting feedback from constituents. The value of different approaches can be discussed with clients, who may decide to use one or more methods simultaneously.

When coaches are asked to observe SMARTER experiments, it is important to look for strengths rather than weaknesses. Identifying observable things that go well can assist and empower educational leaders to design new experiments that build on those positive dimensions. If an experiment doesn't go according to plan, notice the ways in which educational leaders are modifying or improvising on their experiments in order to be more successful. Evocative coaches not only affirm this level of autonomy and spontaneous engagement, they recognize it is the only way effective professional learning happens. It is not the role of the coach to decide whether or not the educational leader did a good job. It is also important for coaches not to get attached to the design as sketched out on the design template. If an educational leader does something differently or doesn't do anything at all, that may reflect the creative brilliance of an improvisation *or* that may reflect a resistance to change. Either way, it represents another opportunity for LEAD (listen—empathize—appreciate—design) to work its magic. Through the repeated cycles of the no-fault and strengths-building turns, educational leaders will experience breakthroughs and find ways to make things work.

CONFIRMING COMMITMENT

Forward movement is made possible when educational leaders believe they have what it takes to activate the plans they have made. If educational leaders do not believe they have what it takes to move forward, or if they believe that their circumstances make progress impossible, they will not take action, learn, or grow. Once a SMARTER experiment has been designed and mapped out using the experimental design template, coaches can increase client motivation and movement by confirming both the client's understanding of the design and his or her commitment to seeing it through.

After confirming that educational leaders understand the experiment by having them summarize what they will do in their own words, coaches can check in on the commitment level of the coachee to move forward by asking, "On a scale of 0 to 10, how confident are you that you will conduct this experiment as planned?" If we hear an answer of 7 or above, we can be reasonably confident that the educational leader will follow through on the design. If we hear a lower number, or if the educational leader's affect is not congruent with the number they pick, then we can ask two follow-up questions: "What led you to pick that number and not a lower number?" and "What would make it a higher number?"

The first question invites the coachee to articulate her or his capabilities in service of the learning experiment, and the second invites an investigation into the environmental supports and resources that might contribute to greater success. Both questions communicate the coach's certainty that the leader is already doing some things well and has the ability to design and successfully conduct experiments that will assist her or him to do more things better in the future.

Coaches should encourage educational leaders to modify their experimental designs, resources, or timeline until their confidence is 7 or higher. That usually indicates educational leaders are ready, willing, and able to conduct and learn from an experiment. Lower numbers may indicate they find the experiment to be either too challenging or unimportant. If clients seem intrigued by a particular idea but intimidated by the challenge, keep working with them to make the experiment SMARTER. We want clients to feel stretched but not so far outside their comfort zone as to be anxious and fearful. When educational leaders think about an experiment, we want them to get into the sweet spot where the challenges are stimulating but not overwhelming, where their skills are stretched but not outstripped. Evocative coaches empower educational leaders to take on greater challenges than they might otherwise think are possible but also may encourage a scaling back of experiments that are too far out of reach.

GETTING INTO ACTION

It is the work of evocative coaching to help educational leaders achieve desired outcomes and enhance their quality of life. To do this, coaches must assist coachees to design ways to experiment with changing their behavior. No coaching session is therefore complete until and unless the client comes away with a good understanding of what he or she will do differently in the days and weeks ahead and an agreement has been made as to what specific actions that client will take before the next coaching session. Such homework, which grows out of the SMARTER experiments, assists educational leaders to be more accountable in their path of development and helps coaches to be more supportive and responsive to a coachee's actions over time. Coaches invigorate coachee learning with recognition. By acknowledging what educational leaders have brought to the table, the good work they have done in brainstorming, and their capacity to conduct experiments that will assist them to see their dreams through to fruition, coaches enable educational leaders to move forward and leverage success. Coaches endorse the work, the aspirations, and the experiments and champion the courage, creativity, and possibility that educational leaders are bringing into the world. They honor their coachees' feelings and needs. Coaches let educational leaders know that they believe not only in their ability to be successful but also in the surprising discoveries they will make along the way.

Concerning all acts of initiative and creation, there is one elementary truth, the ignorance of which kills countless ideas and splendid plans: that the moment one definitely commits oneself, then Providence moves too. All sorts of things occur to help one that would never otherwise have occurred. A whole stream of events issues from the decision, raising in one's favor all manner of unforeseen incidents and meetings and material assistance, which no one could have dreamed would come his or her way. I have learned a deep respect for one of Goethe's couplets:

"*Whatever you can do, or dream you can, begin it.*

Boldness has genius, power, and magic in it."

—W. H. Murray (1951, pp. 6–7)

REFLECT AND REFINE

Conducting design experiments represents our best guess as to how things might work better, but the unexpected happens and improvements can always be made. When educational leaders understand that experiments are just that—experiments— then they will approach performance improvement with a sense of freedom and curiosity rather than of pressure and compulsion. They need not wait for the next coaching session to reflect on possible changes and to design new experiments. The experimental design worked out with the coach does not take precedence over client discretion.

Unless coaches have been asked to participate in the experiment, either as observers or as participant-observers, they will receive their information as to how the experiments went from client reports and data sources, such as contemporaneous notes and/or audio or video recordings. These reports and data may come to coaches in the form of interim updates, through e-mails or spot encounters, or as parts of subsequent coaching sessions.

- What went well? Why do you think it went as well as it did?
- What did you learn and how did you grow?
- What surprised you?
- What do you hope to build on going forward?
- How did you feel before, during, and after the experiment?

Coaches and clients review together observational data collected in real time because these are the data that can best serve educational leader learning and growth. These data often prove to be important conversation elements as educational leaders make sense of their experiences, process their feelings, and frame new aspirations for the future.

However the data come, evocative coaches recognize that all data on client activities tell a story and launch a new round of coaching conversations. All that we have learned about LEAD comes back into play. When coachees have a story to tell, coaches listen attentively and explore it from different angles. When clients feel disappointed or frustrated about the results of their experiments, coaches reflect their understanding of those feelings and needs and watch for the golden sigh. They inquire as to the glimmers of hope—what was learned and what can be built upon. When coachees are energized and enthusiastic, coaches offer guesses as to the needs that have been met as well as the strengths, vitalities, and aspirations evident. Once coaches have assisted coachees to process the experiment from a strengths-based perspective, it is time to brainstorm new ideas and design new experiments for continued learning, growth, and change. From there, the process moves back around the Möbius strip, with another twist of capacity creation and building on strengths.

CHOREOGRAPHING THE COACHING DANCE

The coaching dance requires that coaches and clients must come to embody both the presence and artistry of the coaching process and carry themselves as instruments of inspiration. The model of LEAD represents four essential steps of the coaching process, set on a Möbius strip. Yet these steps are not linear or progressive in any simple sense of the word. The underlying relational, emotional, motivational, cultural, and political dynamics of educational leaders at work are as complicated as any human endeavor. So coaches learn to notice and respond to those dynamics in adaptive ways. We learn to dance with our clients, iteratively moving around and around the dance floor with LEAD generating ever-higher levels of professional mastery and maturity. We learn when to push and when to pull. We learn not only to expect the unexpected but to leverage the unexpected for creativity, growth, and change. We learn to bring out the best in educational leaders, regardless of where they start in terms of competence, experience, willingness, and vision. By engaging educational leaders in the dance of self-directed learning and performance improvement through evocative coaching, we enable them to more fully rise to the challenge of creating schools and school systems where learning is job one for the youngest students to the oldest person on staff.

At first, as with all dances, these steps may feel unfamiliar, awkward, and confusing. We may be rather clumsy and stilted in their application. Toes can get stepped on; we trip; we do not always get the timing just right. That dynamic may occasion discouragement and prompt some to give up. If we hang in there, however, with lightheartedness and a sense of humor, practicing the dance steps until the choreography begins to take shape in our minds and in our interactions with the educational leaders we coach, all this begins to change. As time goes on, we become more graceful and light on our feet as we go through the motions. Things begin to shift in our conversations and in our presence with others. When we know the choreography, we become undercover agents of transformational change. Clients may not realize what we are doing or how it is happening. We hope they have the sense of doing it themselves because new attitudes and actions have been evoked from within. They begin to notice more lightness in their step and to feel more hopeful as they experience more success in their schools and districts.

To successfully and enjoyably dance with someone, one must know not only the steps of the dance and have a sense of their progression, flow, and destination, one must also be in sync with one's partner. We once knew a man who loved to dance the tango. When the music began, we noticed he would slip his reading glasses out of his pocket and put them on. Curious, we asked why he did that. He explained that to do this dance well requires a close read of his partner's facial expressions and movements. So it is with coaching. It requires a close read of our partner so we can make adjustments to the tone and style of what we are bringing to the coaching conversation. Where are we starting? How are we moving? What is the rhythm? As the dance advances, it is critical to monitor multiple contingencies in real time. The unexpected happens, and when it does, adjustments must be made to maintain the graceful flow. It is a case of continuously processing in the present. What is going on? What am I doing? What is my partner doing? How can we stay or get back in step? Such questions and sensitivities are essential to making dances work.

That same beauty is possible in evocative coaching conversations. We may not be physically dancing with coachees, but we are moving together through the coaching process in ways that cocreate a new reality. We are not always taking the lead, nor are we always following. We are rather moving back and forth between the different steps, exploring stories, empathizing with feelings and needs, inquiring into strengths, or developing and prototyping designs, intuitively initiating and responding in ways that bring out the best in educational leaders. We want them to feel engaged, intrigued, open, willing, stimulated, supported, and challenged by the conversation. We do not want to be wandering around aimlessly or engaging in a casual chat. We want to know where we are and where we are going. We want to know when it is time to circle back and when it is time to move forward. We want to pick up on and recognize the signals and cues so that things come together and educational leaders realize their full potential. The more we pay attention to the leaders we are coaching and navigate with curiosity, the more evocative coaching becomes.

When coaches trust and practice the process, we increase our ability to make significant contributions to the professional development of educational leaders and to the learning climate of their schools and districts. Evocative coaching does not depend for its effectiveness upon how much time and structure we have available for a coaching conversation. It depends upon our ability to connect and dance with educational leaders in the moment as partners on the never-ending journey of learning how to better lead.

The coach dances with [clients] to facilitate the unleashing of potentials and the experience of change. The dialogue dance creates motivation and energy. . . . It creates readiness for change, the power to change, and the leverage for change. In this dance, new frames of mind are co-created for facilitating that change. The dialogue is a dance around support, celebration, accountability, fun, and actualizing potential. It's a dance for enabling dreams to come true. Do you want to dance?

—L. Michael Hall & Michelle Duval (2005, p. 6)

 ## Key Points in This Chapter

1. Instead of framing goals to be accomplished, evocative coaches assist clients to frame these aspirations as SMARTER experiments, which reduces the fear of failure, increases the fun, and makes learning the primary intention.

2. A SMARTER experiment is **s**pecific, **m**easurable, **a**ttainable, **r**elevant, **t**ime bound, **e**valuated, and **r**efined.

3. The experimental design template invites coachees to frame their learning in terms of an if-then hypothesis that can then be tested.

4. Coachees are invited to tie the current experiment to their larger aspirations, values, or professional standards.

5. Brainstorming is a key skill of design thinking that is used to generate a wide array of possible strategies before picking a smaller subset to enact.

6. Coaches are looking for a confidence level of 7 or higher on the confidence ruler. If it is lower, coaches may look for ways to increase the resources or lower the challenge of the experiment.

7. Evocative coaching is not a set of steps to be followed in a set order but tools to be marshaled in response to the needs of the situation.

 ## Questions for Reflection and Discussion

1. What are the advantages of framing a SMARTER experiment as opposed to a SMART goal?

2. When educational leaders are having a hard time coming up with new ideas, how might coaches help them out?

3. Why is it important for the coachee to put the first idea on the table during brainstorming?

4. What are some good ways to capture the data from SMARTER experiments? Why is this important?

5. How might you assist the coachee to evaluate and refine her or his experiment either during or after it is enacted?

6. How might you frame your own learning aspirations as a coach as an if-then hypothesis? How is this aligned with your personal aspirations or professional standards?

The Dynamic Flow of Change

The point of coaching is to facilitate a leader's growth and change to ever-higher levels in order to support school and district success. That is no small task, and coachees are not always ready, willing, and able to make changes in a particular arena at a particular time. "Progress is a nice word," observed Robert Kennedy, "but change is its motivator and change has its enemies"—a lesson he learned all too well. If coaches and coachees readily engage in the coaching process and have designed an experiment they are eager to try, that's great. If not, this chapter is about what to do next. In this chapter, we explore how coaches assist their clients to balance levels of support and challenge and how they roll with resistance, honor ambivalence, and get out of the way of the client's change process. We will also explore how we might assist clients as they contemplate leading change at the system level.

In many respects, evocative coaching can be framed as a process for shifting inertia. We want educational leaders to understand both themselves and their practices better. Things are the way they are and people are doing what they are doing for a reason. Exploring inertia assists coachees to enter into a new relationship with themselves. If they are not responding to the coaching process and are not doing well in their school or district, then respectfully exploring the attachments and assumptions tethering them to the status quo can begin to shake things loose. Educational leaders who get attached to underperformance do so as the result of a constellation of underlying relational, emotional, motivational, cultural, and political factors. No real progress can be made until they move beyond those factors. Evocative coaching can assist clients to do just that.

Change is difficult. Even if it is for the better, it can be uncomfortable. Our clients' readiness to change can be thought of as a continuum ranging from "I won't" or

"I can't" on the one end, to "I may" in the middle, and "I will" at the opposite end (Prochaska & Norcross, 2002). This range runs from not thinking about changing a behavior, to thinking about it, to planning to change, to testing out ways to do it before we actually start. A coachee's stage of change refers less to his or her outlook on life than to the readiness to change a specific behavior. Educational leaders will typically be in different stages of change for different projects. The more accurately a coach senses a coachee's readiness to change, the more effective and appropriate the coaching strategies can be. The "I won't" people may have dug in their heels because their autonomy needs have been stirred up by the perception someone is telling them what to do or how to do their job. People in the "I can't" stage lack self-efficacy for the things they are being asked to do and have not yet found a strategy they feel confident in implementing. For different reasons, both of these kinds of people are not even contemplating, let alone working on, making a change (Prochaska & Norcross, 2002). Pressuring them to prematurely try new behaviors may set them up for failure and can cause them to withdraw from the coaching process altogether. Shifting instead to designing an awareness experiment in which they explore an avenue of interest to them may move them into the "I may" arena of contemplating change. Understanding the theory of flow may guide us in the design of an awareness or an action experiment that suits the level of challenge the client is ready for.

GETTING INTO FLOW

One way to understand our goal with regard to bringing about motivation and movement in clients is through understanding the dynamics of a process called flow. *Flow* is a term coined by psychologist Mihaly Csikszentmihalyi (1990; pronounced "chick-sent-me-high") as he researched the conditions that made for optimal human experience. He set out to examine what made for peak human performance across a variety of human endeavors. What he learned was that regardless of the domain, whether the performance was in the realm of music, chess, golf, or mountain climbing, the state that performers described when they were at their best was remarkably similar. This state, which he called flow, is the experience of being both fully immersed in and unusually successful with an activity. "Flow is the state in which people are so involved in an activity that nothing else seems to matter; the experience itself is so enjoyable that people will do it even at great cost, for the sheer sake of doing it" (Csikszentmihalyi, 1990, p. 4). A person in flow experiences a feeling of energized and focused attention and a high level of enjoyment and fulfillment. An activity that produces flow has clear goals, and the participant receives direct feedback on progress toward meeting that goal. The participant feels confident and in control of the activity. As a result of the deep concentration associated with being in flow, any worries and concerns the participant has disappear and the subjective experience of time is altered so that she or he hardly notices the passage of time. Not all of these components need to be present together for flow to be experienced, but some combination of them is required.

To reach that state of full engagement, the activity needs to be intrinsically interesting and just within the outside reach of the participant's abilities. If the activity is too challenging, then it is overwhelming and stressful. If the activity is not challenging enough, then it is boring and tedious. The sweet spot—the flow spot—is where the level of challenge perfectly matches the skills, training, strengths, and resources of the performer (Csikszentmihalyi, 2000). Athletes sometimes speak of this experience as being "in the zone." Such flow moments are inherently pleasurable and even timeless. They successfully walk the tightrope between anxiety and boredom, effort and ease, challenge and support. They build on each other to make educational leaders more competent and coaching more evocative. Educational leaders will more fully benefit from their SMARTER experiments when those experiments are designed to help them get into flow. By conducting experiments that are neither too hard nor too easy, but rather perfectly suited for their interests, abilities, and environments, coachees will enhance their willingness to take on even more daring and creative experiments in the future.

Keeping with the metaphor of flow, we draw upon the analogy of a river to explore the dynamics of change. The river of change is sometimes calm, often turbulent, always dynamic and moving. Even when we become frustrated at the seemingly slow pace of change, we can be assured that nothing is ever really staying the same. A Buddhist teaching holds that we never step into the same river twice. Each day, each conversation presents a new opportunity to foster productive change.

THE RAPIDS

Coaches are often called upon to coach educational leaders in the rapids, particularly novice leaders or those struggling with a challenging new leadership assignment. A kayaker entering a narrow passage or shallow water recognizes in that environment the potential for danger. The swiftly moving water and the many boulders, both visible and submerged, pose potentially life-threatening hazards. Well-trained and experienced kayakers may encounter the rapids with a sense of exuberance and enthusiasm, confident in their skills to successfully meet the challenge. Those with less experience, however, may find themselves in the grip of fear. This fear, if it is too intense, may contribute to a debilitating decrease in performance, compounding the danger. It works much the same way with leaders facing a potentially difficult situation. Educational leaders whose skills and resources are equal to the task may feel energized and enthusiastic in anticipation of facing a leadership challenge. Those whose skills and resources come up short may anticipate the same experiment with a sense of anxiety that can interfere with performance and contribute to poorer outcomes all around. Fear has a way of constraining and riveting attention to the source of the fear. That constriction limits the range of options that are considered, creating a potential for a downward spiral of ineffective performances.

The theory of flow suggests two possible courses of action when we find ourselves coaching an educational leader who is overwhelmed, anxious, and afraid, mired in the "I can't" stage of change. The first is to reduce the level of challenge, perhaps by designing experiments with more support and resources and by finding ways to decrease interference and obstacles. Educational leaders generally know what external realities they would like to change, but they do not always realize how their cognitive, physiological, and affective states come into play. What are they focusing on? What voices are they listening to? They may be remembering past failures rather than successes. They may want to control outcomes without paying sufficient attention to the processes involved in getting to those outcomes.

The more interference educational leaders experience from nonsupportive environments—the louder the noise from both external and internal sources—the more educational leaders are up against when it comes to their ability to succeed. Coaches can assist educational leaders to regroup and refocus through a variety of conversational and personal practices. Who can they turn to for support? Who could they collaborate with? What other resources are already available in the system that they could call upon? What resources could they find outside the system? How can they lower the volume on their own negative self-talk? How can they reduce their anxiety, manage their stress, and relax? Assisting coachees to talk through these dynamics can expand their awareness of options in the present moment. By mustering support in these ways, evocative coaches assist educational leaders to be more successful.

The second course of action suggested by the theory of flow is to work on equipping educational leaders with more skills for the task at hand. Coaches can invite leaders to design experiments that help them to learn and practice new skills. What strengths could leaders leverage in developing new skills? How could they arrange their experiments so as to make their weaknesses irrelevant? What training opportunities are available to them? How could they practice new behaviors in small, low-stakes pilot experiments? Our job as evocative coaches is to assist educational leaders to experience moments of flow that become the stuff of wonder and joy.

One day I met with a woman I had been coaching and she handed me a beautifully wrapped gift. Taken aback, I said, "You didn't have to do that!" She replied, "I didn't. It's from my husband." She continued, "When we were on vacation, he said, 'I want to get something for that nice lady who has changed our lives.'" This woman had been dealing with some very difficult staff issues and parent issues, and she had been working herself to death. In our work, we were able to help her move out of a reactive mode and to develop some clear strategies to address these issues. She found that she could have a balance in her life and develop a greater sense of control. Her way of showing up in her life began to shift and it made a difference in how people responded to her. I've found that if you empower the individual, the rest will follow.

—Susan, Early Childhood Consultant

THE DOLDRUMS

Coaches may also find themselves called upon to coach educational leaders in the doldrums, navigating through slow, deep waters. These may be veteran leaders who have been in charge of the same school for a long time. Or they may be those who have cultivated effective strategies for buffering themselves from the demands of seemingly never-ending reform initiatives, adopting a defensive posture toward each new initiative that "this too shall pass." Educational leaders in the doldrums may have skills that outstrip the challenges at hand, which results in boredom and a lack of initiative. They may also be discouraged due to years of pressure and a lack of acknowledgement for their efforts. Through story listening, empathy reflections, appreciative inquiries, and design thinking, we reconnect leaders with their aspirations and increase their awareness of new possibilities. These new possibilities may mean letting go of old strategies developed over the course of a career for resisting directives and attempts to force leaders to change. This letting go does not come easy. It requires us to cultivate an evocative quality of conversation that loosens the moorings and engages these leaders in the quest for educational excellence.

Our ability to engage educational leaders in such evocative conversations depends upon both our presence and our approach. The most important thing to remember as we coach educational leaders in the doldrums is to respect and empathize with their needs and desires. They are not lazy, crazy, stupid, or wrong for feeling the way they feel. We assume a client has a legitimate reason for the stance he or she has adopted. A good interpersonal connection and understanding of leader experiences can reframe negative energy and reawaken positive desire. Story listening and empathy reflections are paramount. By understanding rather than judging coachee lethargy, we increase our chances of hearing the golden sigh, that release of pent-up emotion and nod of recognition. Once we sense that release, we can work more confidently and directly with appreciative inquiries and design thinking. Energy mounts for design conversations, which bolster motivation and make possible new efforts for educational leaders to experience flow.

Following the client's lead, evocative coaches ease their way into such collaborative and cocreative conversations. By remembering that we are in partnership rather than in charge and attending more to the client's feelings than to our own thoughts and opinions, we become genuinely inspired and inspiring. At their best, coaching conversations may feel intense, moving, powerful, deep, and exciting. In these pivotal moments in conversation with coachees about their strengths, opportunities, aspirations, and resources, their feelings, needs, and desires translate into the willingness and ability to change. These moments inspire educational leaders to generate new ideas, to discover new insights, and to uncover new capacities, all of which lead to bold actions that can positively alter their future. When the relationship is right and the necessary supports and scaffolding are aligned, educational leaders appreciate being called to go beyond what they're imagining is possible to increase the odds of success.

A prerequisite [for innovation] is an environment—social but also spatial—in which people know they can experiment, take risks, and explore the full range of their faculties. It does little good [to conduct experiments] in an environment that dooms their efforts from the start. The physical and psychological spaces of an organization work in tandem to define the effectiveness of the people within it.

—Tim Brown (2009, p. 32)

ROLLING WITH RESISTANCE

When we encounter resistance to change, rather than assume there is something wrong with our clients, we roll with the resistance by exploring their readiness to change and examining the dynamics keeping them stuck in the status quo. As evocative coaches, we do not tell educational leaders what to do or push them to get with the program since that is likely to exacerbate their resistance to change. There is a tough-love school of coaching that encourages coaches to press for an outcome, but those outcomes are seldom effective or enduring. Effective and enduring changes require a more evocative approach. Our challenge as coaches is to not grow impatient or insistent with our clients. Our ability to recognize and to accept that they do not intend to change a particular behavior is the key to future possibilities. We do not press them to move forward. Instead we ask them to deepen their knowledge and understanding of both themselves and their task, without judgment, fear, guilt, or blame.

Through the adroit use of the evocative coaching model and our facility with the no-fault and strengths-building turns, we are well equipped to guide educational leaders through the process of exploring and resolving resistance. We might want to explore what stories the educational leaders are telling themselves about what is going on and what is possible. Which of their needs have been stimulated by the prospect of change? How are their strengths, values, and aspirations being engaged or frustrated? We want to explore how we can more fully engage with our coachees as partners and cocreators of aspiration, understand more completely the benefits and concerns they see in the change, and get clients to a point of confidence before actually making the change. When educational leaders resist participating in the design phase of the process, it is a time for coaches to gently and respectfully assist them to explore their inertia. They may be willing to design and engage in an awareness experiment in order to explore either their own reluctance to change or to gather information about how others have approached a similar change. Evocative coaches communicate certainty in the ability of clients to learn and grow. The more we assert our expertise, the more resistance we may provoke. In contrast, the more we affirm our belief in the coachee's ability to learn, the more confident the coachee becomes. The more we dig for the causes of problems, the more trouble we may dig up. The more we search for capacities, the more excited coachees may become.

To move forward, coachees at the "I won't" end of the readiness-to-change continuum need lots of empathy to explore their feelings and needs concerning the change process (Miller & Rollnick, 2002). This is the time to use distinctive reflections to show we understand and respect these feelings and needs. It is not enough to engage with coachees about their feelings alone. To do so can reinforce their resistance. Feelings are valued because they raise awareness and point to the realm of needs. The heart of empathy is to get to the underlying universal needs. That is where the insights that can lead to new perspectives and behaviors are found. We seek to appreciate the beauty of all the needs educational leaders are trying to meet until one rises to the surface as being the most compelling for now. By expressing empathy, coaches elevate readiness and lower resistance to change through facilitating a life-giving connection and make the relational field between coachees and coaches both safe and interesting (Rosenberg, 2003).

Coaches cannot afford to be attached to an outcome. We want educational leaders to find their own answers and to chart their own course so that motivation is high and progress is more likely. If there are consequences for noncompliance with organizational directives, we want to make sure clients are aware of those consequences as they chart their own course of action, but it is ultimately their choice, not ours, as to what they choose to do and not to do. If we are in both a supervisory or evaluative role and a coaching role, it will be important to be explicit when we are fulfilling our supervisory responsibilities and then to be explicit in moving back into our coaching role. It may be our responsibility in our evaluative role to share with clients our assessment of their performance across the areas of an evaluation rubric. Whether a performance evaluation is conducted by us or someone else, we will want to be sure coachees have a clear and accurate knowledge of the potential consequences for failure to improve in a particular area. As coaches, though, we remain clear that the choice of how to proceed remains with the coachee.

To coach successfully, evocative coaches pay close attention to changes in client affect. When a client pulls back, it may be time for more empathy. When a client leans forward, it may be time for more inquiry. There is the sense of keeping just the right amount of tension on the line. Too little tension and coaching becomes little more than a chat; too much tension and coaching becomes a chore. The right amount of tension enables clients to develop their passion and to move forward, often dramatically, in their path of development. Learning to appreciate and value the underlying needs behind resistance talk is a challenging and yet essential part of evocative coaching. Resistance has much to teach us. Pushing back against resistance closes the door on that opportunity. When we find ourselves tempted to confront resistance directly, we often end up provoking more resistance and squandering the chance to dance with coachees through the fire of their negative feelings and unmet needs. The more curious we become about the living energy of their needs, while suspending our judgments, interpretations, assumptions, evaluations, and agendas, the greater the chance of breaking loose a new zone of possibility and hope.

When resistance is high and energy is low, it is time for coaches to change our approach. Whatever we are doing is stimulating the wrong energy and triggering an unproductive response. Backing off from goals that coachees "must" work on is an important first step. Returning to the no-fault turn is the next step. Once we again hear the release of the golden sigh, we come back around to appreciation of the strengths, opportunities, aspirations, and resources that educational leaders can draw upon and build on in the search for possibilities.

The first time I sat down with Ruth, she said, "I don't want to be coached. Don't ask me a bunch of questions, just tell me what to do and I'll do it." Ruth had been assigned to a very challenging school in a tough part of town. She was a wonderful person, but she was a very direct "It's my way or the highway" kind of leader. She was looking to me for that same kind of direction. I was a little taken aback, but after a pause I said, "I'll tell you what, let's split the difference. I'll ask you questions for half the time and we'll brainstorm actions you can take for half our time together." Ruth agreed. Over time, she began to trust the process more and more and to value the insights she had during our sessions. By spring, she said, "I need to know how to do this coaching thing. What book should I read?" Before I knew it, she had organized a book study on coaching among the other principals in the district!

—Paulette, Leadership Coach

HONORING AMBIVALENCE

When our coachees hang back, tap dancing away from challenge and commitment, or if they design experiments only to report procrastinating about putting them into action week after week, we may want to explore their ambivalence.

These are people in the "I may" stage of change. Ambivalence is the felt sense of conflicting feelings about alternative possibilities. It is not that one possibility is good and the other is bad, it is that both possibilities have value and meet different needs. Ambivalence arises as clients come to terms with these competing commitments, attachments, assumptions, and emotions. Until and unless educational leaders are able to sort out and appreciate those dynamics, they are not likely to take effective action. It is a common experience clients may move through as they contemplate their options for performance improvement (Miller & Rollnick, 2002). We want to receive and explore ambivalence as a gift, recognizing there is something valuable to learn from it.

If educational leaders are not choosing to engage with us, we assume they have their reasons for sitting tight and doing just what they are doing. Until those reasons are understood, accepted, and appreciated, no transformation is possible and no improvement is likely. Harvard researchers Kegan and Lahey (2009) assert that we all have a natural immunity to change and that our current mindsets are managing our anxieties and concerns brilliantly—keeping things right where they are and just the way they are for good reasons. They have designed a simple but powerful tool for exploring inertia and overcoming ambivalence: the immunity to change map. In order to move forward in the midst of ambivalence, we must become conscious of how these immune systems are operating. The simplicity of the map, a four-column worksheet based on four questions (see Figure 7.1), belies its sophistication and power in what it invites people to think about. If educational leaders are willing to talk honestly about what is going on with them using the four questions on the map, and if they are willing to test their big assumptions, Kegan and Lahey demonstrate how they can move from being unconsciously "immune" to change to being consciously "released" from the behaviors and strategies that have been holding them back. This tool facilitates coachee understanding of their attachment to the status quo so new options become possible.

OVERCOMING IMMUNITY TO CHANGE

Column One. The first column asks the question, "What are you committed to doing that would make you more successful?" To get on the map, these visible commitments or improvement goals should meet four criteria: (1) they should be viewed as true by the client, (2) they should be viewed as chosen by the client, rather than as assigned or imposed by someone else, (3) they should be viewed as areas where there is room for improvement, and (4) they should be viewed as important by the client. Even educational leaders with great inertia have some awareness of the things they want to do to be successful. These are the things that go in column one.

Column Two. The second column asks the question, "What are you actually doing or not doing that works against those first column commitments?" A principal may state, for example, that observing in classrooms is important (a column one commitment) but that she rarely gets around to it (a column two behavior). What is she doing instead? She may report that her time is spent dealing with discipline, completing paperwork, responding to e-mail, and returning parent phone calls. The more specific and observational the better when it comes to the items in the second column. The point is to notice and become aware of these behaviors, not to figure out what to do about them or why they are happening.

Column Three. The third column asks the question, "What are the hidden or competing commitments that keep the column two behaviors in place?" Here we are trying to increase awareness of and explore the attachments that tether clients to whatever they are doing now. On the one hand, they say they want to do the things in column one. On the other hand, they are actually doing and not doing the things in column two. Why is that? What commitments fuel those column two behaviors? To get at the hidden or competing commitments, Kegan and Lahey suggest clients identify a list of worries in column three that arise when they imagine trying to do just the opposite of the things in column two. These concerns, listed in the worry box, can then be framed as commitments to keep those things the client is worried about from occurring. For example, the principal who is not managing to get into classrooms may report being worried that if paperwork is not completed during the school day, it will stack up and she will have to stay late in the evening to complete it, thus taking time away from her family. Or if the paperwork is not completed on time, she will be reprimanded by someone from the central office. Or she may assume that if she doesn't deal with discipline referrals promptly, students will not learn the lessons the discipline is intended to teach and they will miss more class time than is necessary. And so forth. Column three makes sense of the column two behaviors because they seek to meet legitimate feelings and needs.

Column Four. The fourth column asks the question, "What are the big assumptions that underlie those column three commitments?" In other words, what mindsets keep this system in place? These big assumptions or mindsets, often involving a mix of relational, emotional, motivational, and political factors, make sense of the column three commitments and thus of the column two behaviors. To identify the big assumptions, one can take each item in column three and complete the following sentence: "I assume that if I did not stay committed to _____, then something bad will happen—and not just something a little bad, but something BTB (big-time bad)." Write down that BTB as a big assumption. Such assumptions display a certain view of the world—a certain mindset—and explain how column three commitments help to avoid the BTB conclusion. For example, the principal in our example might assume a reprimand from central office will lead to job loss or that student behavior in her school will get even worse if discipline is not meted out promptly.

At this point, now that we have a much greater understanding of our immunity to change, Kegan and Lahey suggest we are better able to explore the reality of our big assumptions by designing and conducting field tests. How do our fears hold up in the real world? What nuances can we discover? What happens if we push the envelope with a gentle nudge? To answer such questions through field testing, Kegan and Lahey recommend several criteria: The tests must be safe, modest, actionable, researcher-like (interested in getting data, not results), and focused on

FIGURE 7.1   Immunity Map Worksheet

Name: Terri

Date: March 16

COMMITMENT (IMPROVEMENT GOALS)	DOING/NOT DOING INSTEAD (BEHAVIORS THAT WORK AGAINST THE GOALS)	HIDDEN COMPETING COMMITMENTS	BIG ASSUMPTIONS
I am committed to offering the highest quality care and instruction at my center. I am committed to running a successful center so that all of my investments and sacrifices pay off.	I am not collecting payments from the parents in a timely fashion. I accept whatever excuses they offer as to why they cannot pay on time. I do not charge the parents the fees they owe for late pick-up. When I witness teachers speaking harshly to the children or chatting with one another when they are supposed to be with the children, I don't let them know that this behavior is unacceptable and what they should be doing instead.	Worry Box: I'm worried that if I hold people accountable, I will find myself alone. I will be ostracized by the staff and the parents. I won't be invited to birthday parties and baby showers. I am committed to being liked and even adored. I am committed to being included in the lives and celebrations of my teachers and parents.	If I hold teachers accountable for quality teaching, they will resent me and will show that by excluding me and being mean to me. If I hold the parents accountable for their payments and for picking up their children on time, they will think that I am not sympathetic to their struggles and they will move their children to a different center.

Adapted from Kegan, R., & Lahey, L. L. (2009). *Immunity to change: How to overcome it and unlock the potential in yourself and your organization.* Boston, MA: Harvard Business School Press.

only one big assumption at a time. In our example, the principal might try visiting one classroom each morning for a week and seeing if the paperwork becomes unmanageable. After doing a test and collecting data, it is important to generate multiple interpretations of the data in order to decide what facet or facets of the big assumption are worth keeping, what might be revised, and what can be let go. Through repeated testing of our big assumptions in this way, we can release our attachment to the status quo, shift inertia, and facilitate readiness to change.

Clients are not required to figure everything out ahead of time, once and for all. They are encouraged to play with possibilities, trying one or more on for size. If they move in one direction and their energy goes up, they won't be ambivalent for long. They'll be more than ready to design their next experiment and keep the momentum moving in a positive direction. If their energy goes down, listening for stories, offering empathy, and celebrating strengths will eventually assist them to find a new path. By exploring stories, reflecting feelings, understanding needs, appreciating strengths, noticing vitalities, and cultivating aspirations, educational leaders will sooner or later move through ambivalence to engage in the powerful work of design conversations.

I was teaching a continuing education course for owner/operators of early childhood centers that was meeting at a local community college. On the first night a young woman in a gray hoodie with the hood pulled over her head slouched in and slumped into a desk at the back of the room. Thinking that she was a community college student in the wrong room, I went back to inform her of the nature of the class. "Yes, that's the class I am here for," she replied. I was stunned! Although she carried herself as someone much younger, it turned out that Terri was actually in her early thirties and owned a childcare center. She had left a successful career in banking to teach in the center, and when it came up for sale, she had invested her entire life savings to purchase it. Three years later, things were not going well and she was feeling completely demoralized and discouraged. Part of the course was to develop a vision, and as she talked about her hopes and dreams for her center, she began to come back to life before our eyes. The things she dreamed of were wonderful, but she seemed to have no idea how to make them happen. When the course was over, she asked me to be her coach. We ended up working together for a year and a half. A big issue that emerged was that she was having a difficult time with accountability— holding teachers accountable to do their best for students and holding parents accountable for supporting their children and for paying on time. We spent a good bit of time working through the immunity to change map. When we got to the worry box, she revealed that she felt quite worried that if she held people accountable she would end up alone—that she wouldn't be invited to baby showers and birthday parties. In exploring those fears, she recounted that she had grown up the only child of very domineering parents and that she often had felt left out and alone. Once she began to conduct some experiments to test her assumptions, she found that she could hold people accountable without being isolated. Then she was really able to lead the center in a new way toward the dreams she had for it. In our last session together, she said, "Thank you for seeing the good in me and in my work. I feel like I have stepped into my own life in a whole new way!"

—Shelly, Early Childhood Coach

GETTING OUT OF THE WAY

Evocative coaches do not view uncooperative behavior as a sign there's something wrong with the client; instead, we explore whether it is a sign something is wrong with the approach we are taking. Rather than writing someone off as intractable or impossible, we recognize that when things are not going well, it may say more about our approach and our presence than about the capacity of the leader we are coaching. Coaching cannot be productive in the absence of openness, understanding, and mutuality. The more we seek to respectfully understand our coachees' experiences, the more open they become.

It is important for evocative coaches to avoid communication patterns that are incompatible or that interfere with expressing empathy. The more we seek to correct the behavior or attitude of the people we coach, the more caught up we get in playing the game of "Who's right?" In the interest of being helpful, coaches may at times feel the urge to advise, commiserate, console, educate, prod, or correct coachees. Although such behaviors may occasionally be appropriate and useful in coaching conversations, especially when coachees ask for the help, they tend to interfere with the maintenance of a productive coaching space. It is not helpful to judge, label, shame, compare, demand, reward, or punish clients during evocative coaching conversations. To stay in connection with coachees and to promote their full engagement, it is better to listen mindfully and reflectively than to jump in and take the conversation off track.

Our tone of voice, pacing, and comfort with silence as coachees respond to our inquiries are as important to creating this dynamic as what questions we ask. The best inquiries in the world will fail to land correctly if they are asked in the wrong way or with an implied "right" answer. Speaking too quickly after an inquiry is voiced, either to try and help clients respond or to get them to see our point, also diminishes effectiveness. We want coachees to sit with our strengths-based questions and to receive our observations so they sink in and call forth both motivation and movement.

If I want to help [someone to] reduce his defensiveness and become more adaptive, I must try to remove the threat of myself as his potential changer. As long as the atmosphere is threatening, there can be no effective communication. So I must create a climate which is neither critical, evaluative, nor moralizing. It must be an atmosphere of equality and freedom, permissiveness and understanding, acceptance and warmth. It is in this climate and this climate only that the individual feels safe enough to incorporate new experiences and new values into his concept of himself. (Rogers & Farson, 1957, p. 3)

AVOIDING COACHING TRAPS

In order to navigate the coaching space to keep the responsibility for performance and growth with the coachee and to keep the interpersonal space productive to the coaching project, it is important to avoid these six coaching traps that can occasionally snare even the most savvy coaches. We want to stay alert in order to avoid the fix-it trap, the cheerleader trap, the rabbit-hole trap, the hurry-hurry trap, the yes-but trap, and the one-right-way trap. The danger in these traps is that they can usurp responsibility from the coachee, which is where it belongs.

THE FIX-IT TRAP. The fix-it trap comes from the noble urge to help people with their problems. When someone starts telling us about a problem, or when we see someone doing something problematic, many of us have an almost instinctive reaction to reach in and help. But the evocative coaching model challenges us to listen and empathize before we start designing solutions. When someone is stuck, guiding them through a respectful exploration of their feelings and needs rather than trying to pull them out has immeasurable value. It can clarify a client's agenda for coaching (their learning brief), plus it also builds self-responsibility and self-efficacy as we subtly communicate that clients are not helpless victims, they don't need us to fix their problems, and they have what it takes to find their own answers. To avoid falling into this trap, evocative coaches learn to become comfortable with silence and to express empathy using the distinctive empathy reflections discussed in Chapter 4.

THE CHEERLEADER TRAP. The cheerleader trap comes from the equally noble urge to encourage someone. When someone is struggling and expressing doubt that they can be successful as a leader, it is natural to want to say, "Oh, you can do it! I know you can!" But the evocative coaching model again urges us to first empathize with those feelings of frustration and discouragement and the needs that may be behind them before rushing in to cheer people up. Painting over the pain with encouraging words can come across as inauthentic and unbelievable. It can make us sound impatient and demanding, as though we want to ditch the pain and get on with things, which can work against change and cook up resistance. Respecting the pain with empathetic understanding while remaining confident that "success can be arranged" and "the answer is somewhere" communicates a far deeper sense of certainty and possibility. It helps people find the intrinsic motivation to change. This may appear to be a slower process on the surface, but it actually speeds things up in the end. People change for good when they feel good about how their struggles and aspirations are acknowledged.

THE RABBIT-HOLE TRAP. The rabbit-hole trap interferes with the work of the no-fault turn in a very different way than the first two traps. We start out listening for feelings and needs, but we get lost in their energy, intensity, and complexity. This happens when we respond with sympathy rather than empathy. We get so caught up in the other person's emotions that we barely come up for air. The emotional contagion becomes a vicious downward spiral. When this happens, coaching becomes little more than a time for venting or a pity party in which we lose sight of the coaching project altogether. We never end up hearing the golden sigh and never roll into the strengths-building turn. This trap is especially challenging with verbal processors who can seemingly talk forever about their feelings and needs and include many extraneous loops, stories, and sidebar conversations that get us off track and lead nowhere. When this happens, evocative coaches interrupt the rambling with distinctive empathy reflections that bring people back to the matter at hand. We keep people focused on what matters most: the underlying needs they want to better meet through coaching.

THE HURRY-HURRY TRAP. We call this next trap the hurry-hurry trap not just because of the chronic time pressures so many educators are under but also because of the specific urgency we as coaches feel to add value and to have something to show for our work. In our rush to get something—anything—done, we go straight to implementation with little ideation. We jump on the first idea that comes along, roll up our sleeves, and get to work. We do little or no brainstorming; thus we do not invite clients to think outside the box or stretch themselves beyond their comfort zone. The more pressure we are under, with deadlines looming, the more likely it is we will fall into this trap. But hurry-hurry solutions are hardly transformational. At best, they are incremental. At worst, they generate a lot of activity without a lot of real progress.

THE YES-BUT TRAP. When we fall into the yes-but trap, we take too much control and responsibility in the brainstorming phase and end up provoking resistance and push back. It usually goes something like this: A coachee identifies a problem or a situation he wants help with. We make a suggestion. He says, "Yes, but . . ." and tells us why it won't work. So we come up with a different idea. He says, "Yes, but . . ." and tells us he already tried that and it didn't work. So we counter with a third possibility. He says, "Yes, but . . ." and tells us why that won't be feasible either. On and on it goes, like a game of ping-pong. We come up with an idea, and the client shoots it down. The client spends more time debating ideas than doing anything about them. We get the sense we have fallen into this trap when it becomes apparent we are working harder than the coachee to come up with a solution. Coaching becomes a tug-of-war rather than a dynamic dance.

THE ONE-RIGHT-WAY TRAP. The final trap insists upon implementation without inspiration. As new mandates and programs are rolled out, people are required to implement standardized procedures without being given permission to make them their own. We call this the one-right-way trap because this process often claims to draw upon evidence-based best practices. But inflexible and dictatorial mandates inevitably backfire, even when they are research based. When we show up with a compliance mentality, insisting that people do things the "right way" or the "standard way," we rob them of their autonomy and thereby undermine their willingness to change either their behavior or their thinking. Of course, this does not mean we shouldn't be aware of and share best practices, but awareness and sharing are very different energies than insistence and demand. The key is to invite clients to customize standard materials and practices until they work for them. By working with coachees to invent adaptive solutions to the challenges they face, we generate the inspiration, ideation, and implementation that make for successful innovation. Through appreciative inquiry (AI) and design thinking, we give educational leaders the opportunity to become excellent at who they are and what they do.

The way out of these traps, then, means changing approaches—adding variety, using humor, engaging the body, being creative, or adapting our communications and actions to keep the coaching conversation moving forward. That is the dynamic dance of evocative coaching. As we move through conversations with educational leaders, our presence, inquiries, and reflections bring out the best in them and encourage their learning in interesting and informative ways.

COACHING AS A CATALYST FOR SYSTEMS CHANGE

Leading change is part and parcel of what it means to be a leader. All that we have explored about the dynamics of change is amplified as the educational leaders we coach lead change in their schools and districts. Most have sought a leadership role because they hoped to help schools and districts do a better job serving students. Thus, for organizational leaders, personal change projects are inextricably intertwined with organizational change processes. Together the coach and leader can consider applying the evocative coaching process to organizational change. Discerning and listening well to the stories of the organization and extending empathy for the array of feelings and needs stirred up by the prospect of change create the conditions for constructive change. The organizational application of AI provides an engaging and deeply participatory method for cultivating a culture of ongoing inquiry. What starts between coaches and coachees leads to design experiments that spread out like ripples in a pond.

As educational leaders assess the readiness for change within their organizations, they will encounter a complex array of individuals at different levels of readiness that must be accounted for and accommodated. Schlechty (1993) drew an analogy to westward expansion in describing different stances to organizational change, highlighting the differing training and support needs of each group. First, there are the trailblazers who are eager to explore new territory. They need acknowledgement and support for their experimentation as well as recognition that not all experiments will work out exactly as planned. Next are the pioneers who are ready to follow as soon as the territory has been mapped and made somewhat less foreign by the trailblazers. These people need opportunities to hear the stories and legends of trailblazers to be inspired by what is possible. A little later, the settlers come along to inhabit the new territory and make it their home. Less ready to change are the stay-at-homes who are comfortable with the status quo and reluctant to take the risks involved in change. Finally, there will be saboteurs who actively resist change. Change, even change for the better, such as a new or renovated school facility, inevitably means a disruption in patterns of relationships that influence participants' sense of meaning and purpose. Because different individuals and subgroups in an organization will almost certainly be at different stages in their readiness to change, finding flow, rolling with resistance, and honoring ambivalence are all important skills for leading a change process.

STORIES OLD AND NEW

Stories are how we make meaning of our lives. Change, whether personal or organizational, disrupts those stories and our ways of making meaning of our experiences. As change agents, leaders need to create opportunities for stories to be told and honored and for new stories to emerge that make sense of the new reality brought about by organizational change. Just as coaches listen to the stories of educational leaders as a crucial first step in the evocative coaching model, educational leaders need to be invited to listen deeply and well to the stories of those they lead. There are valuable insights to be had that will assist the leaders in designing and implementing experimental designs for organizational growth and improvement.

Stories that emerge from a deep exploration of the school or district data are worth exploring carefully. Adding stories to the review of achievement scores compared to state standards through the paired interviews of the AI process is a good place to start. What can be learned from the stories of students and subgroups of students who are doing well? Where are there pockets of success among subgroups of students who are struggling? There is so much more to explore than just test scores. The data addressing the strengths of the student body, the faculty, and the community will help the leader develop a deeper understanding of the people at the center of his or her organization. A close look at the resources available and how they are being allocated will reveal another set of stories. What are influential forces within the policy environment? What recent changes have been made to policies and why? What curricular changes have been made and what has been the result? Making sense of these data is important whether the leader is new to the school or district or has been there for a long time.

Stories about the climate and culture of the organization also warrant careful attention. The analogy of climate as applied here concerns participant perceptions of the quality of the interpersonal relationships in the organization and how these perceptions influence attitudes and behavior in relation to the core mission of the school or district. We want to pay attention to these conditions since they are likely to influence the change leaders want to design for their schools and systems. Just as meteorologists draw a distinction between the day-to-day fluctuations of weather and the larger and more lasting trends of climate, organizational climate is considered to be a relatively enduring trait of the organization rather than the more immediate emotional reactions to particular events. To extend this analogy, we can imagine the clouds of collective emotion that sometimes seem to settle over a school and remain for a sustained period of time. In some schools, dark clouds seem to fill the sky, heavy with rain and the threat of a storm. In these gloomy schools, energy is low and a collective depression seems to characterize most inter-actions as inhabitants dwell on the organization's many failings. Resentment tends to run high in these schools, which can lead to resistance and outright sabotage of change initiatives. Such schools are frequently targeted for turnaround initiatives, but these initiatives have an uneven track record of success. A recurring storyline in these schools might be a long line of reformers who have come and gone over many years.

In other schools, however, the climate seems to be pleasant and mild, with occasional high, fluffy clouds. These sunny schools are energetic and happy places where the enthusiasm and sense of purpose are contagious. The vibrant school scale (Clement et al., 2015) explores the presence of specific positive attributes, such as curiosity, fun, creativity, play, openness, collaboration, empathy, trust, movement, democratic decision making, and agency, among both adults and students. Coaches seek to assist educational leaders to move their schools and districts toward greater vibrancy through the experimental design process.

Collective efficacy is a particularly potent aspect of school climate that has been found to be powerfully related to student outcomes. Much like individuals, groups adopt beliefs about their capacity for the task at hand that then affect their moti-vation and performance. Faculty members take on beliefs as to whether or not they have what it takes to bring about learning for the particular students they serve (Tschannen-Moran, Salloum, & Goddard, 2014). These beliefs are conveyed through the stories told and retold about the capabilities of the faculty in relation-ship to the challenges presented by the environment and the likelihood of success. If we think of collective emotions in a school as clouds in the atmosphere, we might see collective efficacy beliefs as the wind. When the wind is at our back—when the collective efficacy beliefs among a faculty of educational leaders are high—it can speed our progress and reduce the effort needed to move ahead. Organizational participants have high levels of energy and motivation for adaptation and the pursuit of ever-increasing goals. Persistence in the face of obstacles and resilience in the face of setbacks are both antecedents to and consequences of strong collective efficacy beliefs. In schools where collective efficacy is low, an abiding sense of futility and discouragement presents a strong headwind, making progress difficult. Paying attention to the level of collective efficacy in the school or district our client leads—and the stories that maintain those collective efficacy beliefs—may provide insight into the system's readiness for change. It may also provide grist for the mill in cultivating strategies suited to that particular context. In addition, a focus on strengths and sharing tales of successes can begin to dispel the myths of hopelessness and despair and replace them with hopeful stories that bolster the collective efficacy of all involved. Closely related to collective teacher efficacy are teacher perceptions of academic press and teachers' trust in students. This trio of variables is a potent predictor of student achievement (Hoy, Tarter, & Hoy, 2006).

Culture has to do with the tacit assumptions and underlying values that make a school or district distinctive. While school climate is often studied using survey research methods to capture the collective perceptions of participants, the study of culture typically draws upon qualitative methods to investigate the assumptions and values that influence how people behave. Thus, stories are an essential part of assessing the culture of a school or district (Bolman & Deal, 2013). The following are questions that coach and client may want to explore:

- What do the mission and vision statements convey about what the organization values? To what extent do these statements align with the actual practices of the organization?

- What are the main ceremonies and rituals and what purposes do they serve?

- What are the dominant stories or legends that people tell? What messages do these stories convey?

- What are the principle images or metaphors that people use to describe the organization (e.g., a family, a zoo, a war zone)?

- What are the most potent norms (i.e., do and don'ts) and how are they enforced?

- What kinds of beliefs about students and their families dominate the organization (officially and unofficially)?

- How do humor and play contribute to the organization's culture?

- What messages do the physical environment and the artifacts on display convey?

Change disrupts symbols, attachments, and meanings. People do not resist change itself so much as they resist the disruption of their existing meaning structure. We are all profoundly conservative with respect to our own ways of making sense of the world (Marris, 2014). To explore these disruptions, coach and client can engage in the following exercise. First, the coach and client both draw a vertical line down the middle of a piece of paper. At the top of the first column, write "Meanings," and at the top of the second, write "Attachments." Under the first column, make a list of the things that are most important to you and that give your life a sense of meaning and purpose. Typical examples include family, faith, making a difference, love, success, or the joy of watching a student learn and grow. In reviewing these lists, you might observe that all of these items are of great importance and also that they are all abstractions. For example, *family* is a category, but every family is composed of a very specific set of individuals. Meanings can be expressed only through attachments—attaching love to a particular person or attaching success to a particular set of activities and purposes. Under the label "Attachments" in the second column, review your first column list and briefly note the related attachments.

The disruptions between meanings and attachments can come in three major forms. The first is through substitution, or substituting one role or set of attachments for another. For example, a teacher might move from one grade level to another, or a principal might move from one school to another. The second form of disruption is through evolution, or a gradual change in an individual's significant meanings and attachments over time. This might happen as a teacher transitions to a teacher leadership role and eventually into an administrative position; over time she has less and less direct contact with the students who in her early career were at the heart of how she defined herself. The third and most difficult form of change is loss, or the sudden disruption of the link between a meaning and its attachment. For example, the loss of a title or position may disrupt an individual's ability to express such meanings as competence, success, or achievement. People respond to loss with an array of emotions that can be quite strong at times: sadness, anger, denial, depression, clinging to the past, or ambivalence about moving forward. These are normal human responses to loss. Change agents often interpret these normal responses as irrational resistance or an attack on them or their work. Coaches can assist their clients to recognize that when the people in their school or district respond to organizational change initiatives with anger, sadness, or ambivalence, they are responding in a normal human way. It is not a sign that there is something wrong either with them or the change. It just takes time to process the feelings associated with loss. Simply listening mindfully and closely to the stories people tell is a powerful strategy for assisting them to cope with loss. Human beings need rites of mourning to heal the loss and ease the transition from the known to the unknown. Bolman and Deal (2013) argue that transition rituals must accompany any significant organizational change, providing opportunities to mourn the past and celebrate the future.

Educational institutions are full of divisive structures, of course, but blaming them for our brokenness perpetuates the myth that the outer world is more powerful than the inner.

—Parker Palmer (1998, p. 36)

EXTENDING EMPATHY

There are moments in all schools when the clouds of emotion gather and the winds of efficacy blow. When the high-pressure system of a drive for change meets a low-pressure system of the pull of the status quo, the thunder of conflict resounds. In these stormy moments, empathy is an essential skill for change agents. Fortunately, this is a skill that evocative coaches can assist educational leaders to develop. The empathy a coach extends to a leader assists the leader to extend empathy to followers in turn. When coaches offer empathy to their clients and focus on their underlying needs, they can also invite their clients to consider the underlying needs of the people in the schools and districts they lead. Accepting the feelings stirred up in those who are affected by a change—and understanding the universal human needs underlying those feelings—helps coachees maintain the vital connection between leader and followers during a change process.

Change inevitably stirs up an array of unmet needs as people find their way through the change process. For example, a change initiative may stimulate the need for competence, engendering feelings of anxiety, uncertainty, and disempowerment as people are asked to enact new ways of doing their jobs. Leaders will find that people in their organizations respond to unmet needs in a variety of ways. Teachers and staff members may withdraw through chronic absenteeism or simply quitting, or they may stay on the job but withdraw psychologically, becoming indifferent, passive, and apathetic. They may resist organizational initiatives through deception, putting on a show of compliance but still maintaining their old patterns of behavior. They may engage in outright sabotage of the change objectives, or they may form coalitions to redress the power imbalance (Bolman & Deal, 2013). Districts and schools need to provide training to help people develop the understanding and skills to implement the change initiative effectively and should also offer psychological support to help employees deal with psychic disruptions to their sense of meaning and purpose that change entails.

There may well be conflict between perceived winners and losers in a change initiative. Conflict can be especially potent in schools and districts because the mission of schools is so dear to parents, taxpayers, and communities alike. Schools and districts are also places with limited resources that must be shared between competing interest groups. When it is handled well, conflict can be a constructive force for positive change. When it is handled poorly, however, it can siphon energy from the core mission of a school, leaving participants feeling wounded and as if they are hunkered down in protective feuding encampments.

As coaches work with educational leaders, they need to be aware of the level of conflict in the leaders' working relationships and the extent to which that conflict is handled constructively. Whether there is "hot" conflict, with open animosity between individuals and teams, or "cold" conflict, with individuals stewing in sullen, resentful silences, it will impact a school's or system's readiness and willingness to engage in the change process. The first step is for coaches to offer empathy to the leader for the negative emotions that have been aroused and for the needs that are not being met. From there, coaches work with clients to design experiments for managing conflicts and resolving disputes constructively so they do not continue to drain the school or system of zest, energy, and the focus on the core mission of educating students.

Suppressing conflict and/or insisting people simply defer to authority does not work in the long run. The process of compassionate communication can be an effective tool in managing conflict in a school or organization. The process starts by honoring conflict as an opportunity to learn what is alive in people and to find common ground. All people are trying to meet the same universal needs, regardless of how well their current strategies are working. Compassionate communication steers people away from criticism, blame, personal attacks, and other variations of the game of "Who's right?" People can vigorously debate differing points of view or different approaches to a problematic situation without impugning the integrity or motives of others. The process creates the conditions for constructive conversations to take place. Speaking cleanly and limiting our communication to observations, feelings, needs, and requests opens up the possibility for people to hear each other in new ways. It can aid in clearing up misunderstandings and help leaders and followers to see the beauty of each other's needs (Rosenberg, 2003).

Coaches should assist leaders in considering ways to create opportunities for participation in decision making regarding proposed change initiatives. These might be forums or committees convened specifically for working through issues related to a particular change initiative. Forums are a critical vehicle for adapting new ideas to existing realities. They may take place through meetings designed for the bargaining and negotiation critical to turn disputes into shared agreements (Bolman & Deal, 2013). The coach can assist educational leaders to determine who should be included by assessing each stakeholder group on two criteria: (1) does the group have a stake in the outcome of the decisions? and (2) do its members have expertise that would contribute to a higher-quality decision? (Hoy & Tarter, 2008). If the answer to both questions is no, to include the group would be a waste of its time. If the answer to one but not both questions is yes, the stakeholder or stakeholder group should be involved in the decision-making process with some intentional limits. If the person or group has needed expertise but no stake in the outcome, the leader should seek to gain that expertise in as efficient a way as possible in order to minimize the time commitment for the person or group. For those who have a stake in the decision but no direct expertise, the leader should serve as an educator, providing them information regarding the decision, soliciting their preferences, and making clear how the ultimate decision will be made.

If the stakeholder meets both criteria—relevance and expertise—then the person or group should be involved in a substantive way. Whether the stakeholder should be included in a fully democratic decision-making process depends upon the answer to a third question: Can the stakeholder be trusted to be committed to organizational goals? If not, the involvement of that person or group should be limited by explicit parameters or safeguards. If these stakeholders are teachers and staff, then the coach and leader will want to consider how to bolster their commitment in order to work toward more democratic decision-making processes in the future. Stakeholders who are judged to be committed to organizational goals based on their previous actions and who have expertise to share should be involved in a democratic process in the interest of reaching a higher-quality decision.

As a new principal, Jake was assigned to a middle school where he followed an ineffective school leader who had been there a long, long time. He was young, smart as a whip, and very energetic. He arrived and immediately started burning bridges with the old guard. I was in one of his faculty meetings, and the teachers literally sat with their backs to him. They came in and turned their chairs so that they faced away from him! When I talked with the teachers about this behavior, I found that they had not been treated with respect either. So it was a process of extending mutual respect in order to move forward.

—Allyssa, Leadership Coach

BUILDING ON STRENGTHS

Engagement in ongoing disciplined inquiry to improve one's practice is central to what it means to be a professional. Evocative coaches assist leaders to continually inquire into their practice. It is, in turn, the leader's responsibility to establish a culture of ongoing inquiry throughout his or her organization. This can be done in a more formal way through strategic planning and in a less formal way through action research. We have found the four-I cycle of AI to be a powerful process to structure an inquiry process (Watkins, Mohr, & Kelly, 2011). This process invites participants to first *initiate* the inquiry, making decisions as to topic choice and method, and then to *inquire* into the areas of strength already present in the organization.

From there, participants *imagine* what the organization would look like, sound like, and feel like if it were to build upon the strengths it already has in the area of inquiry, however small, hidden, or latent. Finally, they *innovate* a new way forward to bring the positive images they have imagined into being. Over the past three decades, AI has a grown into a worldwide phenomenon with a robust and growing research base as to its effectiveness as an organizational change process (Cooperrider, 2000; Watkins, Mohr, & Kelly, 2011; Whitney & Trosten-Bloom, 2010).

The AI process fosters engagement with the change process even if the current reality is one of distress, distrust, and pain. It is a deeply participatory process. Rather than taking a small leadership team to an off-site location where they will sit around a single conference table and their conversations will be limited by sharing the "airtime" available around that table, AI encourages the involvement of as many stakeholders as possible. The limitation of speaking time around the conference table is resolved by beginning the process with paired interviews so everyone has time to speak and be heard. By connecting educators with the positive aspects of the stories of their schools and districts, we reawaken the aspiration to reach even higher. By engaging their unique combination of strengths, values, talents, priorities, and sensitivities, educators discover new possibilities and new avenues for moving forward.

INITIATE. In the first phase, *initiate,* participants make decisions about topic choice and method. AI always starts with that first, fateful decision to focus on strengths as opposed to searching for gaps and conducting a root cause analysis of those deficits. Choosing to focus on strengths can feel like a leap of faith, especially the first few times when the participants have not experienced the process for themselves. Despite the skepticism some may bring to the table, there is something compelling about the positive approach of AI. It is not only more fun, it also bolsters the collective efficacy of the group and enhances creativity, and the plans that are made are more likely to be enacted because of the ownership and positive energy generated. The topic choice can be made by the leader and the coach together, or it could involve members of a small group, such as a leadership team or a planning team that represents key stakeholder groups. The team typically starts with a very open-ended inquiry using the generic AI interview protocol. The themes that emerge provide the basis for a larger inquiry involving as many stakeholders as possible. As AI becomes infused into the culture of the organization as a means of ongoing inquiry, smaller groups may self-organize to explore topics of their own choosing.

INQUIRE. The second phase, *inquire,* invites participants to investigate the area of focus. This typically begins with conducting paired interviews in which people share stories and explore their experiences with the area of the inquiry. The design of the interview protocol for discovering relevant instances of strength and success is a crucial part of the process (Watkins, Mohr, & Kelly, 2011). Especially in the early stages of using AI, it can be useful to consult with an experienced AI practitioner to review the protocol. Participants then interview one another in pairs. When the members of one pair have had sufficient time to tell and explore their stories and to appreciate one another's values and wishes, that pair joins with one to three other pairs to form small groups of four to eight. Each person then recounts briefly his or her partner's stories, values, and wishes with the group. As the sharing unfolds, participants identify three to five themes that energize and enliven them. These are shared with the large group, and the themes are then grouped into similar meta-themes for the group as a whole. The identification of these themes is referred to as mapping the positive core of the organization.

IMAGINE. The next phase in the process, *imagine*, involves developing vivid images of what the team, school, or district would look like, sound like, and feel like if it honored fully the themes selected and if the relationships were just as people desired. Participants can remain with the same groups or form new design teams to dialogue around the themes that people are energized about. These small groups develop creative presentations of their desired future and convey their images of that future through drawings, collages, music, or skits. After the groups develop their images of the future, they then capture them in a set of claims for the school or district, framed in the present tense as though those new images were already present and expressed fully in the organization. These claims are sometimes called possibility statements or provocative propositions.

No amount of skillful invention can replace the essential element of imagination.

—Edward Hopper (1981)

INNOVATE. In the fourth phase of the process, *innovate*, small groups convene to design and plan SMARTER experiments around collective change projects in order to move the team, school, or district closer to the beautiful, vivid images that participants developed in the *imagine* phase. People brainstorm action steps, select those steps they most want to enact, designate responsible parties, schedule activities, identify locations, and plan the logistics of getting things done. Strategies over which team members have control are listed as commitments. Strategies that require the involvement, permission, or resources from another party are listed as requests.

Once the group has conducted its experiment, its members should reconvene to make sense of the findings, and the process can begin all over again. It is an iterative, ever-evolving process of organizational learning, growth, and change. Logistically, the four phases of the AI cycle can be completed in a daylong planning and development summit or across several shorter meetings over a longer period of time. Either way, AI provides a constructive way for organizational participants and stakeholders to engage in productive conversations concerning what they want their team, school, or district to be and how they want to move forward.

When Luis was appointed as principal of Meadowbrook High School, I was assigned as his coach to serve as a thinking partner and to help him to be successful. His background was as a police officer, so while he felt confident in his ability to manage discipline, he knew that instruction was an area in which he needed support. Luis eagerly read the books that I suggested he read and watched the videos I recommended as he began to catch a vision for what might be possible. As Luis walked through the school with me, we noticed that while the classrooms were fairly orderly, the instruction lacked rigor. When I asked a student in an English class what she would do with the essay she was working on when she finished, the student said, "We turn them in to our teacher, but our teachers don't have time to grade them." Luis commented that with the desks in rows, whole-group instruction, and worksheets approach we saw, school looked much the way it had when he'd been a student decades before. He was a bit overwhelmed at the prospect of how to turn around the quality of instruction, especially when there were no compelling external pressures, such as a lack of accreditation or high suspension rates, to help him make his case for the need for change. As he and I met to strategize, I suggested that he focus on just one department to be the model and that ramping up the rigor would be the challenge issued to them. He started with the social studies department and was delighted when he visited the classroom of a government teacher, arguably the most boring teacher in the school, who had rearranged the desks in his classroom into triads, with one struggling student in each, and questions for the Friday quiz printed on 5 × 8 cards that required high-level answers rather than the simple recall he had typically asked of students. The students were engaged in lively conversation and the teacher was beaming. Soon the word spread and other teachers wanted the opportunity to try these new methods as well. Every Wednesday was an early release day, and I assisted Luis to carefully prepare for each staff meeting, demonstrating a new instructional strategy or showing a video. I helped him to focus on a relatively narrow set of skills, scripting the critical moves so that Luis modeled the behaviors he was hoping to see from the teachers. Before long, the excitement was contagious and all of the departments in the school were trying new instructional strategies that invited students to engage in higher levels of rigor.

—Janet, Leadership Coach

EVOKING GREATNESS

Key Points in This Chapter

1. Change can be both exhilarating and challenging, whether it is a personal change in one's leadership practice or the spearheading of needed organizational change.

2. Getting educational leaders into the flow zone will enhance motivation, effort, and enjoyment. The coach and the educational leader work to get the leader into flow. This is done by considering whether the leader is in the rapids or in the doldrums and whether he or she needs to adjust the level of skills up or the level of challenge down.

3. Rolling with resistance creates a respectful stance; keeps the responsibility with the client, where it belongs; and keeps the coach out of unproductive power struggles with the client.

4. Honoring ambivalence and exploring the competing commitments behind that ambivalence through the immunity to change map maintains a respectful stance from which to experiment.

5. We want to avoid the fix-it trap, the cheerleader trap, the rabbit-hole trap, the hurry-hurry trap, the yes-but trap, and the one-right-way trap because these traps can usurp responsibility from the coachee.

6. A leader can apply the evocative coaching model to team, school, or district change, thus inspiring ongoing inquiry and lasting change.

Questions for Reflection and Discussion

1. Tell a story about a time when you experienced flow. What was going on? Who was involved? How does your experience align and differ with the description of flow developed by Mihaly Csikszentmihalyi?

2. How could you experience flow more often in your own life and work? What environmental modifications would help you to do so?

3. Imagine a change you'd like to make in your own life. What actions are you avoiding that keep you locked in your current position? What actions do you take that help maintain the status quo? What BTB (big-time bad) things are you worried would come to pass if you started (or stopped) taking those actions? How might you safely test your assumptions?

4. How might you heighten your awareness of your use of communication patterns that interfere with connection? What do you notice about the energy in a conversation when these patterns are present?

5. How can coaches assist educational leaders to work through conflicts productively? Brainstorm six useful ideas.

6. Consider an organizational decision faced by either you or your client. How might the criteria of relevance, expertise, and commitment to organizational goals help guide you in deciding which stakeholders to involve and how?

The Reflective Coach

In this book we have introduced the process of evocative coaching as an effective and enjoyable way to promote learning, growth, and change in educational leaders. Whether our person-centered, no-fault, strengths-based approach challenged your own assumptions and approach to leadership coaching or whether it resonated deeply with your previously held convictions, it is now time to reflect on what we have presented in light of your own experience. In this way you can fashion your own definition of coaching—a definition-in-action—that will clarify, facilitate, and empower your way of being with the leaders you coach.

COACHING THE SELF

Just as we invite educational leaders to reflect on their experiences to generate new stories and design new actions, we take the time to do that for ourselves and for each other. We facilitate our own continuous growth and progress by reading books like this one and reflecting upon our coaching experiences. Donald Schön (1983) coined the term *reflective practitioner* as he made the case that both reflection-*in*-action and reflection-*on*-action are part and parcel of how professionals do their work. Reflective practice involves thoughtfully considering critical incidents in one's own experience and applying professional knowledge to practice. It is through such reflection that artistry enters the work of a professional, taking practice beyond the mere application of technical knowledge. Schön described the far-reaching consequences for schools if they were to truly embrace reflective practice to challenge prevailing knowledge structures. This would require schools to incorporate on-the-spot experiments to explore not only the routines of everyday practice but the central values and principles of the institution.

As coaches we assist educational leaders to become reflective practitioners when we enable them to examine their leadership practices and determine what works best for their schools without judgment or presuppositions. As coaches we become reflective practitioners when we pay attention to our own story; actively engage in self-empathy; inquire into our own strengths, opportunities, aspirations, and resources; and design our own SMARTER experiments for personal and professional growth.

HEARING OUR OWN STORY

Deep story listening is something we can do not just for others but for ourselves as well. How often do we stop and listen to the stories we are telling in our own life? We can listen to our own stories by practicing mindfulness—the nonjudgmental awareness of what is happening in the present moment—throughout the day and in those significant moments right before the start of coaching sessions. When coaches model a mindful presence, clients can emulate that presence in their own leadership practice. We take time to STOP (**s**top, **t**ake a breath, **o**bserve, acknowledge and allow what's here, **p**roceed), both through short pauses in the midst of our coaching sessions and school visits—reflection-*in*-action—and through longer pauses before and after our coaching engagements—reflection-*on*-action.

One way to extend that deep listening to ourselves is through journaling. As a part of this reflective practice, we might consider engaging in the kinds of imaginative story listening exercises that we have invited our coachees to try. For example, after writing the story of one of our coaching experiences from our point of view, we might try writing about that same exchange from the point of view of the coachee. What was the experience like for her or him? What was the coachee feeling and needing as the situation unfolded? Powerful insights can come from seeing an experience from another vantage point. We might also explore the decision points in the coaching conversation. How might have things shifted, for better or for worse, had we made a different decision at a critical point in the exchange? Playing that out on paper can help us to become aware of the many decision points that a single coaching session holds. It may invite us to prepare for future coaching sessions by anticipating these decision points and outlining some of the key questions we want to explore in advance so fewer decisions are made on the fly. Finally, we can explore the lesson points from the stories of our coaching session. If this story were a fable, what would the moral be?

SELF-EMPATHY

Every time someone tells us a story about his or her life or we step back to reflect and organize our thoughts, we have the opportunity to connect with both the facts and the feelings of the situation. In addition to noticing the emotions that are showing up in our clients, we can notice the emotions and physical sensations showing up in us as we listen to our clients' stories. An awareness of our own feelings and needs is crucial if we want to be an empathic presence with the leaders we coach. Being mindful of our own energy and emotional reactions in relation to the leaders we are working with can be done in the moment (reflection-*in*-action) or outside of coaching sessions (reflection-*on*-action) in order to facilitate our competence and development as coaches. It can be done alone or with a mentor coach. The more we know about what is going on with us, the less we will allow our own experiences, feelings, opinions, and worries to get in the way of our being present in the moment.

Although coaches recognize the importance of creating a generative relational space with clients, it is sometimes difficult to maintain a calm, safe, judgment-free posture in the face of a client who seems to be doing more harm than good. It becomes even more difficult when those behaviors persist in spite of a coach's best efforts to support self-responsibility and behavior change. When conversations with educational leaders trigger an emotional response in us and we start viewing our coachees as irritating or uncooperative, it helps to notice the things we are saying to ourselves and then to explore the underlying feelings and needs. What are we really feeling when we think a client is being uncooperative? Coaches may be more invested in an outcome than the coachee. We may want to push hard to make change happen. It is important to remember that this can interfere with empathy and provoke resistance to change. Such promotional efforts are usually counterproductive because they encourage resistance talk rather than change talk, hindering the advancement of the client's agenda and the work of coaching in general. Although we may be momentarily frustrated with a client, this may say more about us than about the client. Becoming curious about the needs that are motivating coachee behaviors can begin to shift things in a positive direction. Recognizing that both poor leadership behaviors and poor engagement with the coaching process are expressions, however unfortunate, of a client's unmet needs can facilitate empathy and relieve frustration. Change is not likely until and unless the needs of coachees are fully and respectfully recognized and expressed.

When we find it difficult to empathize with clients, it may mean we are not receiving enough empathy in our own lives. Since coaches should not expect or demand empathy from our coachees, we must be sure to get it from other sources. Regular self-empathy and mutual empathy with significant others are essential practices for authentic coaching presence. By connecting deeply with and understanding our own feelings and needs, coaches grow our empathy skills and open the way for relational authenticity with others. Here, too, journaling can be a powerful strategy to become aware of both our feelings and the needs behind them. One useful exercise in this regard is to create an "I" diagram on the journal page. Above the top horizontal line, write the facts of the situation as they appear to you, attempting to avoid evaluations, judgments, diagnoses, or blame. To the left of the vertical line, write down your thoughts about the situation under the heading "The story

I'm telling myself." This helps you to remember the story of your thoughts and recollections are but one version of reality. To the right of the vertical line, under the heading "The heart of the matter," capture your feelings and needs, making use of the lists presented in Chapter 4. Finally, below the lower horizontal line, write the requests you make of yourself and of others as to how to move forward.

It is not possible to coach masterfully when overwhelmed, fatigued, stressed, burned out, or despairing. Therefore, self-care on the part of the coach is an essential aspect of coaching effectiveness. Mindfulness contributes to the cultivation of our strengths through taking the opportunity to quiet our mental chatter. Paying attention to the rhythm of energy out and energy in, of work and rest, is a critical part of self-management for conveying coaching presence. The more things we do that fill us with energy, the more likely it is we can serve as inspiring role models for the educational leaders we coach. Unless we are doing the things that make life worth living, including taking adequate time for rest and recovery, it is quite difficult to share renewing energy with others. We pay attention to energy dynamics when we work with clients in designing SMARTER experiments; we attend to those same dynamics when it comes to our own personal and professional practices.

INQUIRING INTO OUR OWN PROFESSIONAL PRACTICE

Our effectiveness as coaches will not only be enhanced by modeling the practice of self-empathy but also by modeling continuous curiosity into our own professional practice. We can always observe ourselves in the moment with metacognitive, or "thinking about our thinking," awareness. This awareness is likely to be more explicit when things are going either worse or better than expected. We can also invest in our own learning by using one of the observation tools described below and designing our own SMARTER experiments around the questions we bring to our practice.

SELF-OBSERVATION

Self-reflection can be facilitated with appreciative observation tools like those we offered in the inquiry phase of the evocative coaching process. To make such observations, coaches may want to solicit the permission of a client to audio and/or video record one or more coaching sessions. We want to be clear with the client that this is for our own learning and growth as a coach and we will delete the recording after we have finished reviewing it. We review the recordings and search for vitalities that enhance the coaching dynamic. These vitalities are the things we want to broaden and build on in our professional practice as coaches. Several self-observation tools are available for download at www.SchoolTransformation.com, or coaches may want to construct their own around their particular learning focus.

Notes and Written Debriefs. Taking notes during coaching sessions is a practice many coaches find helpful to capture the most salient points and any agreements for actions on the part of the coach or the client. It can help to convey a sense of seriousness about the process and the commitments made. If the coaching session is face-to-face, however, it is important that note-taking is not so extensive as to be intrusive of the coaching dynamic and rapport between coach and client. In addition to taking notes during the coaching session, it may be helpful for the coach to take 5–10 minutes immediately after the coaching session for a written debrief. Creating such debriefs assists with continuity from one session to the next. The coach may document such dynamics as those listed below.

COACH DEBRIEF

- What did I notice?
- When were energies high?
- How did I feel during the session?
- What questions got a reaction?
- What promises were made?
- What would I like to build upon and develop in the next session?
- What would I like to explore further?

Charting Talk Time. For a coaching session to be truly evocative, we want the coachee to do more talking than the coach. The leaders we coach have greater opportunities for meaning-making and ultimately take more responsibility for their learning if we encourage them to do more of the talking. In service of this objective, coaches are encouraged to adopt a WAIT and SEE attitude; that is, to ask ourselves, "Why am I talking?" and to remind ourselves to stop explaining everything. When the client is talking, it represents a measure of vitality. One simple way to find out what proportion of the conversation coaches and coachees talk is to review an audio recording of the session and tally minute-by-minute totals of who was speaking. This can be done in two-second intervals or in terms of "idea chunks." See Figure 8.1 for an example from a coaching session that Meredith conducted with Carmen, an assistant principal in her first year at the high school level.

FIGURE 8.1   Charting Talk Time

Charting Talk Time

Coach: <u>Meredith</u>   Coachee: <u>Carmen</u>

Date of Conference: <u>March 5</u>   Time of Conference: <u>4:00</u>

MINUTE	COACHEE	TOTAL	SILENCE	COACH	TOTAL
0:00	### ### ### ///	18		###-///	8
1:00	### //	7		### ### ###-//	17
2:00	### ### ###-/	16	/	###-/	6
3:00	### ### ###-///	18		###-////	9
4:00	### ### ###-////	19		###	5
5:00	### ### ### ### ###-###	30			0
6:00	### ### ### //	17		### ###-/	11
7:00	### ### ###	15		### ###	10
8:00	### ### ### ### ###-////	29			0
9:00	### ### ### ###-///	23		###-/	6
10:00	### ### ###	15		### ### ###-//	17
11:00	### ###-////	14		### ### ###-///	18
12:00	//	2	/	### ### ### ###-/	21
13:00	###	5	.//	### ### ### ###	20
14:00	### ### ###	15	//	//	2
15:00	### ### ### ### ###	25		///	3
16:00	### ###-//	12	/	### ###-/	11
17:00	### ### ###-/	16		###-///	8
18:00	### ###-/	11		### ###-///	13
19:00	///	3		### ### ### ###-//	22
20:00	###	5	/	### ### ###-///	18
21:00	### ###-////	14	//	###-//	7
22:00	### ###-///	13		### ###-/	11
23:00	###-///	8	/	### ###-//	12
24:00	### ### ### ### ###-###	30			0
25:00	### ### ###-//	17	//	###-////	9
26:00	### ### ###-//	17		### ###	10
27:00	### ### ###	15		### ### ///	13

MINUTE	COACHEE	TOTAL	SILENCE	COACH	TOTAL
28:00	////-////	10	/	////-//// ///	13
29:00	////-////-////-////-//	22		////	4
30:00	////-////-////-////-////-////	29			0
31:00	////-////-////-////	20		////-///	8
32:00	////-////-////-////-///	23		/	1
33:00	////-////-////	15		////-////	10
34:00	////-////	10	//	////-////-///	13
35:00	////-////-////-////-////-//	27		/	1
Total		585 (62%)	17 (2%)		337 (36%)

After a creative energy check, I asked Carmen about an area of emerging growth that she would like to explore. Carmen explained that one of her responsibilities was to oversee special education for her grade level. She and another of the new assistant principals were both feeling some frustration at the absence of established procedures, so that 504 and IEP meetings were handled quite differently at each grade level. After listening to what she described, I offered Carmen some empathy reflections about the frustration she was experiencing as well as for the embarrassment she felt when teachers complained to her about the lack of consistency. Afterwards, I invited her to retell the story from the standpoint of Helen, an older assistant principal who was charged with the oversight of special education for the whole building. Initially, Carmen was a bit shy and needed a little coaxing to speak from Helen's perspective. Before long, though, she really became engaged and spoke passionately from Helen's point of view. When we concluded the role play, Carmen shared the insights that had come to her from playing with the story in that way. She realized that this was Helen's first year with the responsibility for the oversight of special education for the whole building and that she was still finding her way in this leadership position. Carmen decided to modify her approach to developing a new set of standardized procedures to be sensitive to what she perceived might be Helen's response, while still making plans to move the initiative forward.

—Meredith, Leadership Coach

Charting Coach Behaviors. Throughout this book we have identified numerous behaviors coaches may use in their work with educational leaders. Some of the more important include attentive listening, asking questions, offering reflections, clarifying focus, brainstorming ideas, designing actions, and celebrating progress. There are many others. The International Coach Federation (2008b), for example, has identified eleven core coaching competencies, and the International Association of Coaching (2009) has identified nine coaching masteries. To become more aware of our behaviors during coaching sessions, we can record a coaching session, identify the behaviors we want to notice, and then chart our behaviors in one- or two-minute time intervals. There is no one right balance of behaviors that coaches are trying to achieve in every coaching conversation. Our goal is to be aware of and responsive to the needs of the leaders we are coaching, in their complex contexts, making just-in-time moves that meet client needs and evoke engagement.

Figure 8.2 provides an example of how one coach charted her behaviors. The ten categories at the top of the chart (listening, questioning, presenting, reflecting, clarifying, brainstorming, designing, identifying resources, celebrating, and using humor) reflect the behaviors that Rachel wanted to observe in her coaching session with Hasan, an experienced middle school principal. By charting her behaviors in two-minute increments, Rachel noticed how her role shifted during different portions of the coaching conversation.

> What I noticed as a charted my coaching behaviors was that I did a lot of listening throughout, which I was pleased to see. I was genuinely interested in Hasan's desire to instill in his teachers a more entrepreneurial spirit and to take greater ownership for their students' learning. He was concerned that once teachers had referred a student to special education or for other kinds of support, their sense of responsibility for that student seemed to diminish. The questions I asked really seemed to get him thinking. When we got to the brainstorming, he came up with a lot of interesting ideas, beyond what he had been thinking before our session. He decided to focus on telling stories of teachers who had evidenced this entrepreneurial spirit and also to talk about the ownership he took in caring for the teachers' wellbeing. I took the initiative to capture these ideas on the experimental design template. He seemed quite pleased to leave the session with a concrete plan for implementing this new initiative. There was a really positive and productive spirit throughout, even though it didn't show up as humor, per se. Although I didn't do much celebrating, it didn't seem to be needed in this case because he had such a clear idea of what he wanted to think through.

Many other behaviors can also be charted. Through self-observation and charting our behaviors, we gain an opportunity to reflect on our contribution and role in coaching conversations.

FIGURE 8.2 Charting Coach Behaviors

Charting Coach Behaviors

Coach: Rachel

Coachee: Hasan

Date of Conference: 2/25

Time of Conference: 1:30 – 2:14

TIME INTERVAL	1. LISTENING	2. QUESTIONING	3. PRESENTING	4. REFLECTING	5. CLARIFYING	6. BRAINSTORMING	7. DESIGNING EXPERIMENT	8. IDENTIFYING RESOURCES	9. CELEBRATING	10: HUMOR
2	𝍸/	𝍸///	𝍸//		///				/	
4	𝍸𝍸𝍸𝍸𝍸𝍸𝍸///			//	//					
6	𝍸𝍸𝍸𝍸𝍸///	////			///					
8	𝍸𝍸𝍸𝍸////	𝍸𝍸			//					
10	𝍸𝍸𝍸𝍸𝍸////	////			///					
12	𝍸𝍸𝍸𝍸𝍸///	𝍸////								
14	𝍸𝍸𝍸///	//	𝍸𝍸/	//						
16	𝍸𝍸𝍸𝍸//	////	𝍸		///					
18	𝍸𝍸𝍸𝍸𝍸/	𝍸𝍸//							/	
20	𝍸𝍸𝍸𝍸𝍸𝍸𝍸///				//					

(Continued)

FIGURE 8.2 (Continued)

TIME INTERVAL	1. LISTENING	2. QUESTIONING	3. PRESENTING	4. REFLECTING	5. CLARIFYING	6. BRAINSTORMING	7. DESIGNING EXPERIMENT	8. IDENTIFYING RESOURCES	9. CELEBRATING	10. HUMOR
22	####-####-####-####-I	####-####-####								
24	####-####-####-####-I	II	II							
26	####-I	II	####-####-II	III						
28	II	####-III	##	III		####-####-III				
30	####-####-####-I	####-####-II	IIII							
32	####-####-####-##	####-II	####-I				####-II			
34	####-####-III		####-####-I	IIII						
36	####-####-II		####-####-####-####-####-III							
38	####-####-I		I		I		####-####-####-II			
40	####-I		II			####-####-II	III	####		
42	####-####-####-####-####	I		II	I				I	
44	II		II							
46										
Total	462 (60%)	102 (13%)	99 (13%)	18 (2%)	22 (3%)	26 (3%)	27 (4%)	5 (1%)	3 (0%)	0

Noticing Evocative Coaching Style Points. To illuminate the evocative coaching process, we have identified two loops (the no-fault turn and the strengths-building turn) and the four steps of LEAD (listen—empathize—appreciate—design). Now we add 16 style points as observable dimensions of the evocative coaching dance. Although we recognize the limitations of numbered diagrams, which imply a far more linear form than evocative coaching conversations ever actually take, we nevertheless see value as reflective practitioners to sketching out the style points in this way.

LOOP I: The No-Fault Turn	LOOP II: The Strengths-Building Turn
Step 1: Story Listening	**Step 3: Appreciative Inquiry**
1. Establishing Rapport	7. Discovering Strengths
2. Celebrating Progress	8. Exploring Opportunities
3. Exploring Stories	9. Framing Aspirations
4. Attentive Listening	10. Identifying Resources
Step 2: Expressing Empathy	**Step 4: Design Thinking**
5. Offering Empathy Reflections	11. Brainstorming Ideas
The Learning Brief	12. Designing a SMARTER Experiment
6. Clarifying the Focus	13. Confirming Commitment
	14. Rolling With Resistance
	15. Exploring Systemic Change
	16. Session Feedback

In Figure 8.3, you can see how Ryan used the 16 style points to observe and reflect on a coaching conversation he had with Julia. Julia was a new elementary school principal who had been appointed unexpectedly the last week of August after the previous principal left suddenly. Ryan observed,

> Watching the recording, I noted again how unsure of herself Julia had seemed at the start of the conversation. Through inviting her to tell her story of this unexpected promotion, she began to seem less wary. As she told her story, I listened for the underlying values in what she shared and then made some empathy guesses about her feelings and needs. This is when there was a shift in the energy in the conversation. As we assessed the strengths she brought to this position, her body position shifted and she became more relaxed and sort of leaned in. The aspiration she wanted to focus on was how to make her faculty meetings more collaborative. The former principal had used a lot of one-way communication in these meetings, which left the faculty fairly disengaged and passive. Brainstorming various ideas and then settling on an agenda for her first faculty meeting seemed to be a very positive step for Julia.

FIGURE 8.3 Evocative Coaching Style Points

Evocative Coaching Style Points

Coach: <u>Ryan</u>　　　　　　　Date: <u>September 7</u>

Coachee: <u>Julia</u>　　Time of Conference: <u>3:30</u>

ELEMENTS	OBSERVED	NOTES
Establishing Rapport *Creative energy check-in*	Yes _X_ No ____	The creative energy check-in broke the ice and helped set a positive tone.
Celebrating Progress *"How did you grow?"*	Yes ____ No _X_	She was so unsure of herself and nervous when we began that I missed the chance to celebrate progress.
Exploring Stories	Yes _X_ No ____	Telling her story of how she was appointed to this position is when she really became engaged.
Attentive Listening	Yes _X_ No ____	I felt I was being a good listener and evoking her capabilities, but when she asked specific questions I reverted to giving advice.
Empathy Reflections	Yes _X_ No ____	Articulating her need for organization and purpose helped her realize why she has been so nervous and flustered. Once we addressed that, she really settled down and was able to plan.
Clarifying Focus *The learning brief*	Yes _X_ No ____	The learning brief seemed easy, but there were details that needed to be clarified.
Discovering Strengths	Yes _X_ No ____	Once we did an assessment of the strengths she brought to the task, her affect changed and she seemed more confident and engaged.
Exploring Opportunities	Yes _X_ No ____	She needed reassurance that it was OK for her to do things differently from the previous principal.
Framing Aspirations	Yes _X_ No ____	Analyzing her previous experiences helped her see how she could make her faculty meetings more collaborative.
Identifying Resources	Yes _X_ No ____	Taking stock of the resources she had available helped her to relax and begin to be more excited about her ideas.
Brainstorming Ideas	Yes _X_ No ____	The brainstorming was difficult because we kept getting sidetracked discussing the ideas before coming back to brainstorming.

ELEMENTS	OBSERVED	NOTES
Designing a SMARTER Experiment	Yes __X__ No ____	She struggled a bit to frame an if-then statement. It was important to take the time for her to have the focus, organization, and clear thinking in place prior to setting the meeting agenda.
Confirming Commitment *The confidence ruler*	Yes __X__ No ____	The two follow-up questions led to identifying some additional supports that increased her confidence.
Rolling With Resistance	Yes __X__ No ____	She was definitely in the rapids when we began but got more confident as we came up with a concrete plan.
Exploring Systemic Change	Yes _____ No__X__	Next time we might begin to think about how to involve her leadership team in the development of the agenda.
Session Feedback	Yes __X__ No ____	She said she was grateful and that she felt less stressed and more ready for her first faculty meeting.

Noticing Body Language. To get a sense of how well you are responding to an educational leader in the moment and facilitating her or his flow, you might request permission to video record a coaching conversation. This can feel threatening to some coachees, so do this only after you have a high degree of trust established in the coaching relationship. Remember to explain it is for your own learning and growth and will be deleted afterwards. While the experience is recent enough that it is still fresh in your mind, watch the video with the sound turned off. Pay attention to both your own body language and that of the coachee to see what this might reveal about how each of you was feeling during various segments of the coaching conversation. Observe actions, reactions, adaptations, repetitions, facial expressions, inclinations, shifts, accommodations, and other salient factors. Look for evidence of vitality. When did you see shining eyes and smiling faces? What were you pleased with and what would you like to do more of in future coaching sessions? Ryan continued his reflection on his session with Julia, noting that

> there were a couple of occasions during the coaching conversation when I noticed Julia become defensive, and by recognizing those moments, I was able to adapt my responses to guide our conversation back into the strengths-building turn. The first occurred when I gave Julia what I thought was an authentic, specific compliment. I noticed immediately that she got really quiet, seemed to physically draw back from the table, and said only, "Yeah," in response. When I noticed her reaction, I wasn't sure if I had seemed inauthentic or if I was talking too much. So I switched back to one of the structured appreciative inquiry questions, and Julia reengaged in the

conversation, leaning forward again and making eye contact with me. Towards the end of our coaching conversation, I saw Julia's wall of defensiveness come up again when I forgot my role as evocative coach and started making suggestions. Julia had been discussing an idea she had for how to organize her faculty meeting. I was excited about the idea and I jumped in with some suggestions for how to make it work. Julia was immediately resistant—she leaned back in her chair, folded her arms, and explained why my suggestion wouldn't work. As soon as I realized what was happening, I acknowledged the constraints she had raised and asked her about her ideas for implementation. I watched as Julia visibly relaxed and began working out how she might bring her idea to fruition. This exchange taught me a lot about coaching. Julia's resistance to my well-intended but meddling suggestion was immediate and visceral. Just as immediate, however, was her relaxation and reengagement in the process when I backed off, invited her to think it through further, and positively affirmed her intent.

ASKING FOR FEEDBACK

Because coaching promotes educational leader development within a learning partnership, it is important for coaches to solicit feedback from clients. This feedback is important both for our own learning and because it enables us to adapt the coaching process to better support the learning and growth of the leaders we are working with. Asking coachees to share insights and to make suggestions on how the coaching process can become more productive and enjoyable increases their sense of engagement and their autonomy and responsibility. Unless we ask clients directly for such feedback, however, they may not often tell us how they would like the coaching to be different. Soliciting honest input at periodic intervals during the coaching program builds the coaching relationship by making it clear to clients that we are devoted to their success and that we will do whatever it takes to facilitate that success. Appreciative inquiries such as the following can therefore move the relationship forward in positive directions:

- What is the best experience you've had so far through the coaching process?

- What do you value most about our coaching relationship?

- What about our process has helped you to reach your goals and move forward?

- If you had three wishes for our coaching relationship, wishes that would help the relationship serve you better, what would they be?

We become better coaches when our clients articulate the kind of approaches and dynamics that are most motivating and impactful. By asking clients to talk about the things that are working well and that they would like more of, we reduce the likelihood they will act out their resistance to change by undermining the coaching process itself. By focusing on positive experiences, values, conditions, and wishes regarding what coachees like and want rather than what they do not like or want, coaches and clients are empowered to be honest in the mutual pursuit of making the coaching relationship as productive and as enjoyable as possible.

As coachees are sharing their thoughts in response to a request for feedback, listen for what is unspoken but conveyed in their tone and hesitations. Ask for clarification when you suspect there may be uncomfortable or hard feelings. Use empathy reflections to better understand their feelings and needs. Remind clients that they can send you feedback at any time and you will always take their suggestions seriously. Encourage the use of e-mail or written notes to communicate postsession thoughts.

When we receive suggestions or criticisms, we should be prepared to act on them wisely. Thank coachees for the input and use it to grow stronger as a coach. Take notes and follow up on the points raised as soon as possible. Avoid the urge to explain your actions or intentions. Review audio and video recordings of coaching sessions to get a sense of the dynamics the coachee has raised. Without violating confidentiality, it may also help to talk with a mentor coach or other coaching colleagues about points of concern. As with all evocative coaching, the goal is to build on the things that are working well and outgrow the things that are working less well. Letting clients know how we are seeking to use their concerns to improve our coaching supports trust and models the very frame of learning, growth, and change that we want coachees to bring to their leadership practices. Modeling an attitude of openness and lack of defensiveness may be as powerful as anything we do as coaches.

Designing Our Own SMARTER Experiments

Once we have inquired into our own coaching practices, we can use the same design-thinking process for the professional development we use to evoke and support the professional development of our clients. We can design experiments to test the hypotheses that undergird our practice as coaches.

1. Take stock of your strengths as a coach by taking the VIA or another assessment, asking for feedback from your clients, and/or through reflecting on your experience.

2. Frame a larger aspiration of who you are and how you work as a coach.

3. Identify near-term opportunities that support your aspiration.

4. Brainstorm ideas for realizing those outcomes. Be creative! Go for quantity, not quality.

5. Select one to three ideas you would like to experiment with to strengthen your coaching presence and practice.

6. Frame a hypothesis, articulating an if-then statement about the outcome you expect from the behaviors you plan to try.

7. Design a SMARTER experiment around those ideas using the experimental design template to clarify and document the details of the experiment.

8. Explore the personal and professional resources available to support the experiment.

9. Conduct the experiment.

10. Collect data through notes, written debriefs, recordings, and/or feedback.

11. Reflect on the story the data tell through deliberation, writing in a journal, and/or talking with a mentor coach or coaching colleague.

12. Notice the feelings and needs stimulated by the experiment.

13. Inquire into strengths and vitalities that can be built on in the future.

14. Design new experiments based upon the results of past experiments.

Learning and professional growth for evocative coaches never stops. Just as with educational leaders, it is a lifelong journey. Even the best talents can benefit from formal training and mentoring, followed by years of practice, more training, and more mentoring to improve mastery. Coaches can continue to build their skills by reading books on coaching, perhaps through engaging with coaching colleagues in a book study. Attending workshops and conferences on coaching, including events sponsored by professional education and coaching associations, is another good way to continue our learning and growth. Coach training programs are also available, including one specifically designed for evocative coaching (for more information, go to www.SchoolTransformation.com).

PROFESSIONAL COACHING CODE OF ETHICS

Because the work that coaches do with people may place clients in a vulnerable position, the coaching profession is guided by a set of professional ethics. The field of coaching is self-governing, and there are a number of coaching organizations that have articulated standards and ethical codes of conduct. Two of the best known are the International Coach Federation (ICF; 2008a) and the International Association of Coaching (IAC; 2003). On its website, the IAC notes that coaches are expected to "maintain high standards of competence" in their work and to "uphold standards of ethical conduct that reflect well on the individual coach as well as the profession at large." To that end, evocative coaches are expected to uphold the following minimum standards of conduct and practice, adapted from the IAC and ICF ethical codes:

An Ethical Code for Coaches

1. Coaches will carefully explain and strive to ensure that, prior to or at the initial meeting, coachees understand the nature of coaching, the nature and limits of confidentiality, and any other terms of the coaching agreement or contract.

2. Coaches will always act with integrity and represent ourselves in an honest and fair manner, being cognizant of our particular competencies and limitations.

3. Trust and responsibility are at the heart of the coaching profession. It is expected that coaches will treat clients with dignity and respect and be aware of cultural differences and the coachee's right to autonomy, privacy, and confidentiality.

4. We do not knowingly engage in behavior that is harassing or demeaning to persons with whom we interact in our work.

5. Because our professional judgments and actions may affect the lives of others, we are alert to and guard against personal, financial, social, organizational, or political factors that might lead to misuse of our influence.

6. It is recommended that we appropriately document our work in order to facilitate provision of services later by us or by other professionals, to ensure accountability, and to meet other legal requirements or agreements.

7. We maintain confidentiality when creating, storing, accessing, transferring, and disposing of records under our authority in accordance with professional standards and any applicable laws and agreements.

8. Coaches take precautions to ensure and maintain the confidentiality of information communicated through the use of the telephone, voice mail, computers, e-mail, texting, social media, facsimile machines, and other information technology sources.

9. Coaches do not share confidential information with others without obtaining the prior consent of the educational leader or unless the disclosure cannot be avoided. Furthermore, coaches share information only to the extent necessary to achieve the purposes of the consultation. Coaches inform educational leaders about such disclosures and review their possible ramifications.

10. Coaches must notify the appropriate authorities if educational leaders disclose they are harming or endangering themselves or others or that they intend to harm or endanger themselves or others.

11. Coaches respect the client's right to terminate the coaching relationship at any point during the process, subject to the provisions of the agreement or contract. Coaches will be alert to indications the coachee is no longer benefiting from the coaching relationship and will discuss with the client terminating the relationship on that basis, including making appropriate referrals to other coaches or professional services.

CONCLUSION

Evocative coaching seeks to facilitate self-directed learning based upon the inherent interests and abilities of individual clients. We want educational leaders to discover and freely choose to use the methods and approaches that work best in their schools and districts, using the LEAD process we have described in this book. Then, and only then, will those methods come alive and take root. Then, and only then, will we have called forth motivation and movement in educational leaders, through our conversations and way of being with them, so they achieve desired outcomes and enhance their quality of life. By exploring motivation and facilitating movement, by building trust, understanding feelings, identifying strengths, crafting visions, brainstorming ideas, and designing experiments, evocative coaches assist educational leaders to become the professionals they always hoped to be. To do all of this, evocative coaches leverage the secret sauce of connection, generosity, and joy. The dynamics of evocative coaching begin to radiate out and spiral upward as people aspire to new heights and celebrate small victories along the way.

We have witnessed how LEAD can become a tool for making all the other leadership tools work. The skills behind this process take time to master. We are so much more accustomed to giving advice and promoting ideas, and we think of that as being so much more efficient, that even the thought of doing otherwise can be unsettling. Yet the evocative coaching model promises to be both more effective and more efficient in the long run. It enables educational leaders to engage fully in their developmental paths and to leap forward in their professional masteries. When educational leaders see coaching sessions as stimulating opportunities to reflect on their experiences, to share their feelings, to meet their needs, and to generate new ideas for moving forward, then coaching fulfills its potential as a powerful catalyst for change.

Key Points in This Chapter

1. Self-reflection and self-care are essential for evocative coaches.

2. To remain sharp, evocative coaches find ways to listen to and play with their own stories; engage in self-empathy; examine their strengths, opportunities, aspirations, and resources; and design their own SMARTER experiments.

3. Asking coachees for feedback at the end of a coaching session or between sessions provides valuable information for the coach's continued learning and growth.

4. Coaches are attuned to the professional ethics of coaching.

5. The opportunity we have as evocative coaches is to reconnect with ourselves and others in the noble work of making a positive difference in the lives of students, families, and communities.

Questions for Reflection and Discussion

1. Recall and tell a story about a wonderful experience you had coaching someone—a time when you felt really pleased by the quality of the connection and what grew out of your work together.

2. What helps you to offer yourself empathy? How are you feeling right now? Have you noticed an improvement in your capacity to articulate your feelings and needs as you have been practicing self-empathy?

3. What needs have been met as you have read this book and engaged with the ideas it presents? What feelings have been stimulated?

4. What are your preferred strategies for reflection? Do you like to keep a journal, converse with a mentor coach, take time for silence, or do something else? Describe how you might strengthen your current practices.

5. What self-observations would you consider using in your own professional development as a coach? What would you like to learn?

6. Which coaching behaviors come most naturally to you? Which ones are most challenging? How can you play more to your strengths in coaching?

7. What are your learning aspirations in relationship to coaching? What are three strategies you might try in pursuit of your learning goals?

8. What is one experiment that you would like to conduct to strengthen your presence and practice as an evocative coach in the next month? Consider each of these questions:

   a. On a scale of 0 to 10, how willing are you to implement the evocative coaching model? What led you to pick that number?

   b. On a scale of 0 to 10, how important would you say it is for you to implement the evocative coaching model? Why didn't you pick a lower number?

   c. On a scale of 0 to 10, how confident are you that you can implement the evocative coaching model? What would it take to make that number higher?

Appendix

Evocative Coaching Principles, Questions, and Reflections

Evocative Coaching Principles

ADULT LEARNING PRINCIPLES
RELEVANT TO EVOCATIVE COACHING

- Adults are autonomous and self-directed.

- Adult learning builds on a wide variety of previous experiences, knowledge, mental models, self-direction, interests, resources, and competencies.

- Adults want to know the relevance of the content to be learned to their goals and roles before they will invest the attention and effort needed for new learning.

- Adults are focused on solutions. Instead of being interested in knowledge for its own sake, adult learning seeks immediate application and problem solving.

- Adult learning needs to be facilitated rather than directed. Adults want to be treated as equals and shown respect both for what they know and how they prefer to learn.

- Adults need specific, behavioral feedback that is free of evaluative or judgmental opinions.

- Adults need follow-up support to continue and to advance their learning over time.

HUMANISTIC PSYCHOLOGY PRINCIPLES
RELEVANT TO EVOCATIVE COACHING

- People are inherently creative and capable.

- The human brain is hardwired to enjoy novelty and growth, which explains the inherent joy of learning.

- Learning takes place when people actively take responsibility for constructing meaning from their experiences, either confirming or changing what they already know.

- The meanings people construct determine the actions they take.

- Every person is unique, yet all people have the same universal needs.

- Empathy, mutuality, and connection make people more cooperative and open people up to change.

- The more people know about their values, strengths, resources, and abilities, the stronger their motivation and the more effective their changes will be.

PRINCIPLES OF COACHING PRESENCE

The International Coach Federation (2008b) defines coaching presence as the "ability to be fully conscious and create a spontaneous relationship with the client, employing a style that is open, flexible, and confident" (p. 2). To this end, the ICF indicates that a professional coach

- is present and flexible during the coaching process, "dancing" in the moment;

- accesses her or his own intuition and trusts that inner knowing—"goes with the gut";

- is open to not knowing and takes risks;

- sees many ways to work with the client and chooses in the moment what is most effective;

- uses humor effectively to create lightness and energy;

- confidently shifts perspectives and experiments with new possibilities for his or her own action; and

- demonstrates confidence in working with strong emotions and can self-manage and not be overpowered by or enmeshed in the emotions of the coachee.

PRINCIPLES OF EVOCATIVE COACHING

- Give clients our full, undivided attention.

- Maintain an upbeat, energetic, and positive attitude at all times.

- Accept and meet clients where they are right now, without making them wrong.

- Ask and trust clients to take charge of their own learning and growth.

- Ensure that clients are talking more than we are.

- Enable clients to appreciate the positive value of their own experiences.

- Harness the strengths clients have to meet challenges and overcome obstacles.

- Reframe difficulties and challenges as opportunities to learn and grow.

- Invite clients to discover possibilities and find answers for themselves.

- Dialogue with clients regarding their higher purposes.

- Assist clients to draw up personal blueprints for professional mastery.

- Support clients in brainstorming and trying new ways of doing things.

- Collaborate with clients to design and conduct appropriate learning experiments.

- Inspire and challenge clients to go beyond what they would do alone.

MINDFULNESS PRACTICES BEFORE A COACHING SESSION

- Close your eyes and take three deep, slow breaths. Notice your breath as it moves in and out. Breathing in and out through the nose is more calming and centering than mouth breathing because it stimulates and soothes the vagus nerve, the main pathway of the rest-and-recover nervous system.

- Stretch and savor the feeling of stretching.

- Set a timer for one minute. Close your eyes and become aware of your breathing. Become aware of the places where your body touches and is supported by your chair and the floor. Become aware of the sounds in your environment.

- As you walk to meet with your coachee, choose to walk mindfully. Notice your feet striking the ground. Notice the movement of your limbs. Notice the weight of anything you might be carrying.

- Set aside your papers; turn away from your computer, tablet, or phone; and look out the window, noticing whatever physical or emotional sensations come up in response.

- Say out loud any of the following statements, letting their message sink in:
    - I am grateful for this opportunity to connect and make a difference.
    - I intend to evoke trust, rapport, and positive energy.
    - I have an opportunity to make a pivotal contribution.
    - I am open to and curious about what will unfold.

- Ask yourself any of the following questions:
  - Where am I?
  - What is going on around me?
  - What do I notice that is unexpected or surprising?
  - What am I thinking about?
  - What am I feeling?
  - How can I enhance my experience of coaching?
- Smile as you recall your coaching client's signature strengths and contributions.
- Do whatever other activities bring you into the present moment and prepare you for coaching. (Adapted from Moore, Tschannen-Moran, & Jackson, 2015)

STOP

Stop.

Take a breath.

Observe, acknowledge, and allow what's here.

Proceed. (Brown & Olson, 2015, p. 36)

CREATIVE ENERGY CHECK

- If your energy right now was a weather condition, how would you describe it?
- What song could be the theme song for your day today?
- What color might capture how you feel right now?
- If you were an animal, what animal would you be right now?
- What object in your school reflects how you are right now?
- What three adjectives might describe how you're feeling right now?
- How would you describe your energy right now, on a scale of 0 to 10?
- What's especially present for you in this moment?
- What is stirring inside you right now?
- What physical sensations are you most aware of right now?
- How would you describe your mood right now?
- What's alive for you or energizing you right now?

THE TWO TURNS, FOUR STEPS, AND SIXTEEN STYLE POINTS OF EVOCATIVE COACHING

The Evocative Coaching Dance

LOOP I—The No-Fault Turn	LOOP II—The Strengths-Building Turn
Step 1: Story Listening	**Step 3: Appreciative Inquiry**
1. Establishing Rapport	7. Discovering Strengths
2. Celebrating Progress	8. Exploring Opportunities
3. Exploring Stories	9. Framing Aspirations
4. Attentive Listening	10. Identifying Resources
Step 2: Expressing Empathy	**Step 4: Design Thinking**
5. Offering Empathy Reflections	11. Brainstorming Ideas
The Learning Brief	12. Designing a SMARTER Experiment
6. Clarifying the Focus	13. Confirming Commitment
	14. Rolling With Resistance
	15. Exploring Systemic Change
	16. Session Feedback

STORY-LISTENING PRINCIPLES, QUESTIONS, AND REFLECTIONS

- The map is not the territory; the story is not the experience.
- Stories help people make sense of experience and move people to action.
- The questions we ask determine the stories we hear.
- Mindful listening means listening with calm energy, an open mind, and focused attention.
- Silence encourages clients to think deeply and understand themselves more fully.
- Reflections help clients to see themselves in a new light.

PROMPTS FOR EVOKING STORIES

- Tell me the story of how you came to be an educator.
- Tell me the story of how you came to lead this particular school or district.
- Tell me a story that illustrates what has been working well for you.

- Tell me a story about a time when you handled a tough situation well.

- Tell me a story about a time when you made a real contribution.

- Tell me a story that illustrates how your core values came through in an important way.

- Tell me a story that illustrates what you love most about your work.

- Tell me a story about a time when you had a lot of fun in your work.

- Tell me a story about an experience as an educator that taught you a valuable lesson.

- Tell me a story about a time when you felt respected as an educational leader.

- Tell me a story about a time when you tried something new.

- Tell me a story that illustrates what helps you to be your very best.

- What hopes did you have for this meeting or initiative?

- What parts of the experience can we celebrate?

- What skills were you using well?

- What approaches were working in some ways?

- What helped you to get through it?

- What might have happened if you had chosen to do something differently?

- What would you say is the moral of the story?

- How can you build on this experience for even better results next time?

When coaching educational leaders, it is also important to invite stories about their schools or districts that can lead to the same kinds of fruitful insights.

- Tell me a story of a time when the school/district faced a significant challenge and was successful in meeting that challenge.

- Tell me the story of someone who is considered a hero in this school/district. What are the traits this community values in him or her?

- Tell me a story of a time when a change initiative went surprisingly well.

- Tell me a story about a time when this school/district celebrated an outstanding achievement.

- Tell me a story about an important decision that this school community faced and how that decision was made.

- Tell me a story of a time when an important conflict divided the staff or the community and how the conflict was ultimately resolved.

- Tell me a story about a time when the school/district was deeply engaged with its community. What was the engagement about, who were the key actors, and how did it turn out?

- Tell me a story about someone who joined the school community and became a real leader.

- Tell me the story of something really funny that happened here—a time when people were playful or shared a good laugh together.

LISTEN FOR ATTRIBUTIONS

- What is the overarching theme? Does it lie more with threat or opportunity?

- Where is the locus of control? Does it lie more with the leader or more on blaming others?

- How is the problem defined? Does it frame others as enemies or allies?

- What is happening with energy? Is it diminishing or increasing?

- What is happening with values? Are they being honored or compromised?

- What is happening with needs? Are they being met, denied, or sacrificed?

- What is the language of potential? Does it lie more with sufficiency or more with lack?

- How is the objective defined? Does it lie more with metrics or morale?

LISTENING FOR STORY VARIANTS

- Imagine vantage points: "Who else?" How might others tell this story?

- Imagine pivot points: "How else?" How might things have gone if you had done one thing differently at any point?

- Imagine lesson points: "What else?" What other lessons can this story teach us?

TAKE A WAIT AND SEE ATTITUDE

WAIT—**W**hy **a**m **I t**alking? (Stevens, 2005, p. 161)

SEE—**S**top **e**xplaining **e**verything

Expressing Empathy Principles, Questions, and Reflections

- Enable clients to compassionately reflect on their own experiences.

- Seek to connect rather than to correct.

- Read, respect, and work with clients' emotions as guideposts to their truth.

- Offer empathy reflections or empathy guesses to see if you understand client feelings and needs.

- Get comfortable with messy feelings; don't rush clients when they feel ambivalent or stuck.

- Communicate confidence in coachee capacities and respect for their intentions.

USE DISTINCTIVE REFLECTIONS WITH COMPASSIONATE COMMUNICATION

- Make observations rather than evaluations.

- Reflect feelings rather than feelings infused with thoughts.

- Reflect underlying, universal needs rather than particular strategies.

- Make requests rather than demands.

AVOID COMMUNICATION PATTERNS THAT INTERFERE WITH EXPRESSING EMPATHY

- Advising or problem solving: "Let me tell you how I think you should handle this."

- Commiserating: "Oh, you poor thing."

- Consoling or reassuring: "There now, it'll be all right."

- Correcting: "That's not how it happened."

- Denying choice or responsibility: "There was nothing you could have done."

- Diagnostic labels: "You must have ADHD."

- Educating: "This could turn into a very positive experience for you if you just . . ."

- Enemy images: "You'd better watch yourself; he's out to get you."

- Explaining: "I would have come by, but . . ."

- Guilt trips: "You should have known better—look at the mess you've made!"

- Making comparisons: "If you were just more like _____."

- Making demands: "You don't have a choice. Do it or else!"

- Moralistic judgments: "What a terrible thing to do!"

- One-upping: "That's nothing; wait till you hear what happened to me."

- Interrogating: "How long has this been going on?"

- Prodding: "Cheer up. Get over it. It's time to move on."

- Rewards and punishments: "If you do that, you'll be in big trouble."

- Stepping over: "Well, let's not talk about that just now."

- Storytelling: "That reminds me of the time . . ."

THE FOUR DS OF DISCONNECTION

DIAGNOSE: judge, label, criticize; e.g., "The problem with you is that . . ."

DESERVE: e.g., "She deserved what she got." "I don't deserve this."

DENY responsibility for one's actions and feelings; e.g., "You made me angry . . ." "I had no choice."

DEMAND: e.g., "You should (have to, must, ought to, are supposed to) . . ." "You can't do that." (Gill, Leu, & Morin, 2009)

LOOP II

PARAMETERS OF THE LEARNING BRIEF

- What is the learning focus?
  - What is the overarching focus of the coaching relationship?
  - What topic or subject area holds the most potential?
  - What is the learning focus of this particular coaching conversation?
  - What are the benchmarks for measuring progress?
  - What are the objectives to be realized?

- How will the coach and client work together?
  - What is the role of the coach?
  - What is expected of the client?
  - How will conversations take place?
  - Who will initiate what?
  - How will observations be arranged?
  - How long will the relationship last?

Appreciative Inquiry Principles, Questions, and Reflections

GENERIC APPRECIATIVE INTERVIEW PROTOCOL

1. **Best Experiences.** "Tell me about your best experience of leading a group of people to a positive outcome—a time when your contribution and way of being assisted the group to accomplish a significant challenge that they might not have accomplished without your leadership. Who was involved? What challenges were you facing? What strengths, values, and capabilities allowed you to be successful in that situation? Describe the experience in detail."

2. **Core Values.** "Tell me about the things that matter most to you, that you value most deeply about yourself, your work, and your relationships. How are these expressed in your life and work?"

3. **Supporting Conditions.** "Recall a time when you worked or played in an environment where you were really at your best. What were the particular aspects of that context that brought out the best in you? Were there particular people, policies, or resources that seemed to matter most? How did you grow and what qualities emerged under those conditions?"

4. **Three Wishes.** "Tell me about your hopes and dreams for the future. If you had three wishes that would make this school/district a more vibrant and positive learning environment, what would they be?"

APPRECIATIVE QUESTIONS TO EXPLORE OPPORTUNITIES

- What opportunities do you see for yourself and your school/district in the coming year?

- What would you like to see more of in your school/district?

- What results do you think are most important?

- What new directions excite you right now?

- What are the best things that could happen in your school/district in the near future?

- What initiatives are working well and need to be strengthened and built upon?

- What would you like your leadership to look like a few months from now?

- What new skills would you like to cultivate moving forward? What opportunities are there to gain those skills?

- What would you like to pay more attention to in your school/district?

- What things are most important to you right now? In life? In work?

- What would you like more of in your life? How is that linked to your work?

- What things can you imagine doing differently?

- What changes would excite and inspire you?

- What changes do you think your teachers, parents, or students would really appreciate?

- What has worked for you in other settings that you can draw on in this situation?

- How would you describe your intentions over the next few months? What would your life be like if you realized those intentions? How would that feel?

- What do you think are the best possible outcomes of our work together?

APPRECIATIVE QUESTIONS TO BUILD ENERGY AND ENTHUSIASM FOR CHANGE

- What is working with your approach? What else is working? What else?

- What talents and abilities are serving you well? What else?

- What's the best thing that's happening now? What else?

- What fills you with energy and hope? What else?

- What enables you to do as well as you are doing? What else?

- What is the positive intent of your actions? What else?

- What would success look like? What else would it look like?

- What was the best part of this experience? What else?

- What stands out for you as a shining success? What else?

- What can you celebrate about what happened here? What else?

- Who do you remember as being particularly engaged? What was happening at the time?

- What values are reflected in how you handled this situation? What else?

- How did this situation connect with your sense of purpose? How else?

- What needs did this situation meet for you? What else?

- What needs did this situation meet for your students? What else?

- What enabled this situation to be as successful as it was? What else?

- When did you feel most comfortable and confident? When else?

- What things did you have in place that helped you to be successful? What else?

- What could assist you to be even more successful the next time? What else?

- What resources do you have available? What else?

- What has worked for you in other settings that you can draw on in this situation? What else?

APPRECIATIVE QUESTIONS TO REFRAME DIFFICULT OR TRYING EXPERIENCES

- Tell me how you got through this and what's possible now.

- What did you try that worked, even if only a little bit?

- How did this experience make a positive contribution to your development?

- What's the silver lining here?

- When, if ever, did things start to go better and look up?

- How else can you describe this situation?

- What was the best thing you did in this situation, no matter how small?

- What values did you hold true to even though it was a tough situation?

- How did you manage to keep things from getting any worse?

APPRECIATIVE QUESTIONS THAT FRAME ASPIRATIONS

- Values: "What are my principles? What do I stand for?"

- Outcomes: "What do I need? What do I want?"

- Strengths: "What am I good at? What makes me feel strong?"

- Behaviors: "What activities do I aspire to do consistently?"

- Motivators: "Why does this matter a lot to me right now?"

- Environments: "What support team and structures will facilitate success?"

FRAMING ASPIRATIONS AS PROVOCATIVE POSSIBILITIES

- Grounded: Building on the best of current reality

- Daring: Boldly stretching the status quo

- Desired: Reflecting what we want to move toward, not what we want to move away from

- Palpable: Sensing the future in the present, as if it was already happening

- Participatory: Involving all relevant stakeholders

EXPLORING RESOURCES

- Financial resources

- Human resources

- Technology resources

- Cultural resources

- Material resources

- Recovery resources

DESIGN-THINKING PRINCIPLES, QUESTIONS, AND REFLECTIONS

- Innovation = Inspiration + Ideation + Implementation.

- Invite clients to cocreate new possibilities through brainstorming.

- Make clear that our ideas are not prescriptions to be followed but options to be considered (among many others).

- Assist clients to choose possibilities they find intrinsically interesting and valuable.

- Harness client strengths to meet challenges and overcome obstacles.

- Design either awareness and/or behavior-change experiments depending upon client readiness to change.

- Ensure clients have strong confidence in their ability to complete the experiment.

Designing SMARTER Experiments (**s**pecific, **m**easurable, **a**ttainable, **r**elevant, **t**ime bound, **e**valuated, and **r**efined).

- Hypothesis: An assertion that you want test or explore

- Procedures: How the experiment will be conducted

- Materials: Things you will need to conduct the experiment

- Data Recording: How the observations will be recorded in real time

- Observations: What happens when the experiment is conducted

- Conclusions: What insights emerged as data were reviewed in relation to the hypothesis

BASIC PROTOCOLS FOR BRAINSTORMING

- Set a minimum number of possibilities to generate.

- Set a time limit to keep things moving rapidly.

- Go for quantity rather than quality.

- Encourage wild and exaggerated possibilities.

- Build on the possibilities put forth by others.

- Combine and expand upon possibilities.

- Withhold judgment or evaluation of possibilities.

QUESTIONS TO HELP PRIORITIZE AND CHOOSE IDEAS

- Which ideas stand out as the best ideas?

- Which ideas might have the greatest impact?

- Which ideas build on what you are already doing well?

- Which ideas would require you to learn new skills?

- What makes the ideas you are considering worth pursuing?

- What attracts you to certain ideas?

- What would it take to succeed with the ideas you are considering?

- How do the ideas you are considering compare to other approaches?

- What strengths might you leverage?

- When have you tried something like this before?

- Which ideas would be easy for you to work with successfully?

- Which ideas would push you the most?

- Which ideas would be the most fun?

- Which ideas do you want to try first?

QUESTIONS TO CONFIRM IMPORTANCE, READINESS, AND CONFIDENCE

- On a scale of 0 to 10, how confident are you that you will conduct this experiment at this time?

Follow-Up Questions

- What led you to pick that number and not a lower number?

- What would make it a higher number?

QUESTIONS FOR REFLECTING AND REFINING

- What went well? Why do you think it went as well as it did?

- How did you grow and what did you learn?

- What surprised you?

- What do you hope to build on going forward?

- How did you feel before, during, and after the experiment? What needs were stirred up or met?

QUESTIONS FOR HONORING AMBIVALENCE AND ROLLING WITH RESISTANCE

- How do you see the possibilities before you? How else might you see them?

- How do you know what you know about the possibilities before you? How could you test what you know?

- What choices are you facing? How else might you describe those choices?

- Who could you talk with about your quandary? Who else could you talk with?

- What do you know for sure about your options? What don't you know?

- Where do you feel the possibilities in your body? What can you learn from that?

- What needs are you trying to meet? What else? What else?

- What values would you honor by going one direction? By going another? And another?

- What benefits do you see to one course of action? To another? And another?

- What concerns do you have regarding one possibility? Regarding another? And another?

- What strengths would be called upon if you went one way? If you went the other?

- How do you feel when you contemplate going one way? Going another way?

- On a scale of 0 to 10, how strongly do you feel about doing one thing? About doing another?

AVOIDING COACHING TRAPS

- The fix-it trap

- The cheerleader trap

- The rabbit-hole trap

- The hurry-hurry trap

- The yes-but trap

- The one-right-way trap

QUESTIONS FOR SYSTEMS CHANGE

- What do the mission and vision statements convey about what the organization values? To what extent do these statements align with the actual practices of the organization?

- What are the main ceremonies and rituals and what purposes do they serve?

- What are the dominant stories or legends that people tell? What messages do these stories convey?

- What are the principle images or metaphors that people use to describe the organization (e.g., a family, a zoo, a war zone)?

- What are the most potent norms (i.e., do's and dont's) and how are they enforced?

- What kinds of beliefs about students and their families dominate the organization (officially and unofficially)?

- What reward systems are in place? What messages do they send in terms of activities or accomplishments that are valued and those that are not?

- What language dominates everyday discourse (e.g. buzzwords, cliques, catchphrases)?

- Are there identifiable subcultures in the organization? How are they differentiated? Are they in conflict or harmony? What impacts do these subcultures have on the organization? What functions do these groupings serve for their members? Is the overall effect on the organization positive or negative?

- How do humor and play contribute to the organization's culture?

- What messages do the physical environment and the artifacts on display convey?

- What story does the school or district website tell?

THE REFLECTIVE COACH

QUESTIONS FOR REFLECTION FOLLOWING A COACHING SESSION

- What did I notice?

- When were energies high?

- How did I feel during the session?

- What questions got a reaction?

- What promises were made?

- What would I like to build upon and develop in the next session?

- What would I like to explore further?

QUESTIONS REQUESTING FEEDBACK FROM A COACHEE

- What is the best experience you've had so far through the coaching process?

- What do you value most about our coaching relationship?

- What about our process has helped you to reach your goals and move forward?

- If you had three wishes for our coaching relationship, wishes that would help the relationship serve you better, what would they be?

References

Adams, M. (2004). *Change your questions change your life: 7 powerful tools for life and work.* San Francisco, CA: Berrett-Koehler.

The American Heritage Dictionary (5th ed.). (2012). Boston, MA: Houghton Mifflin Company.

Avital, M., & Boland, R. J. (2007). Managing as designing with a positive lens. In M. Avital, R. J. Boland, & D. L. Cooperrider (Eds.), *Advances in appreciative inquiry: Designing information and organizations with a positive lens* (Vol. 2, pp. 3–14). Oxford, UK: Elsevier Science.

Bennis, W., & Nanus, B. (1985). *Leaders: The strategies for taking charge.* New York, NY: Harper & Row.

Bolman, L. G. & Deal, T. E. (2013). *Reframing organizations: Artistry, choice, and leadership.* San Francisco, CA: Jossey-Bass.

Borwick, I. (1969, Jan.). Team improvement laboratory. *Personnel Journal,* 18–24.

Brown, T. (2009). *Change by design: How design thinking transforms organizations and inspires innovation.* New York, NY: HarperCollins.

Brown, V., & Olson, K. (2015). *The mindful school leader: Practices to transform your leadership and school.* Thousand Oaks, CA: Corwin.

Buckingham, M. (2007). *Go put your strengths to work: 6 powerful steps to achieve outstanding performance.* New York, NY: The Free Press.

Clement, D., Feldstein, L., Hockaday, M., & Tschannen-Moran, M. (2015). *The vibrant school scale.* Paper presented at the annual meeting of the University Council for Educational Administration, San Diego, California.

Cooperrider, D. L. (2000). Positive image, positive action: The affirmative basis of organizing. In D. L. Cooperrider, P. F. Sorensen Jr., D. Whitney, & T. F. Yaeger (Eds.), *Appreciative inquiry: Rethinking human organization toward a positive theory of change* (pp. 29–53). Champaign, IL: Stipes.

Council of Chief State School Officers. (2015). *Model principal supervisor professional standards 2015.* Washington, DC: CCSSO.

Csikszentmihalyi, M. (1990). *Flow: The psychology of optimal experience.* New York, NY: Harper & Row.

Csikszentmihalyi, M. (2000). *Beyond boredom and anxiety.* San Francisco, CA: Jossey-Bass.

de Saint-Exupéry, A. (1950). *The wisdom of the sands.* New York, NY: Harcourt Brace and Company.

Damasio, A. (2010). *Self comes to mind: Constructing the conscious brain.* New York, NY: Random House.

de Waal, F. (2009). *The age of empathy: Nature's lessons for a kinder society.* New York, NY: Harmony Books.

Drake, D. B. (2008). Thrice upon a time: Narrative structure and psychology as a platform for coaching. In D. B. Drake, D. Brennan, & K. Gørtz, *The philosophy and practice of coaching: Insights and issues for a new era* (pp. 51–72). San Francisco, CA: Jossey-Bass.

Fredrickson, B. L. (2009). *Positivity: Groundbreaking research reveals how to embrace the hidden strength of positive emotions, overcome negativity, and thrive.* New York, NY: Crown.

Freire, P. (2000). *Pedagogy of the oppressed: 30th anniversary edition.* New York, NY: Continuum International Publishing Group.

Gallwey, W. T. (2000). *The inner game of work.* New York, NY: Random House.

Gill, R., Leu, L., & Morin, J. (2009). Nonviolent Communication Toolkit for Facilitators: Interactive activities and awareness exercises based on 18 key concepts for the development of NVC skills and consciousness. Available at http://nvctoolkit.org/

Hall, L. M., & Duval, M. (2004). *Meta-coaching volume I: Coaching change for higher levels of success and transformation.* Clifton, CO: Neuro-Semantics.

Hall, L. M., & Duval, M. (2005). *Meta-coaching volume II: Coaching change for transformational change.* Clifton, CO: Neuro-Semantics.

Haven, K. F. (2007). *Story proof: The science behind the startling power of story.* Westport, CT: Libraries Unlimited.

Hoy, W. K., & Tarter, C. J. (2007). *Administrators solving the problems of practice: Decision-making, concepts, cases and consequences* (3rd ed.). Boston, MA: Allyn and Bacon.

Hoy, W. K., Tarter, C. J., & Hoy, A. W. (2008). Academic optimism of schools: A force for student achievement. *American Educational Research Journal, 43,* 425–446.

International Association of Coaching. (2003). IAC ethical principles. Retrieved from https://certifiedcoach.org/about/ethics/#code

International Association of Coaching. (2009). IAC coaching masteries overview. Retrieved from https://certifiedcoach.org/certification-and-development/the-coaching-masteries/

International Coach Federation. (2008a). ICF code of ethics. Retrieved from https://coachfederation.org/about/ethics.aspx?ItemNumber=4045&navItemNumber=4046

International Coach Federation. (2008b). ICF professional coaching core competencies. Retrieved from https://coachfederation.org/credential/landing.cfm?ItemNumber=2206

Jaworski, J. (1998). *Synchronicity: The inner path of leadership.* San Francisco, CA: Berrett-Koehler.

Jones, D. (2001). Celebrate what's right with the world. [DVD]. St. Paul, MN: Star Thrower Distribution.

Jordan, J. V. (2004). Therapists' authenticity. In J. V. Jordan, M. Walker, & L. M. Hartling (Eds.), *The complexity of connection: Writings from the Stone Center's Jean Baker Miller Training Institute* (pp. 64–89). New York: Guilford.

Jung, C. G. (1962). Modern psychology offers a possibility of understanding. In R. Wilhelm, *The secret of the golden flower: A Chinese book of life* (pp. 75–137). San Diego, CA: Harcourt Harvest Books.

Kabat-Zinn, J. (2012). *Mindfulness for beginners.* Louisville, CO: Sounds True.

Kegan, R., & Lahey, L. L. (2009). *Immunity to change: How to overcome it and unlock the potential in yourself and your organization.* Boston, MA: Harvard Business School Press.

Kelm, J. B. (2005). *Appreciative living: The principles of appreciative inquiry in personal life.* Wake Forest, NC: Venet.

Kise, J. A. G. (2006). *Differentiated coaching: A framework for helping teachers change.* Thousand Oaks, CA: Corwin Press.

Knight, J. (2007). *Instructional coaching: A partnership approach to improving instruction.* Thousand Oaks, CA: Corwin Press.

Knowles, M. S., Holton, E. F., & Swanson, R. A. (2005). *The adult learner: The definitive classic in adult education and human resource development.* Houston, TX: Gulf Publishing Company.

Marris, P. (2014). *Loss and Change: Revised Edition.* Florence, Kentucky: Routledge.

Maslow, A. H. (1968). *Toward a psychology of being.* Princeton, NJ: Van Nostrand.

Miller, W. R., & Rollnick, S. (2002). *Motivational interviewing: Preparing people for change* (2nd ed). New York, NY: The Guilford Press.

Moore, M., Tschannen-Moran, B., & Jackson, E. (2015). *Coaching psychology manual* (2nd ed.). Philadelphia, PA: Lippincott Williams & Wilkins.

Murray, W. H. (1951). *The Scottish Himalayan expedition.* London, UK: J. M. Dent & Sons Ltd.

Palmer, P. (1998). *The courage to teach: Exploring the inner landscape of a teacher's life.* San Francisco, CA: Jossey-Bass.

Pearsall, P. (1998). *The heart's code: Tapping the wisdom and power of our heart energy.* New York, NY: Broadway Books.

Peterson, C., & Seligman, M. E. P. (2004). *Character strengths and virtues: A handbook and classification.* New York, NY: Oxford University Press.

Pink, D. (2005). *A whole new mind: Moving from the information age to the conceptual age.* New York, NY: Penguin Books.

Prochaska, J. O., & Norcross, J. C. (2002). Stages of change. In J. C. Norcross (Ed.), *Psychotherapy relationships that work* (pp. 303–313). New York, NY: Oxford University Press.

Rock, D., & Page, L. J. (2009). *Coaching with the brain in mind: Foundations for practice.* Hoboken, NJ: John Wiley & Sons.

Rogers, C. (1980). *A way of being.* New York, NY: Houghton Mifflin.

Rogers, C. (1989). *On becoming a person: A therapist's view of psychotherapy.* New York, NY: Mariner Books.

Rogers, C., & Farson, R. E. (1957). *Active listening.* Chicago, IL: The University of Chicago Industrial Relations Center. Retrieved from www.gordontraining.com/artman2/uploads/1/ActiveListening_RogersFarson.pdf

Rosenberg, M. B. (2003). *Nonviolent communication: A language of life.* Encinitas, CA: PuddleDancer Press.

Roughton, R. (1981, April). Hartford: CT: Newsletter of the Older Friends Group. ©PAIRS, 1990. Retrieved from http://www.chsn.org.uk/media/files/HandoutonListening.pdf

Rumi. (2004). *Rumi: Selected poems.* (Coleman Barks, Trans.). New York, NY: Penguin Books.

Rushdie, S. (1993). *The Rushdie Letters: Freedom to speak, freedom to write.* Kerry Ireland: Brandon Book Publishers. pp. 13–24.

Scharmer, C. O. (2007). *Theory U: Leading from the future as it emerges.* Cambridge, MA: Society for Organizational Learning.

Schlechty, P. C. (1993). On the frontier of school reform with trailblazers, pioneers, and settlers, *Journal of Staff Development, 14,* 46–51.

Schön, D. A. (1983). *The reflective practitioner: How professionals think in action*. Cambridge, MA: Basic Books.

Senge, P., Scharmer, C. O., Jaworski, J., & Flowers, B. S. (2004). *Presence: An exploration of profound change in people, organizations, and society*. New York, NY: Doubleday.

Senge, P. M. (2006). *The fifth discipline: The art & practice of the learning organization*. New York, NY: Doubleday.

Senge, P. M., Cambron-McCabe, N., Lucas, T., Smith, B., Dutton, J., & Kleiner, K. (2000). *Schools that learn: A fifth discipline fieldbook for educators, parents, and everyone who cares about education*. New York, NY: Doubleday.

Silsbee, D. (2008). *Presence-based coaching: Cultivating self-generative leaders through mind, body, and heart*. San Francisco, CA: Jossey-Bass.

Stevens, N. (2005). *Learn to coach: The skills you need to coach for personal and professional development*, Oxford, UK: How To Books Ltd.

Stober, D. R. (2006). Coaching from a humanistic perspective. In Stober, D. R., & Grant, A. M. (Eds.), *Evidence based coaching handbook* (pp. 17–50). Hoboken, NJ: John Wiley & Sons.

Stone, D., Patton, B., & Heen, S. (1999). *Difficult conversations: How to discuss what matters most*. New York, NY: Penguin.

Tschannen-Moran, M. (2014). *Trust matters: leadership for successful schools* (2nd ed.). San Francisco, CA: Jossey-Bass.

Tschannen-Moran, M., Salloum, S. J., & Goddard, R. D. (2014). Context matters: The influence of collective beliefs and norms. In H. Fives & M. G. Gill (Eds.), *International Handbook of Research on Teachers' Beliefs* (pp. 301–316). New York, NY: Routledge.

Watkins, J. M., Mohr, B. J., & Kelly, R. (2011). *Appreciative inquiry: Change at the speed of imagination* (2nd ed.). San Francisco, CA: Pfeiffer.

Wheatley, M. J. (2002). *Turning to one another: Simple conversations to restore hope to the future*. San Francisco, CA: Berrett-Koehler.

Whitney, D., & Trosten-Bloom, A. (2010). *The power of appreciative inquiry: A practical guide to positive change* (2nd ed.). San Francisco, CA: Berrett-Koehler Publishers, Inc.

Zandee, D. P. (2008). The poetics of organizational design: How words may inspire worlds. In M. Avital, R. J. Boland, & D. L. Cooperrider (Eds.), *Advances in appreciative inquiry: Designing information and organizations with a positive lens* (Vol. 2, pp. 131–146). Oxford, UK: Elsevier Science.

Zander, R., & Zander, B. (2000). *The art of possibility*. New York, NY: Penguin Putnam.

Zeus, P., & Skiffington, S. (2000). *The complete guide to coaching at work*. New York, NY: McGraw-Hill.

Zhang, P. (2007). Toward a positive design theory: Principles for designing motivating information and communication technology. In M. Avital, R. J. Boland, & D. L. Cooperrider (Eds.), *Advances in appreciative inquiry: Designing information and organizations with a positive lens* (Vol. 2, pp. 45–74). Oxford, UK: Elsevier Science.

Index

organizational-based inquiry, 159, 204–205
reflective practices, 203, 205
story listening, 12
strengths-based inquiry, 107
Hoy, A. W., 162
Hoy, W. K., 159
Humanistic psychology principles, 189–190
Human resources, 117–118, 201
Humor, 32, 205
Hurry-hurry trap, 155, 204

Ideation, 121, 155
Imaginative story listening, 12, 63–66, 170
Immunity to change, xi, 149–152, 151 (figure)
Implementation, 121, 155, 156
Incentives, 7, 14, 16–17, 21
Initial coaching session, 37–38
"Initiate-inquire-imagine-innovate"
    process, 163–166
Inspiration, 121–122, 156
Instruction, 14, 16–17
Integrity, 28
Intent, 49
Intention, 21, 22, 72–73, 73 (figure)
International Association of
    Coaching (IAC), x, 7, 176, 184
International Coach Federation (ICF), x, 7, 23,
    176, 184, 190
Interpersonal dynamics, 31–33, 35–36, 51
Interview protocol, 108–109, 198–200
Intonation, 34
Intuition, 23, 60–61

Jackson, E., 25, 192
Jaworski, J., 63
    see also Senge, P. M.
Jones, D., 100
Jordan, J. V., 22
Journaling, 170, 171–172
Judgmental evaluations, 73 (figure), 74–76,
    87, 88–89 (figure)
Jung, Carl G., 103

Kabat-Zinn, J., 23
Kegan, R., xi, 60, 86, 149,
    150–151, 151 (figure)
Kelly, R., 115, 132, 163, 164, 165
Kelm, J. B., 102
Kennedy, Robert, 141
Kise, J. A. G., 91
Kleiner, K.
    see Senge, P. M.
Knight, J., 55, 70, 130
Knowles, M. S., 16
Krishnamurti, Jiddu, 78

Lahey, L. L., xi, 60, 86, 149,
    150–151, 151 (figure)
Language usage, 79, 80–81 (figure), 86
Lateral relationships, 35–36
Laughter, 32, 205
Leadership coaching, 3–4
Leadership platforms, 116–117
LEAD (listen, empathize,
    appreciate, design) model
    basic concepts, 11–15
    benefits, 5, 186
    dynamic processes, 136–138
    Möbius strip model, 11 (figure), 41 (figure),
        95 (figure)
    no-fault turn, 42–44, 133, 179, 193
    strengths-building turn, 95–96,
        133, 179, 193
    style points, 179, 193
Learning brief, 97–98, 179, 193, 197
Lesson points, 66
Leu, L., 77, 197
Levels of stories, 50
Lewin, Kurt, xi
Life-giving connections, 7–8, 42, 148
Listening skills
    appreciative inquiry, 61, 63–64, 156–160
    attentive listening, 11–12, 22, 30, 56–63
    deep listening, 170
    imaginative story listening, 12, 63–66, 170
    LEAD (listen, empathize, appreciate,
        design) model, 11 (figure), 11–12,
        41 (figure), 179, 193
    story listening, 6, 12, 42–43, 45–48, 50,
        63–66, 156–160, 170, 193–195
    style points, 179
    see also Compassionate communication
Listing, Johann, 41
Lucas, T.
    see Senge, P. M.

Marris, P., 160
Maslow, A. H., 82
Material resources, 118, 201
Maybe-so stories, 64
McKay, Sarah, 74
Meanings and attachments, 160
Mentors, 4, 4 (figure), 36–37
Miller, W. R., 92, 147, 149
Mindfulness/mindful coaching, 6–7, 21, 23–26,
    170–172, 191–192
Mnemonic devices, 48
Möbius, August Ferdinand, 41
Möbius strip model, 11, 11 (figure), 41 (figure),
    41–42, 95 (figure), 96, 136
Mohr, B. J., 115, 132, 163, 164, 165

Moore, M., 25, 192
Moralistic judgments, 75
Morin, J., 77, 197
Motivation
    adult learners, 17
    appreciative inquiry, 14, 99–100, 108, 110, 116
    calm assurance, 32
    causal attributions, 87
    coaching benefits, 4, 8, 10, 22, 122, 186
    coaching conversations, 145
    collective efficacy, 158–159
    design-thinking process, 133–134
    empathetic understanding, 70, 155
    feedback, 182–183
    heartfelt connections, 72
    incentives, 7
    interpersonal dynamics, 136–137, 141–142
    nonjudgmental behaviors, 27
    openness to possibilities, 33, 53
    resistance to change, 147, 150
    self-empathy, 170–171
    story listening, 51, 53–54, 56
    strengths-based inquiry, 96, 153
    trust and rapport, 42
    universal human needs, 82–83
Murray, W. H., 135
Mutual empathy, 171
Myers-Brigg personality assessment tool, 110

Nanus, B., 103
Needs
    adult learners, 16–17, 189
    appreciative inquiry, 13, 99
    benevolence, 27
    change processes, 156–157, 161–162
    coachable stories, 51, 56
    coaching traps, 154–155, 204
    compassionate communication, 73 (figure),
        80–81 (figure), 81, 81–87, 90–92,
        137–138, 161–162
    distinctive reflections, 78–79, 196
    empathetic understanding, 70–72
    faux feelings, 87, 88–89 (figure)
    moments of silence, 24
    no-fault turn, 43
    openness, 28–29
    reflective practices, 78–79, 183
    resistance to change, 145–150, 203–204
    self-empathy, 171–172
    SMARTER experiments, 135–136
    story listening, 6, 12–13, 47, 59, 156–157
    strategic thinking, 76–77
    trust and rapport, 37–38
    universal human needs, 16–17, 82–87,
        85 (figure), 88–89 (figure), 161–162

vitality, 111
    see also Feelings
Negative emotions, 74
Negativity, 12
Neuroscience research, 48, 72
No-fault turn, 42–44, 133, 148, 179, 193
Nonjudgmental awareness
    attentive listening, 57, 59–60
    coaching conversations, 5
    creativity, 9, 15
    mindfulness, 6, 23–24, 170–172
    safe environments, 27, 43–44
    supervisory challenges, 36
Nonviolent Communication (NVC)
    model, xi, 13, 72
Norcross, J. C., 7, 142
Note-taking, 173

Observations, 73 (figure), 78, 111–112,
    172–173, 176, 179, 181–182
Obstacles, 49
Olson, K., 24, 192
One-right-way trap, 156, 204
Ongoing disciplined inquiry, 163–166
Open-ended questions, 13–14, 53–54, 55, 107,
    193–195
Open listening, 59–60
Openness, 28–29, 33
Openness to possibility, 33, 43–44
Opportunities, 112–114
Optimism, 33
Organizational change, 156–162, 204–205

Pacing, 34
Page, L. J., 48, 104
Palmer, P., 56, 161
Pascal, Blaise, 71
Patton, B., 57
Pearsall, P., 72
Peer coaching, 37
Performance anxiety, 9
Performance coaching, x
Personal disclosure, 29
Personality assessment tools, 110
Perspective-taking practices, 65
Peterson, C., 110
Pink, D., 50
Pity, 70
Pivot points, 66
Playfulness, 32, 205
Poetic principle of appreciative inquiry,
    101 (figure), 103, 115–116
Points of view, 64–65
Positive behaviors, 27–28, 33, 42–44
Positive inquiry, 13–14, 101–103

CORWIN
LEADERSHIP

Simon T. Bailey & Marceta F. Reilly

On providing a simple, sustainable framework that will help you move your school from mediocrity to brilliance.

Edie L. Holcomb

Use data to construct an equitable learning environment, develop instruction, and empower effective PL communities.

Debbie Silver & Dedra Stafford

Equip educators to develop resilient and mindful learners primed for academic growth and personal success.

Peter Gamwell & Jane Daly

A fresh perspective on how to nurture creativity, innovation, leadership, and engagement.

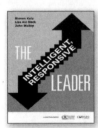

Steven Katz, Lisa Ain Dack, & John Malloy

Leverage the oppositional forces of top-down expectations and bottom-up experience to create an intelligent, responsive school.

Lyn Sharratt & Beate Planche

A resource-rich guide that provides a strategic path to achieving sustainable communities of deep learners.

Peter M. DeWitt

Meet stakeholders where they are, motivate them to improve, and model how to do it.